ERASMUS
OF CHRISTENDOM

"Roland Bainton, Titus Street Professor Emeritus
of Ecclesiastical History, Yale University, is not
only the leading American authority on the Reformation, but also a distinguished writer. His
award-winning book *Here I Stand* (Abingdon,
1957) has been acclaimed as the best Luther
biography. Now this companion volume on
Erasmus shows many of the same extraordinary
qualities: Mr. Bainton has mastered the prodigious amount of literature on Erasmus, but he
wears his scholarship lightly. His colourful
portrait will give inspiration and enjoyment to
readers even if they are not specialists in the
history of Humanism."

Felix Hirsch, *Library Journal*, 1969

ERASMUS
OF CHRISTENDOM

*

Roland H. Bainton

COLLINS
FONTANA LIBRARY
Theology & Philosophy

First published by Charles Scribner's Sons, New York, 1969

First published in Great Britain
by William Collins Sons & Co. Ltd.,
London, 1969

First issued in the Fontana Library of Theology & Philosophy, 1972
Second Impression October 1977

Copyright © Roland H. Bainton 1969

Made and printed in Great Britain by
William Collins Sons & Co. Ltd., Glasgow

To the memory of

RUTH WOODRUFF BAINTON

Love dwelt in her heart, kindness on her lips
and laughter in her eyes.

Illustrations Acknowledgments—Plates

*

1 By permission of the Syndics of the Cambridge University Library.

2 Royal Library, Windsor Castle, Berkshire. Reproduced by gracious permission of Her Majesty The Queen.

3 Harold Mattingly, *Roman Imperial Coinage* (London, 1926).

4 Royal Library, Windsor Castle, Berkshire. Reproduced by gracious permission of Her Majesty The Queen.

5 and 10 respectively: Vol. II of *Albrecht Dürer* by E. Panofsky, Plate 65, "Portrait of Frederick the Wise" and Plate 305, "Portrait of Erasmus of Rotterdam" (Princeton University Press, 1943). Plate 5 is from the Staatliche Museen, Berlin.

6 Custody of the Lord Chamberlain, St. James's Palace, London. Reproduced by gracious permission of Her Majesty The Queen. Photograph from the Bettmann Archive.

7 Courtesy of the Bibliothèque de l'Université Catholique, Louvain. Paul Naster, *Les Médailles Italiennes d'Adrien VI*, Scrinium Lovaniense, edited by E. van Cauwenbergh (Louvain, 1966).

8 Louvain, Librairie Universitaire Uystpruyst. Henry de Vocht, *Literae ad Franciscum Craneveldium*, Humanistica Lovaniensia I (Louvain, 1928).

9 Zentralbibliothek, Zürich. Lithograph from the painting by Hans Asper.

11 Direktion der Staatlichen Graphischen Sammlung, München.

12 Oeffentliche Kunstsammlung Kunstmuseum, Basel.

Preface

*

THIS Biography is an expansion of five lectures delivered on the L. P. Stone Foundation at Princeton Theological Seminary during February 1967. A briefer version was given earlier as a Menno Simons Lecture at Bethel College, North Newton, Kansas.

Erasmus of Rotterdam has never had his due. The reason is in part that he founded no church to perpetuate his memory. In consequence he has lagged far behind with respect to a critical edition of his *opera omnia*, behind not only the major reformers, Luther, Calvin, Zwingli, and Melanchthon, but even the minor reformers, Caspar Schwenkfeld and the Anabaptists. The correspondence has indeed been magnificently edited by the Allens and the *Ausgewählte Schriften* by the Holborns, but of the total output only a little else has received this distinction. A critical edition of the entire corpus has been undertaken only at long last, and not by a church but by the Royal Dutch Academy out of national pride of which Erasmus was entirely devoid.

Neither has Erasmus had his due on the score of interpretation. Rejected by the Catholics as subversive and by the Protestants as evasive he has fallen chiefly into the hands of the rationalists who have appreciated him chiefly for his satire on contemporary superstitions. In recent years a spate of monographs has redressed the balance, but the results have not been gathered into a single volume. To encompass so much is a brash endeavour here launched under the aegis of Dame Folly.

I have long been drawn to Erasmus on a number of counts. I share his aversion to contention, his abhorrence of war, his wistful scepticism with respect to that which transcends the verifiable; at the same time I am warmed by the glow of his piety. I am convinced of the soundness of the place assigned by him to the classical alongside of the Judaeo-Christian in the heritage of the Western world. I relish his whimsicality and satire. I endorse his conviction that language is still the best medium for the transmission of thought, language not merely read but heard with cadence and rhythm as well as clarity and precision.

Yet I should probably never have undertaken this assignment were Erasmus lacking in contemporary relevance. He is important for the dialogue which he desired never to see closed between Catholics and Protestants. He is important for the strategy of reform, violent or non-violent. He was resolved to abstain from violence alike of word and deed, but was not sure that significant reform could be achieved *sine tumultu*. He would neither incite nor abet it. The more intolerant grew the contenders, the more he recoiled and strove to mediate. He ended as the battered liberal. Can it ever be otherwise? This is precisely the problem of our time.

R. H. B.

New Haven, Connecticut
Winter 1968

Contents

*

List of Illustrations

*

Plates

Line-Blocks in Text

List of Illustrations

CHAPTER ONE

Monasticism: Holland

*

ERASMUS of Rotterdam is today the best known of the humanists of the sixteenth century, though his reputation rests for the most part on a single work, a little fantasy written for diversion, called *The Praise of Folly*, which in later life he regretted having published. In his own day he enjoyed an unparalleled popularity and for solider reasons. No man in Europe had so many friends in high places in Church, state, and school. He was invited to take up his residence in the entourage of crowned and mitred heads, of kings and emperors, burgomasters and town councillors, cardinals and popes. Henry VIII sent him a pressing invitation in his own hand and Erasmus insisted that Henry knew enough Latin to have composed it himself and not merely to have copied the draft of a secretary. Francis I sent an appeal to come to Paris signed in huge letters FRANÇOYS (see p. 15). The letter is extant in the library of the university of Basel. Charles of the Netherlands and Spain, later the emperor, made Erasmus an imperial councillor on a pension. Margaret, the regent in the Low Countries, cut it off to force Erasmus to come back from Basel to her domains. The King of Hungary, the Archbishop of Canterbury, the Cardinal Primate of Spain – all would have been honoured to have him in their midst. Pope Leo would gladly have him come to Rome and Pope Hadrian was urgent in his invitations. The university centres, Cambridge and

Oxford, Louvain, Basel, and Vienna, likewise strove for his presence. These were, of course, the days when potentates vied with one another to enhance their reputations by assembling at their courts astrologers, musicians, poets, artists, fools, and scholars. But less exalted folk were also devoted to Erasmus. Oecolampadius, who assisted him in the publication of his New Testament at Basel, framed a letter from him and hung it over his desk until it was stolen by another admirer. One of the printers in the Netherlands, desiring to see Erasmus before his departure for Basel, went to Antwerp. Learning that he was instead at Louvain, the man walked all night only to arrive an hour and a half too late. There is only one person recorded not to have been eager to have Erasmus as a guest. Dame Alice, the second wife of Thomas More, understood no Latin, Erasmus no English. She did not relish a guest for a month at a time who was forever joking with her husband in an unknown tongue.[1]

What was the secret of his appeal? No doubt in a measure his charm, urbanity, and wit which could mollify opponents in personal encounter, but above all his prodigious erudition directed towards the realization of the aspirations of his age. This was the period of the Renaissance and the Reformation. Both were movements of reform. Unlike many of the revolutionary movements of the twentieth century they looked with no disdain upon the past, but sought to correct the immediate past by return to a past more remote. For the Renaissance this meant classical antiquity, for the Reformation the gospel. The glory of Greece, the grandeur of Rome, the grace of Galilee should repristinate society and revivify the Church. This programme appeared to some to contain incompatibles. There were churchmen who looked with disdain upon pagan letters and literati who scorned the

Cher et bon amy. Nous auons donne charge a nostre cher et bien
ame messire Claude Cantiuncula, present porteur, de vous dire et
declairer aucunes choses de par nous; desquelles vous prions
tresaffectueusement le croyre, et y adjouster entiere foy, comme
feriez a nostre propre personne. Cher et bon amy, nostre Seigneur
vous ait en sa garde.

Escript a Sainct Germain en laye le viime jour de Julliet.

Je vous auertys que sy vous voules venyr, que vous seres le byen
venu.

Francoys

(The transliteration is from *EE* V, 1375, p. 307.)

tomes of the theologians. Erasmus sought to hold the two
in conjunction. He was in this respect no innovator.
Syntheses of the Christian and classical had been
attempted long before by Augustine, by Aquinas, by
Dante. Erasmus essayed the task afresh, not in order to
systematize theology, but in order to give substance to a
reform. He would purge the Church and refashion the
world. At first he was highly optimistic as to the possi-

bility of a revival through the dissemination of the literature of Christian and classical antiquity. His greatest instrument was education and the great tool of education was the printing press. No man laboured so arduously to bring learning abreast of technology. His incense was the odour of printer's ink.

The mark of the Parisian printer Badius on the title page of a work of Erasmus.

The stupendous programme which he envisioned did not appear fatuous in the sixteenth century because of an interlude of peace in Church and state. The heresies of the Middle Ages had been suppressed. From the twelfth century on, sectarian and heretical movements had plagued the Church. The Albigenses, Waldenses, Fraticelli, Hussites, and Wycliffites had threatened to disrupt the structure of Christendom. In Spain ecclesiastical and national unity was menaced by the presence of the Jews and the Moors. By 1500, the danger had been relatively surmounted. The moderate Hussites had been contained, the Wycliffites (called Lollards) driven underground, and the Waldenses driven to the highest ground habitable on the Alpine slopes. The Jews had been expelled from Spain and the Moors conquered. The Inquisition could afford to relax and be tolerant of the airing of doubts.

In this atmosphere arose a movement of reform in the Church which today is called in French *évangélisme*, that is to say, a return to the evangel, the religion of the New Testament. Though without organization, the movement had representatives in all lands: in France, Lefèvre; in England, Colet; in Spain, Ximenes; in Holland, Gansfort; in Germany, Geiler of Kaisersberg. But no man so epitomized this reform in its many aspects as did Erasmus of Rotterdam.

His campaign for the purification of the Church induced attacks upon contemporary thought and practice. He had three great aversions. The first was obscurantism. He inveighed against many of the contemporary scholastics because they were not open to the study of the pagan classics nor to the spirit of critical inquiry. The second was paganism. Some scholars in his period were so addicted to the classics as to discard the essential Christian heritage. The third he called Judaism, or again Pharisaism or legalism, that is to say, the effort to ensure salvation through the meticulous observance of external rules as to food, dress, vigils, and the like. At this point the monks were the particular, though not the exclusive (or indiscriminate), butt of his attack. On the ethical side he naturally upbraided clerical concubinage, but his strictures were more severe against cruelty, whether on the part of the Church against heretics, the state against thieves, or rulers against each other.

Optimism as to the possibility of reform by education was buoyed in the early sixteenth century by a comparative lull in warfare. The Wars of the Roses ended in England with the accession of Henry VII. After the invasion of Italy by Charles VIII in 1494, the powers were mainly sparring until the major conflicts of the 1520's. Cardinal Wolsey in 1518 brought to pass in the Treaty of London a basis for universal peace not only between England and France but among all the European powers. The proponents of reform by education were in those days jubilating with lyrical optimism and their poet laureate was Erasmus.

The mood was of short duration. The Protestant Reformation emerged to shatter the structure of the Church. The wars between the empire and France embroiled Europe in new convulsions, while the Turks threatened to capture Vienna. Erasmus, ever the prophet of peace, pleaded, exhorted, and essayed the role of mediator with fruitless persistence. He drew fire from both sides in the controversies and ended his days as both the arbiter and the outlaw of Christendom.

Erasmus was a man of moderation partly because he perceived the ambiguities of all things human. There is an appropriateness in the ambiguity attending the date of his birth. Was it in 1466 or 1469? His most direct statements give the year as 1466, but some references look to 1469 and still other dates. A modern scholar argues for the later date, as better explaining the sequence of the early studies. Another scholar replies that this sequence cannot be determined with precision. The question is of supreme importance for determining when to have the commemoration. The Swiss have settled for the prior

date and celebrated the event in 1966. The Dutch prefer
the later year and scheduled their observance in 1969. As
a genuine Erasmian, I would postpone solution of the
problem to the judgment day, though in the interim, and
tentatively, I would accept the more precise statements of
Erasmus in favour of 1466.[2]

Erasmus was a Hollander. There is no doubt about
that and he spoke with pride of his native land, which he
called sometimes Hollandia and sometimes Batavia.
"The inhabitants of this area," he said, "were described
in antiquity as rude and rustic. They are not so today,
unless rustic be taken to mean hardy. This folk is without
guile, humane and benevolent, free from belligerence and
truculence. Its only vice is indulgence in the pleasures of
the table, perhaps because the land is so abundant with
lush meadows and marshes replete with fowl. No comparable area is so populous and urbanized. The homes
display an opulent elegance, for our navigators touch on
the ports of the world. The number of those distinguished
in letters is not great, perhaps because the life is too easy
and perhaps because this people consider integrity more
estimable than erudition."[3]

A biographical *Compendium*, attributed to Erasmus,
gives the following account of his parentage and birth.
His father, Gerhard or Geert, was the ninth son in a
family which fastened on him as the one who should
enter the priesthood. He was living, with a view to
marriage, with Margaret, the daughter of a physician.
His family so harassed him that he left Margaret pregnant
and went to Rome, supporting himself there by copying
manuscripts, for he was a learned man. The family sent
him word that she had died. In grief he took orders.
Returning home he discovered the deception, but was
faithful to his vows and did not return to Margaret,

though helping with the support of the child. This is the
story on which Charles Reade based his novel *The Cloister
and the Hearth*. The chief difficulty with the tale is that it
makes no mention of Peter, a brother older than Erasmus
by nearly three years. For this reason, plus other dis-
crepancies and differences of style, modern scholars are
dubious as to the authenticity of this *Compendium*.
Erasmus himself in 1523, when it was composed, had no
motive for concealing the facts. In the circles in which he
then moved none knew his father and for himself he had
been relieved by a papal dispensation from the disabilities
of illegitimacy. In asking for it he was entirely frank,
informing the pope that he was born of an unlawful and,
"as he feared, a sacrilegious union."[4]

His first schooling, we learn from reliable sources, was
at Gouda under a certain Peter Winkel. For a year the lad
was a chorister at Utrecht, presumably under the great
organist Obrecht.[5] Why Erasmus remained for only a
year we do not know. Perhaps because his voice did not
qualify. In later life it was weak. At any rate, the mother
took him, together with his brother Peter, and placed the
two in the school at Deventer. This meant a journey of
around a hundred miles and one wonders why she did not
select a school less distant. The reason was probably that
Deventer was the intellectual centre of the land. More
books were printed here than anywhere else in the Low
Countries, and more in the Low Countries than in
England, France, and Spain.[6]

Deventer was impregnated by the spirit of the *Devotio
Moderna*, the "modern piety" of the Brethren of the
Common Life. The movement originated two hundred
years before the time of Erasmus under the impact of
Gerard Groote (died 1340) of Deventer, who gathered a
following dedicated both to the contemplative and to the

Deventer in the sixteenth century.

active life. They lived in a community under a regimen like that of the monks, calling for fasts, vigils, reading, and prayer, privately and in common, interspersed by long periods of silence unrelieved by boisterous levity. The Brethren went out into the world to care for the sick and the poor and, above all, to teach children. Sometimes they established schools of their own, sometimes planted their members here and there as teachers in existing institutions. Their support came not from alms, but from labour, whether manual or literary, in particular from the copying of manuscripts, which continued to be in demand for some time after the invention of printing. This was work also in which the Sisters could engage, for there were houses also of a branch for women.

The movement called itself modern, but the modernity

lay rather in the area of zeal than of dogma.[7] The teaching
of the Church was accepted and discussion of her tenets
deprecated. Thomas à Kempis, the best known of the
Brethren, in his *Imitation of Christ* declared that the
"Trinity is better pleased by adoration than by speculation"[8] and he looked askance upon addiction to study.
There was thus an anti-intellectualistic strain in the
movement. The stress was placed upon piety and
deportment. The piety was marked by a heartfelt, lyrical
devotion to Jesus, with undeviating endeavour to follow
in his steps rather than to merge the self in the abyss of
the godhead. The Brethren were consequently fond of the
Latin mystics, Bernard and Bonaventura, rather than of
the German mystics, Eckhart, Suso, and Tauler.[9] Nor did
they conceive of piety as consisting in tearful dissolution
before the wounds of Christ. The following prayer to
Jesus by Thomas à Kempis turns upon the teaching and
example of the Master.[10]

Lord Jesus Christ, who art the light, true, eternal and un-
changing, who didst deign to descend to the prison of this
world to dispel the shadows of human ignorance and show us
the way to the land of eternal brightness, hear the prayers of
my humility, and by Thine immense mercy instil into me
that divine light which Thou hast promised to the world and
ordered to be preached to all peoples, that I may know Thy
way throughout my earthly pilgrimage. Thou art the mirror
of life, the torch of all holiness. . . . Thou hast set Thyself
before me as an example for living. . . . be Thou my joy, the
sweetness of my soul. Dwell Thou with me and I with Thee,
with all the world shut out. Be Thou my teacher, my Master,
and may Thy teaching be my wisdom.

One observes that there is no reference to Christ as the
propitiator. He is the enlightener, the exemplar, the
beloved companion, and the Lord.

One of the most persistent notes in the piety of the Brethren was inwardness. "Learn to despise the outward. Direct thyself to the inward and thou shalt see the kingdom of God come within thee."[11] "Strive to withdraw thy heart from all love of the visible and transfer it to the invisible."[12] Inwardness admits of no compulsion, and objection to constraint militates against lifelong vows which constrain the monk to go through exercises in which the mind perchance no longer believes and to which the heart no longer responds. To go on repeating by rote is the utter stultification of piety. The movement at the outset dispensed with lifelong vows, but such was the pressure from the older orders, who feared lest the more flexible rule would undercut their own recruiting, that one branch of the Brethren yielded and joined the Augustinian Canons Regular. Others, however, stoutly held out for their freedom.[13]

The ethical concern of the Brethren made some of them hospitable to the writings of classical antiquity. Gerard Groote in his writings cited nineteen classical authors as over against twenty-one Christian. He was particularly attracted to the moralists Seneca and Cicero.[14] The disposition to draw upon the pagan preparation for the gospel received a great impetus from the Italian Renaissance. Rudolf Agricola, trained at Groningen in the atmosphere of the Brethren, went to Italy and was there imbued with Petrarch's ideal of elegant diction, to be employed, however, only in the service of religion. For Agricola the cultivation of the soul, man's immortal component, was to be undertaken by way of erudition leading to the tranquil and unshakable seat of wisdom.[15] To this end he acquired proficiency not only in Latin, of course, but also in Greek and Hebrew. Erasmus, when twelve years old, heard him speak at Deventer. A younger

man than Agricola was his friend Alexander Hegius of
like aspirations. While Agricola wrote about education,
Hegius practised it as head of the school at Deventer.
Erasmus, in his last year there as a scholar, heard him
lecture on special days. For both men Erasmus entertained a high regard and found in their example a
tremendous confirmation for his own later battle on
behalf of a broader study of the humanities, the more so
because these men could not be reproached with any
deviation from the faith, from the Church, or even from
the Brethren. Agricola was buried in the cowl of a
Franciscan.[16]

One observes thus two strands in the tradition of the
Brethren. The one represented by à Kempis was fearful
lest any sort of learning might wither the spirit. The
other, stemming from Groote and flowering in Agricola
and Hegius, could appropriate the classical heritage. The
two attitudes were to conflict. Erasmus was to champion
the liberal wing while retaining essentially the piety of
à Kempis.

The educational system at Deventer, when Erasmus
entered, had not yet felt the force of the new currents.
The methods of instruction were still medieval, failing
to make proper use of printed texts and relying instead
for the teaching of Latin on the memorization of
mnemonic verses embodying the rules of grammar.
Erasmus felt that the best way to learn a language is to
memorize a modicum of rules and then to steep oneself
in its literature. He learned Horace and Terence by heart.
Why he should have done so with such enthusiasm and
so little encouragement he could explain only by saying
that he was impelled by some elementary drive. "An
occult force of nature drove me to the humanities."[17]
Erasmus was a predestinarian, not with regard to man's

destiny, as was Luther, but with regard to man's endowment.

The school days at Deventer were terminated by the death of the father and mother within a year of each other through the plague .Erasmus and his brother came then under the tutelage of their old school teacher at Gouda, Peter Winkel. Apparently he had little feeling or understanding of Erasmus' literary exploits, for when the lad wrote him a letter in his most polished Latin style, Peter told him next time to enclose a commentary.[18] What to do for the boys was a problem. They were orphans, the illegitimate sons of a priest, and the funds which the father had left for them had dwindled. If they wanted to be scholars, and if they were poor, the only hope appeared to lie through some form of monasticism. Peter arranged to send them to a school of the Brethren at Bois-le-Duc. There they stayed for two years. Erasmus considered this time the least profitable of his whole career. The Brethren in that particular house were certainly not in the tradition of Groote, let alone of Agricola and Hegius.

At the end of the period the boys felt ripe for the university and wished to go, even though penniless. Others had managed it somehow. But Winkel evidently thought they would be more secure in a monastic order. The boys resisted taking perpetual vows and in so doing were entirely in line with Groote and those of the Brethren who had refused to be incorporated. In after years Erasmus regretted that he had not identified himself with the original branch. Then, why did he not? Presumably because he had just spent two years with them at Bois-le-Duc where the inmates did not share his interests. A strong inducement for joining the Augustinian Canons at Steyn was that they had a good library. Luther entered the monastery to save his soul by good works, Erasmus to enlighten his mind by good books. He was then sixteen years of age.[19]

The year of the novitiate appears to have been to his taste particularly because he was granted unusual latitude. He was not required to keep the vigils, which interrupted his sleep, nor to observe the fasts by eating only fish, which upset his digestion. God had equipped him with an acute mind and a fastidious stomach, which churned at the smell of salt fish, a very inconvenient trait in a land where salt fish was a staple of the daily diet. With regard to all of his idiosyncrasies he was treated with indulgence and he felt that the monastic life had much in its favour.[20] One recalls the experience of Martin Luther, who said that during the first year in the monastery the Devil is relatively quiet. At the end of the year Erasmus took the vows.

A modern historian contends that throughout Erasmus' entire monastic period the devil was quiet and that the story of resistance to taking the vows was a later fabrication designed to secure a dispensation under the plea of duress from monastic obligations.[21] Support for this assumption is found in the fact that Erasmus is known to have reworked a tract written in the monastery against the monks who discountenanced pagan literature. The work was first published in 1522 some thirty years after the original composition. An earlier draft has been edited by this historian who feels that the subsequent revision has sharpened the strictures. But this is not at all apparent. True that in the first version Erasmus does not speak of the decline of the Church, but he does speak of the decline of the age, in which the Church is included. True that in the earlier version he impugns only obscurantists in general, but in the later mentions specifically the

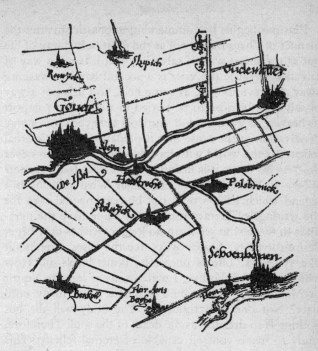

Gouda and Steyn.

Franciscans and Dominicans. This means that he had become more discriminating, for he had no criticism of his own order, the Augustinians. A second and more pertinent piece of evidence is adduced in that while in the monastery Erasmus wrote a tract, *On Contempt of the World*, with praises of monasticism. A concluding chapter largely nullifies what has preceded.[22] The modern historian says that this must have been added thirty years later.

Let us review this composition and then assess its import.

Erasmus begins by commending monasticism after the manner of Chrysostom, not as the most heroic way of life but as the surest way of salvation. But it is not a way of salvation because the vow is a second baptism washing away all previous sins, as some held, and it is not a way of salvation because to be buried in a cowl is a passport to heaven, as even Rudolf Agricola believed. It is a way of salvation in the sense that it prepares man for eternal felicity, as the world with its ephemeral values can never do. "As for fame, it is fleeting. Where now is Alexander? Where is Xerxes? Where Hannibal? What remains is a legend which itself would not be remembered save for the writings of literary men. What value have the pyramids to those who see them no longer? Riches only beget desire for more. Beauty wilts like the roses, friends flit like swallows. Life is uncertain, death levels all. How many are there who live, I will not say as long as Nestor or Methuselah, but to be a hundred? How many until sixty? Not one in a thousand! The body will die but nothing is so dreadful as the death of the soul. Therefore, study to make yourself capable of eternal felicity. This you can do best by secreting yourself from the seductions of the world."

Everything thus far could have been said by a Stoic or a Cynic in antiquity. So also could much that follows. But the more specifically Christian notes begin to appear.

Erasmus continues that the preparation of the soul requires separation from the distractions and disturbances of the world. When the poet is seized by the divine madness he must withdraw from the crowd. When the architect or the artist is conceiving some great plan he must be quiet. So is it with the preparation of the soul. Elijah found the Lord, not in the earthquake or the fire, but in the still small voice. "Where did Moses see the burning bush? Not in the cities of Egypt, but on the mount. Where were the Ten Commandments delivered, if not from out the storm cloud brooding on the brow of Sinai? Where was John the Baptist reared, that he should be able with his finger to designate the Lord? Not in palaces, but in the wilderness. How often did our Lord withdraw to desert places apart! So, also, did Pythagoras and Plato. What room is there for meditation amid the disturbances which recently beset our land? We have seen men living on the fodder of cattle and dying of hunger. The monastery offers an asylum of tranquillity."

Erasmus continues:

The monastic life affords liberty, for Cicero said that liberty is the ability to live as you wish. If, then, you wish to be a monk, you have liberty. But above all, monastic life offers the highest felicity. For some this consists in the vision of celestial things. St. Bernard said that the vision of God, should it last but half an hour, yet exceeds every delight of the world. I have myself seen men dissolve in tears of joy, though I confess the experience has never been mine. And to a man of learning what felicity the monastery affords! Here he may read and ruminate and write books. Delights never cease, since books are so varied. For the sources of our faith, turn to the Old Testament and the New. For eloquence to Jerome, Augustine, Arnobius, and Cyprian. Or, if you are more fastidious, to Lactantius, the Christian Cicero. If you wish meatier fare take Albertus Magnus, or Thomas. In books you have the treasures of Holy Writ, the monuments of the prophets and the apostles, the commentators and the doctors. You have the writings of the philosophers and the poets. They are not to be eschewed, for among the noxious plants there are also healing herbs. To be among such writings, with leisure and freedom from fear, is not this to taste the delights of Paradise? Here are roses red and lilies white, here purple violets and the fragrance of sweet thyme. The fruit is delicious and salubrious. Through this garden flows a limpid murmuring stream. In this charming retreat you are free to wander at your pleasure.

For the sake of the monastic life, one who is committed to it should with dry eyes console a weeping mother seeking to dissuade him from his resolve and thrust from him a sister clinging to his neck.

Then in Chapter Twelve comes an epilogue which certainly qualifies, if indeed it does not nullify, the tract itself. "I see," says Erasmus to his imaginary reader, "that you are packing your bags to enter the monastery. Let me warn you not to be too precipitant. Do not let yourself down a well from which you cannot get out." Then follows an account of how contemporary monasticism had declined from the primitive period of the early centuries. "Many now," Erasmus continues, "enter the monastery and the monastic life for improper reasons. One has been jilted, another frightened by sickness into taking a vow. Some have been cajoled by parents or tutors who wanted to be rid of them. I would strenuously dissuade a young person from taking a vow which cannot be recalled. Some are induced by superstition and folly, and think they are monks because they have a cord and a cowl. You need not think vows will do you any good if you violate the vow made to Christ in baptism." Erasmus is here making the point that the interior piety of the *Devotio Moderna* would not result automatically from entering the monastery and was quite possible on the outside.

How now is this tract to be understood? Erasmus himself said that the essay was written as a literary composition. This meant something quite specific. The humanists revived the practice of the ancient rhetoricians in assigning to students propositions which they should both defend and refute. The one essay was called a persuasive, the other a dissuasive, *suasoria* and *dissuasoria*. Originally this practice was a device for training lawyers to take either side of a case, and, when the law declined, was continued in the rhetorical schools as an exercise. The danger was obvious that the student might become indifferent to truth. The risk could be avoided if one brief were much stronger than the other, or if the circumstances were varied so that a course defensible in one case would not be in another.[23] Erasmus used both devices. The normal procedure was to write both essays at the same time. Erasmus did this on a later occasion with reference to the war of Pope Julius against Venice, but his *suasoria* for marriage was followed only several years later by the *dissuasoria*. There is reason to believe that the essay *On Contempt of the World* was a *suasoria* in favour of monasticism. The epilogue is the outline of a *dissuasoria*. It may have been added years later. It might perfectly well have been written at the same time.

The essay contains within itself a clear indication that it is a statement of what could be said, of what had been said, in favour of monasticism, and not necessarily of what Erasmus believed, though much indeed need not have been repugnant to his conviction. The alien element is the statement where he urged one committed to the monastic life to console a weeping mother with dry eyes and to repulse a clinging sister.[24] This does not sound like Erasmus at any time. As a matter of fact it has been lifted out of the letter of Jerome to Heliodorus, an ex-soldier, who, having become a monk, then left the cell to become a secular priest. Jerome remonstrated saying: "Should your mother, with ashes on her head and with garments rent, display the breasts that gave you suck, heed her not. Should your father prostrate himself before you, trample on him. With dry eyes fly to the standard of the cross. In such cases cruelty is the only true affection."[25] Jerome himself has often been reproached for the brutality of this passage until it was discovered that in his case also it was rhetoric. He adapted this speech from a *suasoria* in favour of the camp by Seneca the Rhetor, where an army recruit is ready to trample under foot a father who would hold him from the battle.[26] His heartlessness is transferred by Jerome to the *militia Christi*. Erasmus in the present tract takes issue with the saint only in the epilogue. When editing Jerome he refuted him directly, saying that in the saint's day one might so talk to a pagan parent trying to keep a child from becoming a Christian, but certainly not in modern times to a parent restraining a child from becoming a "religious," as if the laity also were not religious.[27]

Clearly, then, what we have here is a *suasoria* in full and a *dissuasoria* in outline. They may well have been written coincidentally. This means that the attitude of Erasmus to monasticism in this early period was discriminating.

But we are not left to conjecture based on the revision of documents real or assumed. We have the letters of Erasmus from the monastic period. These enable us to see that during his six years at Steyn the Devil was not quiet. Erasmus went through both an interior and an exterior crisis. The interior was set up for him, as for Luther, by the fear of death. Erasmus testified that in his youth he had trembled at the very mention of the name of death.[28] But the ground of anxiety was different for the two men. Luther shrank from the sight of a crucifix because the Christ on the cross would some day sit upon a rainbow to consign the damned to eternal perdition. Erasmus shuddered at death because it might cut him off before he could so far progress in virtue as to be "capable of eternal life." The difference is evidenced in the words used by the two men to describe their depressions. Luther called his *Anfechtung*. The word suggests an assault from without, an attack by the Devil. The only hope lay in a conquest from without by Christ, who for us overcame the Devil, Death, and Hell. Erasmus called his depressions *pusillanimitas*,[29] literally, weakness of spirit, faint-heartedness, for which we have the little-used English derivative, pusillanimity. This implies a weakness within, which man can do something to remedy by pulling himself together. In Luther's case moral effort was useless, but not so for Erasmus.

Yet to say to oneself, "brace up," is, after all, not so easy. Erasmus craved the support of others and fastened his affections upon a fellow monk, Servatius Rogers. The opportunities of conversing with him were scant, in view of the religious exercises and the silences imposed by the rule. Erasmus, in tears, poured out his affection in a letter, with an impulsiveness by which Servatius was frightened.[30] The original rule of the Brethren discouraged "too intimate friendships, which are open to the suspicion of carnal affections."[31] Erasmus needed a spiritual father like Staupitz and found one, or, rather, a spiritual mother and she not even a nun. Berthe de Heyen was a wealthy widow who declined to remarry and devoted herself to the nurture of her daughters, who entered the cloister, and to the care of the poor, and to assisting the monks and the Brethren, for whom she built five houses. Her own home was a hostel in which they were assured of entertainment and spiritual counsel. On her death Erasmus wrote to console her daughters. He began by saying that he was so overcome he could scarcely write. Many times he had tried but now for their sake he would overcome his wound. "You, dear sisters, will understand my suffering. When I was left an orphan she consoled me. She lifted me out of my faint-heartedness. She guided me with her counsel. She cared for me as if I had come from her own womb." She had helped, in a measure, with regard to his fear of death, for at the funeral of a young bride who had died suddenly six weeks after her marriage, Berthe alone was composed. "There is no occasion for wailing," she assured Erasmus; "the Lord has given, the Lord has taken away. Blessed be the name of the Lord. If we fight valiantly, great will be our reward, and God will not suffer us to be tempted beyond our strength." Erasmus, therefore, comforted the daughters that their mother had now joined the Apostles and the martyrs, the Virgin and the angels who sing about the throne of the Lamb.[32]

But still this consolation did not quite meet his own needs. If death cut him off would he be fit to sing about the throne of the Lamb? Life is a preparation for death. With renewed ardour Erasmus sank himself in his studies and found them a therapeutic. There was a parallel here to the experience of St. Jerome, who exorcised his temptations by filling his mind with the rigorous discipline of learning Hebrew. And there was also a parallel to Luther, whose evangelical insight dawned as he laboured over the exposition of the Psalms. Study helped because at any rate it meant doing something. But more than that it supplied the need for friendship, not with the living to be sure, but with the immortal dead. Erasmus was better acquainted with Jerome and Seneca than with his own prior. Then, too, it brought contemporary friendships. Fellow monks were stirred to share in the quest, notably William Hermann, for whose poems Erasmus subsequently found a publisher. The circle of friendship went even beyond the walls of Steyn to a neighbouring monastery where lived a like spirit in Cornelius Gerhard. Physical separation in this case necessitated correspondence: happily many of the letters have survived. Here was friendship on a new level, directed not to a person as a person but built upon a common devotion to a quest, greater than either participant. The enthusiasm of the few kindled the many. All the brothers began to devote themselves to study and Steyn was being converted into a veritable university.

At this point came the exterior crisis. The superior intervened. One can well understand why, if all of the monks were following the example of Erasmus in disregarding vigils and fasts. He received an order to put aside his books and lay down his pen. He was constrained, he said, "to rot in idleness." His letters take on a tone of martyrdom.[33] He revenged himself by writing the tract *Antibarbari* (*Against the Barbarians*), approximately in his nineteenth year.[34] Somewhat later the work was recast in the form of a dialogue to make it more diverting.[35] After still further revision it appeared in print in 1520, more than thirty years from the date of the original composition.[36]

The immediate object was to justify the use of pagan learning. At this point Erasmus was no innovator. He had behind him an imposing tradition within the circle of those stemming from the *Devotio Moderna.* Like Groote, Hegius, and Agricola he was taking his stand against the conservatives and in so doing was in line with a venerable tradition within the Church. The early Christians had wrestled with the problem of what to retain from the Jewish and pagan background. Some wished to reject the

Old Testament which enjoined the keeping of the law which the Christians had discarded. Some desired to reject the classics which celebrated the exploits and amours of the gods. The Church decided to retain both with discrimination. Unassimilable elements were allegorized. Erasmus drew from the whole tradition of the Christian defence of the classics while adding spice of his own. "You tell me that we should not read Virgil because he is in hell. Do you think that many Christians are not in hell whose works we read? It is not for us to discuss whether the pagans before Christ were damned. But if I may conjecture, either they are saved or no one is saved. If you want to reject everything pagan you will have to give up the alphabet and the Latin language, and all the arts and crafts." Erasmus was quite right on that score. The technology of the sixteenth century had advanced little beyond that of the Roman Empire. "You say you do not want to be called a Platonist or a Ciceronian but you do not mind being called an Albertist or a Thomist. You say that knowledge puffs up and makes men arrogant. Was that true of Augustine and Jerome? And perhaps, in any case, God, in his economy, has a place for pride, if it be not inordinate. A touch of self-esteem prods the beginner to great endeavours. As for the ancients, we must discriminate. Some things among the pagans are useless, dubious, and harmful. Some are highly serviceable, salutary, and even necessary."

But the objection was not so easily quashed, for the aim of scholarship is knowledge, and how is knowledge of God to be acquired? Christianity asserts that such knowledge comes by way of God's unique self-disclosure in Christ. At a point in time He became incarnate in Christ, whose commission was confirmed by miracles and recorded in books. Their meaning has been elucidated

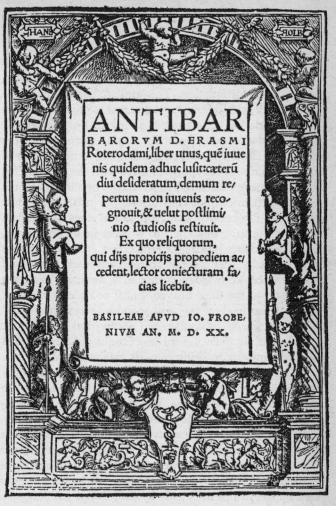

ANTIBAR

BARORVM D. ERASMI
Roterodami, liber unus, quẽ iuue
nis quidem adhuc lusit: cæterũ
diu desideratum, demum re/
pertum non iuuenis reco/
gnouit, & uelut postlimi/
nio studiosis restituit.
Ex quo reliquorum,
qui dijs propicijs propediem ac/
cedent, lector coniecturam fa/
cias licebit.

BASILEAE APVD IO. FROBE/
NIVM AN. M. D. XX.

The title page of the *Antibarbari:* with Holbein's name at the top
and Froben's mark at the bottom.

and formulated by the Church. This revelation is not to be called into question. This Erasmus believed. But the classical world made the approach to God by way of insight and inference. For the pagan, revelation is not so much a deposit as a quest, never ending, never amenable to definitive formulation. This attitude passed over into Christianity with reference, at any rate, to the elucidation of the revelation once and for all given. But the deposit and the quest have been in tension throughout the history of Christian thought, and never more so than in Erasmus himself. He comes to grips with the problem for the first time in this tract. He certainly would not deny the historic revelation, but emphatically he insists that direct revelation has ceased. The Holy Ghost does not sit as a dove on the back of a chair to whisper in anybody's ear, as in the pictures of Gregory the Great. "There are those who ask why they should fritter away their days over books when knowledge comes in a flash, as Paul was caught up to the third heaven. But if you are looking for flashes from heaven you will spend a lifetime waiting." Erasmus himself, of course, had no mystical experiences. "And after all, even if Paul was caught up, nevertheless he told Timothy to bring him his manuscripts."

Knowledge does not come in that way. But how, then? By proceeding from nature to grace, from reason to revelation. This, of course, was the Thomistic methodology. "The pagans, who knew only the light of nature, were not in darkness but were illumined by the 'rays shining from the immortal light' and we may use them as our stairs. For he who tries to scale the battlements of Heaven meets with God's displeasure but he who ascends step by step is not to be cast down." But proceeding step by step does mean that we shall have to be tentative. Erasmus praised the Academics (the Sceptics of antiquity) who "preferred to dispute modestly rather than confidently to affirm." He came close to admitting the charge that "piety depends on faith, but scholarship investigates by arguments and brings everything into question."[37]

Erasmus did not think that the end of the quest was nothing but a point of interrogation. Yet he could discover in history no unbroken ascent in the acquisition of knowledge, and his own period was marked by a decline in erudition, if judged by classical standards. Why should there not be a continuous ascent? The search for an answer led to an examination of the ebb and flow of history. The conclusion was that even the periods of recession may be making unseen gains as winter stores resources for the coming spring. Another significant observation is that one period devotes itself to one phase of truth, another to another. Their findings appear contradictory, but the disharmony could not be more harmonious: *discordia sed nihil concordius*. There is a coincidence of opposites. Here we are verging on the view of Cusa that truth finds its best expression in paradox. Yet if it be thought that this process yields no definite results let it be remembered that the heretics were refuted by the scholars, and much more by the scholars than by the martyrs. By dying for a conviction a man proves only that he is sincere, not that he is right. The truth of his claim must be established by a rigorous examination of its validity. The scholars have therefore benefited the Church more than the martyrs.

Two other writings of the monastic period were programmatic. An essay on peace and war contained already the essential notes of the campaign which Erasmus waged until his death. The tract is significant further as the proof that Erasmus in his pleas for peace was not actuated by ulterior motives in the hope of an emolument from a prince whose policy at the moment called for peace.

The little *Oration on Peace and Discord*[38] begins with themes drawn from classical authors. "Nothing is more agreeable than peace, nothing more frightful than war." Man of all creatures, born without claws, is contrived to live by benevolence. Nature confesses that she seeks to mollify men by conferring upon them alone the gift of tears, that they may grieve over each other's woes; but, alas, ambition, avarice, and petulance have impelled even brothers to assail each other so that there is more concord even among beasts. What serpent ever tried to poison another serpent? Does the lion prey on the lion, the wolf on the wolf? Even the tigers of India preserve concord among themselves. But men, infected by the rabies of discord, devour one another.

This is from Juvenal.

It was not always so, continues Erasmus, for in the Golden Age men dwelt secure, without gold, living joyously from the fruits of the earth. They slept carefree in caves, or in the open. But we, beneath our roofs, toss with anxiety. How much better was their poverty with peace than our opulence with contention! Could they rise from their graves they would think us demented.

This is from Ovid and Seneca.

Consider also the heavens, though they are not inhabited by a rational soul, as some philosophers suppose, nevertheless they keep their orbits in tempered harmony. If this mechanism of the stars cannot endure without peace for a day, let alone forever, how shall we neglect that which is so needful?

This is from Dion of Prusa.[39]

Then come the Christian motifs. Erasmus employs the figure utilized by the apostle Paul of the necessity of co-ordination among the members of the body. The section following in Erasmus is an adaptation of Paul's words: "If I give my body to be burned and have not love, I am as sounding brass and a clanging cymbal": "What good are monastic lacerations of the flesh and a perpetual babbling of the lips?" asks Erasmus. "Those who think they can practise any virtue without peace are the ones whom the Lord called 'whited sepulchers.' Concord enhances, discord vitiates all things. What destroyed Troy? What Carthage? What Corinth and Rome? What if not factional strife? [This theme is prominent in Sallust.] But enough of ancient history," says Erasmus. (Thus far he might only have been writing a literary declamation. From here on he speaks of what he knows.) "What land would be more opulent than ours, if not despoiled by petulant factionalism!" This statement hardly comports with the praise of his countrymen already quoted as free from belligerence and truculence, but the picture which follows is the true one. Holland, for nearly two centuries, had been rent by the strife of two warring factions, the Hoeks (fishermen) and the Kabeljauws[40] (codfish), whose names might have been invented in satire by a Swift or a Voltaire, but there is neither fiction nor satire in what Erasmus goes on to say. He continues:

The fields of our land are rich with harvests, the meadows with cattle, the nearby sea with fish, and affluence abounds. Why does this not suffice us? Tears start as one views the calamities of our time. Harvests are burned, villages given to the flames. Some labourers are killed, some captured, some become fugitives. Women are abused, virgins violated, wives abducted, no road is safe, no path of the sea is clear of this tiger of violence. In the cities famine stalks, justice is buried, laws overthrown, liberty oppressed, all is confusion. Who is not moved to tears by the manifold ways in which men are wiped out, by starvation, hanging, the sword, the wheel – a prey to birds? Debased nobles suffer in battle a death debasing and the common folk fall without number and without name.

Concord binds in a sweet bond, discord disrupts even those who are joined by blood. The one builds cities, the other demolishes; the one creates wealth, the other dissipates. Discord turns men into beasts. Concord unites souls after death with God. I do not exhort you, I do not pray you, I implore you, seek peace.

This tract was more than an academic exercise because peace was imperative for the realization of the programme which Erasmus had come to envision as his vocation – to reform society and the Church through education. The character of his calling took shape in his mind partly through the influence of an Italian; one may say that Erasmus was Italianized before ever he went to Italy. The first of the Italians to affect him was Lorenzo Valla. He was esteemed in the circle of the *Devotio Moderna*, not only as a philologian, but also as an apologist for Christianity. That he could be so understood may surprise the student who associates with Valla the assertion that a harlot is to be preferred to a nun because a nun denies the claims of nature. But one is not to forget that this statement occurs in a dialogue in the mouth of an Epicurean as popularly understood. He is refuted by a Stoic, and the Stoic in turn by a Christian. Which of the three interlocutors did Valla endorse? The Brethren believed that his real opinion was that of the Christian; today one who reads the concluding section, ending in a rhapsody on the Virgin Mary after the manner of St. Bernard, will find it hard to think that this is throughout a mere rhetorical exercise.

Be that as it may, Valla, as a proponent of rhetoric rather than dialectic, influenced Erasmus. The symbol of dialectic was the closed fist because of the close-knit reasoning. The symbol of rhetoric was the open hand which dispenses truth through the art of persuasion, through eloquence, which depends on words – and in this case Latin words. To distinguish their shades of meaning, Valla wrote a tract entitled *Elegantiae*[41] of which Erasmus now made an epitome, arranging the words in alphabetical order as in a dictionary. This was the first venture of Erasmus as a teacher of teachers by providing the tools of the craft.

Valla also sharpened Erasmus' historical sense by correcting the popular misunderstanding of Epicurus whose teaching was supposedly summed up in the maxim, "Eat, drink, and be merry." Epicurus did say that the chief end of life is *hedoné*, which does not mean hedonism. Nor did it mean voluptuousness when Valla translated it as *voluptas*. These words meant rather felicity which could be equated with the Christian beatitude. In this sense Erasmus could call monasticism the true Epicureanism. Valla thus did for Epicurus what Aquinas had done for Aristotle and the Florentine Academy for Plotinus. Another pagan could be regarded as a Christian precursor. Erasmus learned, then, from Valla the role of eloquence, the meaning of words, and the sense of history.

The programme of Erasmus did not conflict with monasticism as such, but the full realization of his dream required that he be not restricted to residence at Steyn. He grew restive, but did not break with the Brethren there who ordained him to the priesthood in 1492. They came later to look upon him as their luminary. Whenever in the region in after years he paid them visits. The prior himself it was, Werner by name, who perceiving the disquiet of Erasmus, suggested that he might be happier as the secretary of a bishop[42] and quite possibly Werner was the one who arranged that Erasmus should enter the service of Henry of Bergen, the bishop of Cambrai. This prelate would have no indisposition to engage the illegitimate son of a priest, seeing that he was himself one of the thirty-six bastards of John, the Lord of Bergen.[43] The bishop needed a secretary to carry on his correspondence with the pope and cardinals among whom he aspired to be enrolled. To receive the red hat he must go to Rome, and Erasmus would be at his side. How exciting to visit Italy, the land of eminent scholars, the land of abundant manuscripts, the land of imperishable memories! *Italia pulcherrima, gloria mundi!* Apparently Erasmus was enjoined to silence until the day of his departure lest he disquiet the monks at Steyn. At any rate he did not confide in his most intimate friend, William Hermann, who sent after him a poem tinged with reproach and avowed envy:

> I must stay and you will go
> To brave the Rhine and Alpine snow.
> To go for you, to stay for me,
> And you will see fair Italy.[44]

CHAPTER TWO

Scholasticism and Eloquence: Paris

*

BUT the longing to see fair Italy was not to be gratified for another decade. The bishop learned without going to Rome that he was not to receive the red hat. A contemporary explained that his funds for bribery were deficient, though this need not be assumed, for he had earlier made himself obnoxious to His Holiness.[1] At any rate the bishop was not made a cardinal and remained at home. Erasmus was retained and assigned routine tasks which he found highly distasteful.[2] Inevitably he was dejected,[3] but happily the bishop was not exacting and gave him some liberty to pursue his own interests. He took advantage of this freedom to examine the library of the Augustinian priory of Groenendael in the forest of Zonia near Brussels and there he discovered works of St. Augustine in manuscript. He was so excited that he took them to bed with him. The monks were amazed and amused that one of their number should go to bed with St. Augustine and could not understand what on earth he found in the saint so to delight him.[4]

Erasmus was consoled not only by thus discovering a friend among the departed but also because he made the acquaintance of a fellow spirit among the living. James Batt, the town secretary of Bergen, after training at the university of Paris, had become the schoolmaster at Bergen, where he had attempted to introduce the humanist studies so dear to Erasmus. The other teachers, addicted to the ancient ways, so harassed him that he resigned to become the secretary to the city. The ire of Erasmus against the "barbarians" was rekindled on hearing this recital and he set himself to rework his earlier polemic, casting it now into the form of a dialogue with Batt as the leading speaker. The scene was laid, as commonly in Renaissance dialogues, in a sylvan retreat. The participants included William Hermann, Erasmus' old friend from Steyn, who had come expressly to meet Batt, together with a physician and the Mayor of Bergen, who brought also his wife and daughters for an outing. He was twitted for injecting nymphs into a Platonic discussion, to which he retorted that they would be the chorus. Batt eloquently recounted his battle with the obscurantists. Hermann proposed that Apollo crown him as a new Hercules and the discussion commenced.[5]

The significance of this scene lies partly in the preponderance of the laity. Over against the two monks were a physician, the town secretary, and the mayor, all with kindred interests. Here was the manifest evidence of the dictum later voiced by Erasmus, "Monasticism is not piety. It is simply a way of living."[6] Batt was of immense service to Erasmus when it came to the business of living. With indefatigable devotion he sought to secure for his friend the means to devote himself exclusively to the training requisite for the role of an educator of educators. The case called for a lifetime endowment as a research scholar. In that day the only possible recourse was to find a Maecenas, or preferably several. Batt assumed the role of mediator in mendicancy, first with the Bishop of Cambrai, and then with Anne of Veere, a wealthy woman to whose service Batt had transferred as tutor to her son Adolf. The hyperbolic effusions of flattery which Erasmus

through Batt addressed to her have ever since been distasteful to the reader, as indeed they were at the time to
Erasmus.[7] He need not have been quite so fulsome as to
set up a triad of Annes, the first the mother of Samuel,
the second the mother of the Virgin Mary, and the third,
Anne of Veere. But let not those with university tenure
or grants from foundations cast the first stone. Besides,
Erasmus could be equally extravagant in praising one
from whom no stipend could be expected. In an admonition to virtue, addressed to young Adolf, Erasmus
introduced an encomium of Batt. How fortunate, he said,
was Philip of Macedon in finding Aristotle as a tutor for
Alexander and even so was the father of Adolf fortunate
in finding a tutor for his son in Batt. What Plato was
to Dionysius, what Socrates was to Alcibiades, what
Seneca was to Nero (where did this comparison put
Adolf?), all this Batt would be to the young De Veere.
Amid all this rhetorical bombast there was a sincere
word for Batt, "the rarest of men, erudite and
irreproachable."[8]

The response of the bishop to Batt's plea was to release
Erasmus that he might attend the university of Paris as a
candidate for the doctorate of theology. His first letter
thence is dated in the fall of 1495. If born in 1466 he was
then 29. Already he was a poet of distinction, well versed
in the Latin classics, notably Terence, Horace, Seneca,
Cicero, and Quintilian. Already he was addicted to St.
Jerome[9] and enthusiastic over St. Augustine. The Bishop
of Cambrai promised financial support for his residence
in Paris,[10] though whether much was paid is doubtful.[11]
At any rate Erasmus was enrolled among the poor
scholars at the Collège de Montaigu at Paris.

This college, founded in 1314, was in a deplorable
state in the year 1483 when the principalship was given to

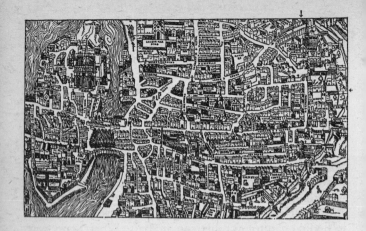

Paris in the sixteenth century, showing the college of Montaigu
(Mon Ecu).

Jean Standonck, who had received his early education
among the Brethren of the Common Life at Gouda. He
had then studied at the universities of Louvain and Paris,
supporting himself as a domestic at the Abbaye de St.
Germain. So little time was free for study that when
candles were available he would work at night. Once he
was badly burned by falling asleep over the flame. On
clear nights he would read under the moon on the tower
of Clovis. By dint of such diligence he acquired first the
master's and then the doctor's degree and lectured at the
Sorbonne on Peter Lombard and Aristotle. His bent was
not towards the classics, though he did not forbid them
to his students. On becoming the principal of Montaigu
he removed the weather cock on the tower and replaced
it with a cross and a lamb. A more ascetic tone was given
to his piety the year before the arrival of Erasmus. When,
at the consecration of the Mass, a certain Jean Langlois

had smashed the chalice by way of denying the real presence, Standonck, commissioned to reclaim him for the faith, had failed. To save his life Langlois abjured, but, being nevertheless condemned to the stake, re-affirmed his heresy. Standonck accompanied him to the pyre, exhorting with such passion that his voice failed. Thereafter for the remainder of his life he imposed upon himself a perpetual fast until he came to resemble a desert saint. His remorse was not that a heretic had been burned, but that a soul had not been saved.[12]

Standonck set himself unremittingly to reform the monasteries and the church of France. Much was amiss. Financial extortion and concubinage were rife.[13] A reforming preacher cried out that the painters were mistaken in portraying the Virgin and John the Baptist on their knees pleading for sinners. "They have quit in disgust," said he.[14] But Standonck was more patient than the Virgin and John the Baptist. To assist in the work of reform he enlisted the services of some of the Brethren of the Common Life, among them Cornelius Gerhard, the old friend of Erasmus. Another was Mombaer, whose devotional manual, the *Rosarium*, may well have influenced the *Spiritual Exercises* of Ignatius Loyola.[15] Erasmus was in lively touch with the whole circle, had frequent conferences with Standonck, and helped with his correspondence.[16]

At the same time Erasmus carried on a little reforma-tory work of his own, though in a different spirit. If Standonck exerted himself to reclaim a heretic already condemned, Erasmus intervened to save one from being condemned. While on a visit to Belgium he had been implored by a tearful girl to deliver her father from the toils of the Inquisition. Erasmus enlisted the help of Batt on the man's behalf and himself appealed to the abbot to impede the inquisitor, who, said Erasmus, was worthier of the stake than his victim.[17] The intervention was successful.

The impact of Standonck on all the varieties of the Reformation of the sixteenth century must have been profound. In the college of which he was the principal, the most prominent leaders of the three great reformatory movements had their training. The first was Erasmus of Rotterdam, the protagonist of the liberal Catholic reform, the second was John Calvin, the champion of the most militant Protestantism, and the third was Ignatius Loyola, who perhaps more than any other gave the edge to the intransigent Catholic reform called the Counter-Reformation.

Of the three Erasmus least resembled the master at the point of rigidity. The regimen at the college of Montaigu proved insufferable. Erasmus was enrolled in the *Collegia Pauperum*, which Standonck, mindful of his own struggles for an education, had established to assist indigent students. They were to do all of the washing, cooking, and scrubbing. The candidates in theology received no food until eleven in the morning when they were given a loaf, the thirtieth part of a pound of butter, some stewed fruit, vegetables cooked without fat, a herring, and two stale eggs purchased at reduced prices. Unruly students were flogged till the blood came.[18] Standonck endeavoured to improve the buildings and control the lice, but they eluded his efforts, according to Erasmus, who in later years reported that the cubicles on the ground floor had rotten plaster and were next to the latrines. The floggings, said he, were savage and the eggs rotten. Many promising students were permanently impaired in mind and body.[19] However much this picture may be overdrawn, Erasmus himself broke down, though we cannot say whether by reason of the privations or the recurrence of malaria. He was cured, so he believed, by the grace of St. Geneviève, the patroness of Paris,[20] and spent the summer recuperating in the household of the Bishop of Cambrai. Then he went back to Steyn, expecting presumably to remain indefinitely, but the Brothers encouraged him to resume his studies at Paris.[21]

He followed their counsel and this time took private lodgings, apparently with financial assistance from the bishop. A little incident of his stay in the boarding house is worth revealing.[22] The mistress punched the maid. When then she came to straighten his room Erasmus suggested that the next time she might pull off the lady's wig and snatch out her hair. He was amazed on returning to his lodging in the afternoon to be informed that the mistress and the maid had been discovered in a tussle amid tufts of hair. The quarrel was composed and he rejoiced not to have been suspected. This was not the first time that he was not perceived to be joking and he did not perceive that he was not perceived to be joking. To compose a quarrel was like him and also to conceal complicity in its inception. A further question of interest is the language in which he communicated with the maid. Did she speak Latin, or he French? She might have known a modicum of Latin to serve any of the thousands of students from all over Europe who were able to communicate with each other and with the French only in this tongue. On the other hand, Erasmus could apparently manage in French. He once wrote a letter in poor French, so he said,[23] and he enjoyed the repartee in French inns.[24] To understand repartee is the ultimate of any language.

Settled in his lodgings Erasmus returned to his studies. They were, of course, theological. Upon his teachers in this discipline Erasmus emptied the vials of scorn. They

Sophistam
spinis.

reminded him of Epimenides of Greek legend who slept
for forty-seven years, except that he did wake up.[25]
Erasmus was not incapable of exaggeration, but in this
instance he was not alone in his strictures. All along, one
scholastic had reproached another with wasting time on
sophisticated trivia.[26] Dorp, later Erasmus' friend in the
Netherlands, said that these theologians would debate
infinitely about infinity and would press a vacuum until
everything about it was vacuous.[27] The eminent Spanish
scholar, Vives, said that to leave the university of Paris
was to emerge from Stýgian darkness.[28] Rabelais, of
course, inundated the *théologastres* with Gargantuan
contempt. The verdict might perhaps have been different
if any of these teachers had been a scholar of distinction.[29]
We know who they were and none was outstanding. On
the other hand not even a keen mind could have made

the current scholasticism palatable to Erasmus. Many of
his strictures fitted precisely one of the most eminent
representatives of the school, who half a century earlier
had taught at Paris, Pierre D'Ailly.

The difficulty lay with the theology itself. It was called
the modern theology and its proponents, the *Moderni*.
This *Theologia Moderna* was remote in its interests from the
Devotio Moderna in which Erasmus had been nurtured.
The theologians of the new school were also philosophers
and their philosophy, called Nominalism, made difficulties
for the faith. They denied the existence of universals,
such as man, horse, or deity. Reality consists only of
particulars related to each other solely by contiguity in
space and time. This being the case no one universal
substance exists to hold the three persons of the Trinity
in unity and they must therefore be regarded as three
gods, that is to say, from the philosophical point of view.
This conclusion was escaped by a dualism between philosophy and theology, couched in terms of a double logic,
or a double mode of knowing.[30] The Nominalist
theologians revelled in conundra set up for theology by
philosophy. Erasmus was not philosophically minded.
Such riddles failed to meet his test for a fruitful discussion
that it must minister to edification and example, to piety
and morality.

Some of the problems engaging the Paris theologians
appeared to Erasmus to be idle because insoluble prior to
the day of judgment to which they should be deferred,
such as the riddles of fate and predestination,[31] and
whether the fire of purgatory is material. Better so to live,
commented Erasmus, as not to get into it, whatever it
may be.[32] These theologians, he added, talk as confidently
of hell as if they had been there.[33] Other questions
appeared idle because without practical bearing, as for

example the distinction between the *generation* of the Son by the Father and the *procession* of the Holy Ghost from the Father and the Son,[34] as the Latins hold, or from the Father alone according to the Greeks. Christ certainly did not bother himself about such questions, said Erasmus. What did the boy Jesus discuss with the doctors in the temple? You may be sure that he did not discuss the squaring of the circle, the *prima materia*, or the *primum mobile*.[35]

Other problems alienated Erasmus because he was at variance with the presuppositions from which they stemmed. The Nominalist theologians made much of the will of God as the ground of all that is and happens. The doctrine of God's omnipotence asserts that God can do whatever He will. In that case can He contradict Himself? Can He make black white? Can He make the past not to have been the past so that a harlot might be a virgin?[36] Can God set aside all the canons of Christian morality? Can He make right wrong? Can He cause a man to hate God? Erasmus perceived that absolute power corrupts even God. There must be some limitation, otherwise all the standards of Christian morality lose their religious undergirding.

Once more, can God do something preposterous as that He should become incarnate not in the man Christ Jesus but in an ass, a cucumber, or a stone?[37] This final question might have prompted serious inquiry in more than one direction. Comparative religion is involved because only Christianity makes the claim that God became incarnate in the form of a man. Other religions do assert that God inhabits animals and objects. Why should not God become incarnate in the bull of Apis, the dog-headed Anubis, the serpent of Aesculapius, the goat of Dionysus? Why not in the black stone of Emesa? And why not in an ass since in the Old Testament God caused Balaam's ass to speak and, in the *Metamorphoses* of Apuleius, the seeker Lucius has his vision of Isis after having been transformed into an ass? The Christian answer to these queries points to the theme dear to the Renaissance of the dignity of man. Erasmus did proclaim the dignity of man but he was not interested in relating this to the incarnation. Sufficient to believe that God did become incarnate in Christ, to believe, to adore, and to imitate.

Another question was whether God can confer upon man the power to create.[38] This also was a live question in the Renaissance which looked upon artists as creators. The concept did not originate with the Renaissance. Peter Lombard said that man cannot create in the same sense as God who makes something out of nothing. Neither can man forgive as God forgives. But in a sense man can forgive and man can create. Aquinas said that it were better to call man not a creator, but a co-creator.[39] The whole question carried with it for Erasmus a touch of arrogance. He had no itch to become a creative writer or a creative scholar. His role was not to create but to transmit the wisdom of the seers and the grace of the Gospel.

Again there were questions on which scholars, if they liked, might sharpen their wits in an esoteric diversion, but they should certainly not disseminate their conundra to the scandal of the faithful. One may say, to be sure, that in a sense the three persons of the Trinity are three gods, that is to say, philosophically speaking, but not theologically. But how will the uninitiated ever grasp this distinction? Simplicity is a criterion for relevance.

From all this we are not to infer that Erasmus rejected scholasticism altogether and learned nothing from the scholastics. Such is not the case. When later he came to write on marriage and divorce he was able to cite not only the Old Testament and the New, the Fathers and the canon lawyers, but also the scholastics *in extenso*. He had read Peter Lombard, Thomas Aquinas, Ockham, Scotus, Bonaventura, D'Ailly, Biel, and Gerson.[40] From beginning to end Erasmus insisted that he was not a foe to scholasticism *in toto*, nor to dialectic.

At the same time we are not to think of him as wholly immersed in theological studies. While in Paris he particularly sought out the circle dedicated to his own enthusiasm for the formation of character through the appropriation afresh of the classical and Christian heritage. There were such persons at Paris and had been for some time. During the middle years of the previous century Guillaume Fichet had taught both rhetoric and theology at the Sorbonne in the belief that the eloquence of the Italian humanists and the theology of the scholastics could be combined.[41] His successor, Robert Gaguin, was a churchman, the general of the Maturins, a humanist who taught rhetoric at the Sorbonne, as Fichet had done before him, a diplomat sent on missions all over Europe by the French crown, a Gallican resisting papal pretensions, and an ardent Frenchman who thought the French and the English could get along no better than the wolf and the lamb.[42] Erasmus sent him a poem accompanied by a letter of fulsome praise. Gaguin was pleased with the poem, but, as for the flattery, told him to drop the nonsense and talk like a man, yet assured him of his friendship, for "a common devotion to learning is the mucilage of affection."[43] Erasmus enlisted Gaguin's influence on behalf of his friend William Hermann, who had been left rueful in the monastery when Erasmus started supposedly for Italy. Now Hermann's poems appeared in a graceful little volume with a commendatory letter by Gaguin and a prefatory commendation by Herasmus (as Erasmus then spelled his name).[44]

Gaguin was responsible also for the first appearance in print of a composition by this same Herasmus. Gaguin had written a history of France. His manuscript did not quite fill out the final quire and he invited the young humanist to utilize the space. This was a delicate assignment, because Gaguin's history of France might be called chauvinistic and such a spirit was utterly alien to the temper of Erasmus. Did he stultify himself in order to get his name into print? See how he handled the case. "The love of country," says Erasmus, "is a noble passion and France is a noble country. Who is more qualified to chant her praise than Gaguin who combines the elegance of Sallust with the felicity of Livy? Alexander, standing at the tomb of Achilles, pronounced him fortunate to have had Homer as his poet and France may count herself fortunate to have Gaguin for her historian. Better to proclaim the glory of our forebears, from the rising of the sun to the going down of the same, than to extend territories. Better to adorn one's country by letters than to erect monuments decorated with spoils. No coins, no pyramids, no statues can so glorify kings as can eloquence. Oh France, receive this eternal monument. Embrace your son Robert Gaguin, the vindicator of your immortality!"[45] This comes close to saying, "My dear Gaguin, France is less honoured by all the military exploits which you recount than by the literary excellence of your recital." One had to be astute to perceive deflation by Erasmus.

Gaguin did not this time protest against the flattery and graciously introduced Erasmus to humanists like the Italian, Fausto Andrelini.[46] After an apprenticeship in law and letters he had come to France in 1489 to teach

eloquence and mathematics at the Sorbonne. He became
the court poet, *poeta regius*, facile in versifying for state
occasions. His witty lectures attracted flocks of students
from the uttermost parts of France and Germany, "*ab
extremis Franciae et Germaniae.*" At the age of twenty-two
he published a volume of amatory verse. He was something of a *bon vivant*, evidently a man of singular charm,
and for Erasmus charm covered a multitude of sins.[47]
He could compose poems like a divine on the Virgin, the
Nativity, and the virtues. Some notes exchanged between
Erasmus and Faustus, apparently at a dull lecture, have
come down to us.

FAUSTUS. I'd like a frugal supper, just flies and ants.

ERASMUS. Do you think I'm an Oedipus to guess the
riddle of your sphinx? I suspect your flies are little birds and
your ants are rabbits.

FAUSTUS. A perfect Oedipus you are. Little birds, yes,
quite small. No rabbits.

ERASMUS. My jocular friend, you made me blush and the
theologian rage. Better not stir up the hornets.

FAUSTUS. Who does not know that Faustus would die for
Erasmus? But let's pay no more attention to this babbler than
an Indian elephant does to a fly. Your envious Faustus.[48]

Some of the allusions elude us, but evidently the friends
liked to banter. Soon Erasmus had more to think about
than jesting with Faustus. Money gave out. Apparently
until now he had received grants from the Bishop of
Cambrai and had been in a position to decline tutoring.
"No monetary consideration shall take me away from
my sacred studies," he wrote in September, 1496.[49]
But hunger flattens lofty pretensions. Erasmus was
forced to take on students and nothing better could ever
have happened to him. He was driven thereby to formulate his educational theory and to commence the prepara-

tion of the educational tools, which with subsequent elaboration were to be among the most enduring of his works. His first pupils were two Germans from Lübeck, Christian and Henry Northoff. He bantered with these lads as if they had been his colleagues. To Christian he wrote in February, 1498, "If you don't break your silence I will call you a scamp, hangman, rascal, rake, criminal, blasphemer, monster, phantom, dung, manure pile, pest, bane, infamy, sycophant, wastrel, jail bird, scourge, cat-o'-nine-tails or any other abuse I can think of. That will make you write even if you are mad. But enough of this nonsense. . . ."[50]

For these and other students Erasmus commenced his treatises on the philosophy and practice of education. They continued to be produced throughout his lifetime, but since his views of education did not alter, the main themes may be treated as a whole. The *Colloquies*, started for the Northoff boys at Paris, circulated in manuscript until 1519 when someone published them without Erasmus' consent. He then promptly produced a version more to his taste and in so doing developed a new literary genre. The *Adages* appeared in rudimentary form in 1500 to be enormously expanded in subsequent editions.[51] The tract on *How to Write Letters* was also commenced at Paris and not published until 1522.[52]

The educational ideal of Erasmus centred on *humanitas*[53] and *pietas*. The first concept was primarily classical, the second Christian. *Humanitas* assumed shape as an ideal at the hands of the Greek Panaitios, who, after the conquest of his country by Rome, became a member of the circle of the conqueror, Scipio Africanus. The teaching of Panaitios was transmitted to subsequent ages by Cicero. *Humanitas* was a translation of the Greek *philanthropia*, not philanthropy, but the love of mankind. Basic was the view of the dignity of man, because he alone of all sentient beings is endowed with reason and with speech, which not only communicates, but also gives shape to ideas in the process of bestowing names. Man thus endowed is worthy of respect and should show respect to his fellows, for man, as Seneca declared, is sacred to man. Human behaviour should conform to the seemly, that which is proper to man's nature. He should treat his kind with civility, strive to maintain concord, and avoid dissension. Should strife arise, let him seek to resolve differences by the arbitrement of reason, and if armed conflict is unavoidable, let it be restrained and let the victor be magnanimous to the vanquished. Such a view seeks to reform by persuasion rather than by compulsion and eschews revolution. It tends thus to become a conservative principle.

The correlative Christian term is *pietas*. Of course *pietas* is also classical. Virgil sings of *pius* Aeneas and we still talk of filial piety. But piety was particularly attached to religion and in the age of Erasmus this meant necessarily the Christian religion. Piety meant reverence, devotion, commitment, and enriched the concept of humanity by the addition of the gentler Christian qualities such as compassion, patience, long-suffering, forgiveness, humility, and self-effacement.

How were these ideals to be inculcated? The answer was through the study of the humanities and the Scriptures. The wisdom of the sages and the grace of the Gospel should shape the mind of the child, which is not corrupted, though capable of corruption unless channelled and disciplined. The classics and the Bible should be taught to men in all walks of life: the prince, the physician, the lawyer, the judge, the architect, the artist, and the merchant as well. Christian Northoff became a merchant.

Verg. Tul. HVMANITAS. Demosth. Hom.

IOANNES FROBENIVS VE-
RAE PHILOSOPHIAE
STVDIOSIS S. D.

En tibi lector optime, Lucij Annæi
Senecæ sanctissimi philosophi lucubrationes omnes, additis etiam
nōnullis, Erasmi Roterodami cura,
si nō ab omnibus, certe ab innume-
ris mendis repurgatæ. In his euol-
uendis si diligēter uersaberis, & lin-
guam tuam reddent expolitiorem,
& uitam emendatiorem. Bene ua-
le, & nostram industriam, tuo fauo
re uicissim adiuua. In indyta Ger-
maniæ Basilea. An. M. D. XV.
Mense Iulio.

ΤΟΥ ΚΑΙΡΟΥ ΙΝΕΜΕΣΙ

HUMANITAS on the title page of Erasmus' edition of Seneca.
Observe Froben's mark of the serpents and the dove.

By what device were the attitudes to be instilled? By way of *eloquentia*,[54] that is, the art of persuasion through pleasing discourse. This art itself had to be taught. With respect to the methods of teaching Erasmus was much influenced by Cicero and Quintilian, and possibly to a degree by the Italian humanists, Filelfo, Vittorino da Feltre, and Poliziano, but probably less by the Italians than by an earlier rector of his own university, Jean Gerson.[55] A comparison is of interest between the ancient rhetorician Quintilian, the medieval doctor Gerson (or one who went by his name), and the Renaissance humanist Erasmus. All were agreed in opposing corporal punishment. Erasmus gives a revolting picture of what he had witnessed. He conceded, however, that if a lad were absolutely incorrigible a flogging might be salutary. But if it were ineffective, then send him back to the plough. Punishment should be rendered as unnecessary as possible by making learning a delight. Work should itself be play, though of course not entirely play. Although the best way to learn a language is by imitation, and this may be fun, still there are a few grammatical rules which must be mastered and learning is hard. Let it be interspersed with play. Quintilian recommended holidays. Gerson allowed games provided they would not encourage avarice, obscenity, or fighting. Erasmus would have no martial exercises and was not interested, like Castiglione, in making athletes. The purpose of games and exercise for Erasmus was to keep in trim for study. If he would make work into play, he tended to make play into work. When later he had a horse he would take a ride in the afternoon, more to clear his head and exercise his horse than for fun. In fact all that he seems to have liked for sheer diversion was an evening sparkling with wit and Burgundy or beguiled by chess.[56] As for dietary regula-

Tyrãnis lu
di magiſtro
rum.

tions Erasmus followed St. Jerome in inveighing against
all those forms of abstinence which impair efficiency for
scholarly pursuits.

All three writers agreed that education should begin
early, certainly not later than the seventh year. Schools
were better than private tutoring, but classes preferably
should not exceed five. The tutor should be as a father to
the lads, having an eye to their individual capacities. The
educational programme should not be differentiated with
an eye to ultimate professions, nor should any account be
taken of national differences. But individual differences
are very important. An elephant cannot receive the same
treatment as an ant. Gerson had in mind monastic schools
when he prescribed almost complete silence at meals. At
night he would have a light always burning in honour of

the Blessed Virgin and to show the way to the rest room. Erasmus counselled that on going to bed a lad should say his prayers, refrain from annoying his neighbours, be charitable in his thought of his fellows, and drowse off over a good book. Quintilian and Erasmus both endorsed visual aids to education. Quintilian suggested ivory letter shapes. Erasmus thought these better than alphabetic arrows used by the English for the young archer. He highly approved of pictures of animals and hunting scenes accompanying the written names.[57]

The above counsels on education were directed naturally to parents and, especially, to teachers. Erasmus wrote also what might be called a little *Manual of Etiquette for Boys*,[58] whether in church, school, or anywhere for that matter. Here are some examples; "A dripping nose is filthy. To wipe it on cap or sleeve betokens a peasant, to rub it off on the arm or elbow is the mark of a vendor of salt herring. [Erasmus churned at the smell of salt herring.] It is not much better to wipe with the hand and then rub on the clothes. Better to use a handkerchief and turn away the head. If you blow through thumb and finger to the ground bury the mucus quickly with your foot. . . . If you have to yawn cover your mouth with the handkerchief or your palm and make the sign of the cross. . . . To laugh at everything is silly. To laugh at nothing is stupid. To laugh at bawdy jokes is dirty. A guffaw which rocks the whole body is not becoming at any age and certainly not for children. A laugh should not sound like the whinny of a horse, nor in laughing should one show the teeth like a dog. The expression of the face can show hilarity." Much of this sounds like the *Instructor* of Clement of Alexandria written in the third century. Evidently manners had not greatly changed.

With regard to the actual programme of studies

Erasmus, as we have seen, trusted less to rules for language than to wide reading. The tract *Antibarbari* (*Against the Barbarians*), already reviewed, contained his defence of the study alike of the classical and Christian literature. In his earlier treatises he spoke only of the Latin authors; later on, after he had gained proficiency, he spoke also of the Greek. He was not worried over the erotic passages in the classics. After all the Old Testament has some very dubious stories unless they are allegorized. Gerson confessed that in his youth he had read Ovid, Terence, the love letters of Abelard and Eloise, and Andreas Capellanus on romantic love.[59] Obviously such reading had not corrupted his morals. Erasmus counselled not rejection but selection and that was one of the reasons why he undertook to cull from the literature of antiquity the gems of wisdom which he called "adages." Many of his examples might well be called "proverbs," or "epigrams." He was not the only one to make such collections. He was slightly anticipated by Polydore Virgil and succeeded by Agrippa of Nettesheim and Sebastian Franck. One wonders at the popularity of proverbs in this period. Was it that men were turning from the art of dying to the art of living? There was no absolute antinomy between the two, of course. The way to die well is to live well. Erasmus both collected maxims and wrote on preparation for death. But there is evident a certain shift of attention in passing from the *Ars Moriendi* to the *Adagia*. Erasmus said himself that the purpose of the adages was to persuade, adorn, and inform.[60]

He began with some eight hundred proverbs in the first edition of 1500 and ended with over five thousand.[61] At first he did little more than collect sayings with brief explanations. He ended by taking some as texts for essays. At the outset he was not in a position to go far beyond the Latin authors. Later he added abundant material from the Greeks. Most of his maxims came from the classics, some from the Bible. The total collection set forth a panoramic picture of the ancient world, pagan and Christian.[62] He has been disparaged because he collected proverbs and did not create them. But how often do literary men create proverbs? A groom rather than a poet is likely to have said, "You can take a horse to water but you can't make him drink." Proverbs like folk songs spring anonymously from the life of the people. The composer makes of the one a symphony, the author makes of the other an essay. The very significance of the proverb lies precisely in this, that it is the distillation of the wisdom of the ages. As such it has a claim to truth because the judgment of all men endowed with reason is sounder than that of a single individual. Here is the ground of the doctrine of natural law, a universal morality, and of natural theology, a universal theology.

Among the proverbs collected by Erasmus a number of expressions have become current in all European tongues, including our own: "To carry off the palm; ——As many men, as many minds;——To champ at the bit . . .;——To leave no stone unturned;——Where there is smoke there is fire;——A necessary evil . . .;——Know yourself;——The mountain labours and brings forth a mouse;——A rare bird . . .;——With one foot in the grave . . .;——Many hands make light work . . .;—— Swallow your own spittle . . .;——To mix fire and water . . .;——To fight with one's own shadow. . . ." In some instances the sentiment survives though the expression has been altered. Erasmus has "to take owls to Athens." We say "to take coals to Newcastle." He takes from Horace the expression "to have hay on the horns." Our form is "to have a chip on the shoulder." He speaks of "a burden to the earth." We speak of "a pain in the neck."[63]

Education for Erasmus did not consist in drawing out of the pupil what was not there. He must first be steeped in the knowledge and wisdom of the ages. Only thereafter is he in a position to express himself. He will first do this through speech by imitation. For that reason it is of the utmost importance that those who teach him should speak correctly. But what was correct Latin? There were great controversies on that subject in which Erasmus was later to be embroiled and to which we shall return. There was also the question of how to pronounce Latin and Greek, and that too is a subject for later consideration.

Even more important than pronunciation was the meaning of words. Erasmus both edited the *Elegantiae* of Valla and brought out his own *De Copia Verborum* (*On the Arsenal of Words*). Let them be used with precision, said Erasmus. Study their connotations in particular settings. Take the word obscene: what is its meaning? This depends largely on usage, for nothing is unclean of itself. *Cacare* (shit) is obscene. *Venter* (belly) is permissible to mention but not to display. Avoid words which are offensive in usage.[64] Some words, said Erasmus, need only to be mentioned to convey their meaning. Others call for an explanation. Of such is the word *bellum* (war). (One would have thought the meaning in this instance to be perfectly obvious, but Erasmus could not miss a chance to dilate on the subject.)

Then came practice in conversation. As an aid at this point, Erasmus, while in Paris, commenced his *Colloquies*, at first little exercises with half a dozen ways to say "good morning, goodbye," and so on. The collection might have been altogether pedestrian save that Erasmus was unable to touch anything without leaving his stamp. In one exercise a speaker says, "Would you be kind enough to set a day for me to call." The other answers, "I don't set dates for my friends, but only for those with whom I don't get along." Another example has more sting:

First Speaker. From what coop or cave did you come?
Second. From the Collège de Montaigu.
First. Then I suppose you are full of learning.
Second. No, lice.[65]

In later years, as the *Adages* became essays, so the *Colloquies* became dialogues. The dialogue form, already used by Erasmus in the *Antibarbari*, was a popular literary device in the Renaissance perhaps by reason of its very ambiguities. Already in antiquity it had been argumentative with Plato and Cicero, satirical with Lucian. The basic assumption was that truth exists and is attainable through the matching of minds in rational discourse. But those who are profoundly convinced that they already have the truth will readily turn the dialogue into the diatribe and the satire into invective. In the Renaissance the dialogue was sometimes used as an educational expedient for teaching Latin conversation. It could also be a device for insinuating unpopular opinions without assuming responsibility, with the risk of being suspected of this very trick when actually innocent. In Erasmus all of the varieties appear and are often blended. But whatever the form, the spirit is that of open-minded reasonable interchange, devoid of malice and reviling, with occasional lapses.[66]

The epistle was another form of composition exceedingly popular in his day. Literary men published their letters: Poliziano, Budé, Sadoleto, Bembo, and Erasmus himself. He produced a tract on how to write letters, the

VALE. MAX. · AVL. GELL. · HORATIVS · OVIDIVS

VIRGILIVS · SALLVSTIVS

QVINTILIA · M. CICERO

DESYDE
RII ERASMI RO
terodami de duplici Copia
Verború, ac Rerú Có
mentarij duo.
Ab Authore ipso ꝗ diligen=
tissime recogniti, ac locis
pleriscꝫ nó infoeli=
citer aucti

Epistola Eras. Ro. ad Iacobum
Vuimphelingú Selestatinú

Argentorati, ex Aedibus Hulde
richi Morardi Anno. M.D.
Mense Ianuario. XXI.

Title page of *De Copia Verborum* with representations of the Latin classical authors. The selection was undoubtedly made by the editor. Erasmus would scarcely have omitted Livy and Seneca.

De Conscribendis Epistolis, in which, as in the *Colloquies*, he gives numerous examples of salutation, conclusions, and treatments of particular themes such as consolation.

Into this tract on letter writing Erasmus inserted an example of the declamation which, as we have seen, took the form of the persuasive and dissuasive. The theme in this instance was matrimony. The persuasive was addressed to a young man who alone could transmit the family name, the dissuasive to an aspiring scholar who might fare better if unencumbered with domestic responsibilities. The defence of marriage has at points an autobiographical ring. Erasmus had, of course, no personal knowledge of the delights of marriage, but he did know the sting of birth without benefit of matrimony. Here is an abridgement:[67]

Marriage was sanctioned by Christ at Cana. It is sanctioned by nature and condemned by heretics. It was instituted not by Lycurgus, Moses, or Solon, but by the Founder of the universe, for God said, "It is not good for man to be alone," and He created Eve, not out of mud, as in the case of Adam, but from his rib that none should be closer and dearer than a wife. After the flood God told man "to be fruitful and multiply." Should not marriage be honoured above all the sacraments because it was the first to be instituted, and by God Himself? The other sacraments were established on earth, this one in paradise; the others as a remedy, this one as fellowship in felicity. The others were ordained for fallen nature, but this one for nature unspoiled. If human laws are revered how much more the law of marriage which we receive from Him who gave us life?

The excitation of Venus, which is necessary for marriage, is from nature and whatever is of nature is pure and holy. The most holy manner of life, pure and chaste, is marriage. You point out that Christ was not married. True, but we are not to imitate him in everything. We can't be born of a virgin as

he was. You reply that the apostles were not married. Some
were not, but they lived at a time of persecution when their
mission as evangelists was difficult to combine with matrimony, but we live in an age when moral integrity is nowhere
better exemplified than in marriage. Let them prate as they
will of the status of monks and virgins. Those who under the
pretext of celibacy live in licence might better be castrated. I
would like to see permission given to priests and monks to
marry, especially when there is such a horde of priests among
whom chastity is rare. How much better to make concubines
into wives and openly acknowledge the partners now held in
infamy! How much better to have children to love and rear
religiously, as legitimate offspring of whom there is no need
to be ashamed and who in turn will honour their sires! I think
the bishops would long since have given this permission if
they did not derive more income from the taxes on concubines
than they could reap from wives.

Some persons may be celibate, as some fields may be
fallow, but if all were celibate there would be no human race
and consequently no celibates and no virgins. The laws of
princes punish unprovoked abortion and contraception, but
how much difference is there between destroying that which
has been started and not letting it get started? To endanger
the life of an unborn child is a capital offence. But how does
this differ from dedicating oneself to perpetual sterility? Why
refrain from that which God instituted, nature sanctions,
reason persuades, divine and human laws approve, the consent
of all nations endorses and to which the highest examples
exhort? What more sweet than to live with her with whom you
are united in body and soul, who talks with you in secret
affection, to whom you have committed all your faith and
your fortune? What in all nature is lovelier? You are bound to
friends in affection. How much more to a wife in the highest
love, with union of the body, the bond of the sacrament and
the sharing of your goods! In other friendships how much
there is of simulation and perfidy! Friends flit like swallows.
Few continue to the end. But a wife is faithful and only death

dissolves marriage, if indeed it does. If you suffer adversity, you have one who will console you and try to make your trouble her own. If you stay at home you have a respite from the tedium of solitude. If you are away you long for a kiss. Absent you desire, returning you rejoice. By marriage the number of your loved ones is increased. You acquire another father and mother. What more charming than to have a little Aeneas who will cherish you in your old age and in whom you are reborn! You say, "Your children may die." But do you think you will have no sorrows if you are celibate? Nothing is more safe, felicitous, tranquil, pleasant and lovable than marriage.

The tutoring to which necessity drove Erasmus brought unexpected good fortune, not only because it induced him to prepare educational manuals, but much more because it enlarged his circle of friends. The first pupils were German. Then came several English youths. To an Englishman, Robert Fisher, Erasmus dedicated the tract *On Letter Writing*, and the *Adages* to Lord Mountjoy. He was a young nobleman of substance who invited Erasmus as his guest to visit England.[68]

CHAPTER THREE

Neoplatonism and Piety:
England: The Netherlands: The Enchiridion

*

ERASMUS crossed the channel in the early summer of 1499. To a friend in Italy he wrote a trifle apologetically that he would have seen him there had he not been wafted to England by Lord Mountjoy, "so gracious and charming a youth that I would follow him to hell."[1] Mountjoy took him instead to his paradisiacal country estate at Bedwell in Hertfordshire. Erasmus' report to Fausto Andrelini suggests that the young cleric was making the easy descent to Avernus. He wrote "Erasmus, you know, has become almost a good hunter, not the worst rider, an elegant courtier. You should come too. Why should a man of your delicate nose wax old amid Gallic scum? If you knew Britain's charms you would come with winged feet and if the gout impeded you would wish yourself a Daedalus. To take one point, the nymphs are of divine beauty, charming and gracious, and especially there is that most admirable custom of kissing at every turn. If you should but once taste how sweet, how fragrant are these kisses you would wish to spend not ten years, like Solon, in England but every day until your death. We will joke some more when we get together."[2]

In appraising this letter one should be aware that the "admirable custom of kissing at every turn" was in this period actually English, but not continental. One must also bear in mind that Erasmus had an uncommon faculty of accommodating himself to the taste of his correspondent and Faustus was a gay blade. In after years Erasmus discountenanced kissing as unsanitary and commended Archbishop Warham for not wasting his time on the chase.[3] In any case Erasmus was not for long diverted by the pastimes of the English aristocracy. In the autumn he was at Oxford, living in the house of the Augustinian Canons, to whom he belonged.

Speedily he began forming lifelong friendships with some of the most accomplished and later to be among the most eminent men in England. John Colet, subsequently the Dean of St. Paul's, was then lecturing at the university on the epistles of St. Paul. Erasmus introduced himself by way of a letter. Colet replied that he knew him already by reputation, having read while in Paris his encomium of Gaguin's history and had at once perceived him to be well versed in literature.[4] Colet did not say theology and evidently regarded Erasmus as a man of letters. As a scholar and person Colet made a deep impression. He was an aristocrat, son of the Lord Mayor of London. He had travelled in Italy, was well versed in the best of the classics, in the Church Fathers, in the civil and canon law. He dressed simply, ate sparingly, and avoided banquets where conversation with sparkling ladies threatened to revive propensities which he had struggled to suppress. Though he would have wished all Christians to be unwed like himself, he conceded that he had nowhere met more unblemished characters than among the married and from among them he chose the directors of the school which he was later to found.[5]

Already at Oxford this young man – he was about thirty – showed how seriously he took points of religious belief. He had arranged a dinner party for a few selected guests among whom Erasmus was invited as a "poet," that is, a literary man. The discussion centred on the nature of the sin of Cain because of which God refused to accept his sacrifice. Colet in defending his view was carried away "with holy zeal and invested with a sublime majesty." Erasmus, who abhorred a heated discussion as much as a German stove, broke in as a poet to relate a diverting story which he professed to have discovered in some ancient authority. In this version, Cain with guile approached the angel with the flaming sword guarding the gate of Paradise in order to wheedle and needle him into passing out some of the luxuriant seeds of Eden. What would God care? inquired Cain. He had forbidden only the apples on one tree. Besides, did the guardian relish his task? From an angel God had made him into an executioner performing the duty assigned on earth to dogs. To keep men out of Paradise the sentinel must himself forgo the delights alike of Paradise and earth, and earth is wondrous fair with vast oceans, lofty mountains, secluded vales, rivulets leaping down rocky declivities. There are thousands of trees with lush foliage and perennial fruits. Man is indeed plagued by disease, but there is nothing which ingenuity and industry cannot surmount. Why then deprive himself of such charms, and why refuse a few paltry seeds to those who already have so many? The angel is seduced and Cain achieves such an abundant yield that God is jealous and plagues him with ants, weevils, toads, caterpillars, mice, locusts, swine, hail, and tornado, and Cain's propitiatory offering is rejected.[6]

Presumably the company was amused. Did they realize that Erasmus had turned the myth of Eden into the myth of Prometheus?

On another point the discussion between Colet and Erasmus was conducted without heat and without levity. Colet could not bring himself to believe that when Christ prayed, "Remove this cup from me,"[7] he was referring to his death upon the cross, since he had come to earth with the express purpose of laying down his life. As a matter of fact Colet was following John's gospel where Jesus says, "Now is my soul troubled and what shall I say, 'Father save me from this hour'? No, for this purpose I have come to this hour."[8] But how then explain the prayer in the other gospels that the cup might be taken from him? Colet interpreted the cup to mean the agony that Christ would experience in witnessing the crime of the Jews. Erasmus regarded this explanation as altogether far-fetched and whether or no the gospels could be harmonized, he would hold to the simple meaning that Christ in his human nature shrank from the pangs of death.[9]

Colet was not the only one who gave to Erasmus a new impetus on this his first visit to England. There were three who like Colet had visited Italy, and there, unlike him, had learned some Greek. They were William

Grocyn, William Latimer, and Thomas Linacre.[10] Erasmus must have met them all in London, for they were not at Oxford during his stay. Grocyn had earlier taught Greek at Oxford, but at the time was lecturing in London on the writings of Dionysius the Areopagite, a Neoplatonic writer of the sixth century, popularly identified with that Dionysius who accompanied St. Paul when he spoke on the Areopagus at Athens. Grocyn at first accepted the legend but having been persuaded of its spuriousness, whether independently or through the critique of Valla, had then the integrity to come before his audience and frankly confess his mistake.[11]

William Latimer is a more obscure figure, of importance perhaps chiefly because he tutored Cardinal Reginald Pole. From his own pen nothing is extant save his letters to Erasmus. Linacre was a medical humanist, to be physician to Henry VIII, and founder of the Royal College of Surgeons. He had spent six years in Italy and had acquired a mastery of Greek from native Greeks there resident, so that he was himself able to produce a Greek grammar and to translate ancient medical writers. In his last years Linacre gave up medicine for the Church and then for the first time read the gospels. On so doing he exclaimed, "Either this is not the gospel or we are not Christians."

Still another among the young English humanists acquainted with Greek was Thomas More who had acquired his knowledge not in Italy like the others, but at Oxford under the tutelage of Grocyn. Erasmus was drawn to More by piety and wit. More was a gay saint, as disciplined as the most conscientious monk, yet with merriment of countenance and a relish for pranks.[12] The rogue took Erasmus for a stroll and then, without warning, dropped in on the household of the children of

Henry VII. There was the princess Margaret, just under ten, later to be the Queen of Scots. And there was Mary, only four, destined to be the bride of Louis XII of France. Arthur was absent. Edmund was a baby. There stood the future Henry VIII, not quite nine, marked already, said Erasmus "by a certain regal bearing and loftiness combined with singular graciousness."[13] More presented a literary offering. Prince Henry none too graciously asked Erasmus what he had to present. On the way back the mischievous More received due chiding and Erasmus set himself at once to write a poem in praise of England and of England's king Henry VII, "skilled in war, lover of peace, indulgent to others, strict with himself, more sublime than Caesar, more generous than Maecenas [a gentle hint]. Here is my Apollo, the father of the age of gold." The boy Henry was lauded as the image of his father.[14]

How much did Erasmus owe to this new circle of friends? His chief debt was personal. He was exhilarated by their approbation and uplifted by their example. These men were not the illegitimate sons of an obscure priest, but scions of the aristocracy, men of substance, yet ready to forfeit station and reputation for what they deemed to be true and right. Grocyn had not recoiled from a public retraction. Linacre was candid in confessing that he had not grasped the import of the gospel. Colet was later to risk the wrath of Henry VIII, and what More did all the world knows.

They gave also a new turn to the studies of Erasmus by impressing upon him the necessity of mastering the Greek language. He had indeed learned the rudiments before coming to England[15] and the first edition of the *Adages*, published in 1500 in Paris, had already several quotations in the Greek tongue. On his return to Paris

Erasmus declared that he would the more readily spend money for Greek books than for clothes.[16]

The English circle affected Erasmus likewise in the realm of ideas. They were enthusiasts for the revival of Neoplatonism. During the Middle Ages the great purveyor of that tradition was Dionysius the Areopagite. Colet wrote a treatise upon his writings and Grocyn took them as the subject of his lectures, as we noted. His doubt as to the apostolic origin of these compositions did not need to entail a rejection of their teaching, and Colet, so far as we know, never entertained any doubt.[17] But more influential on the English circle than the medieval transmission was the revival of original Neoplatonism through the academy at Florence, headed by Ficino and Pico. Colet had corresponded with Ficino. More translated a life of Pico and Pico's letter to his nephew. For the second time Erasmus was italianized without going to Italy: first when in Holland he came to know Valla, now in England when he was first drawn into the orbit of the Florentines. In the dedication of the first edition of the *Adagia* to Lord Mountjoy, Erasmus referred to Pico as "endowed with a certain divine felicity of temper [*ingenium*]."[18] In listening to the lectures of Colet, Erasmus averred that "he could hear Plato himself speaking."[19] This is rather a startling statement since Colet was lecturing on Paul.

In assessing the measure of Platonism imbibed by Erasmus we must distinguish three levels of the Platonic tradition. The first of course was Plato, the second Neoplatonism, and the third Florentine Neoplatonism. All three had in common a dualism of matter and spirit. The material world is but a shadow of the world of ideas. Man is a duality composed of body and spirit. The body is a tomb, or at any rate a prison, of the spirit, which can in a measure be emancipated in ecstasy. Immortality consists in the liberation of spirit from body. Plato held that the world of sense came into being by the shaping up of formless matter. Neoplatonism explained the origin rather in terms of emanations proceeding in a downward progress from unity to multiplicity, from spirit to matter. The Aristotelian static classification of God, celestial beings, men, animals, plants, and minerals thus became a ladder of descent, but might also be a ladder of ascent, for man at the centre, combining the below and the above, might sink to the one or rise to the other until, purified and illumined, he might be united in rapture with the Ineffable One. Florentine Neoplatonism was interested in addition in the recovery of unity in philosophy and religion, in reconciling Aristotle and Plato, and in drawing together the world religions, under the aegis of Christianity to be sure, but by reason of common elements. Adumbrations of the doctrine of the Trinity were discovered in the occult lore of the Orient, the Zoroastrian and Sibylline Oracles, in the supposedly Christian corpus of Hermes Trismegistus, and again in the Jewish Cabala with its number symbolism and triads.

Erasmus found only selected elements congenial in this tradition. He, too, was hospitable to the pious heathen, but by reason of their moral idealism. He regarded oriental occultism with its number speculations and trinitarian foreshadowings as sheer fantasy. He was not interested in the problem of how the world came into being. Enough for him that the Church's teaching declared it to have been created out of nothing. As for immortality, he believed in the resurrection of the body rather than in the disembodiment of the spirit. Occasionally he manifested interest in religious ecstasy but could not claim it for himself. What Erasmus did derive from this whole tradition was a reinforcement of his own religion of inwardness. For him also man was composed of body and spirit, though sometimes, like the Alexandrian fathers, he had a three-fold division of body, soul, and spirit; usually, however, only two. He did not regard the body as wholly evil and for that matter the Platonists were of course not Manichean dualists. So long as the spirit is in the body they agreed that the claims of the body are not to be denied. But bodily acts and usages, if not conjoined with devout inner attitudes, are vain. Such a view could easily lead to a disparagement of all of the external rites of the Church, including her very institutional structure. So far Erasmus would not go, but others in his wake were to outdo him.

The Neoplatonic revival did not create but reinforced and gave a new tinge to that spirituality which Erasmus had already inherited from other strands in the Christian tradition. The *Devotio Moderna* had, of course, always demanded the fervent rather than the formal. Whereas in Germany the Reformation began as a protest against indulgences, in Holland the focus was on the spiritualizing of the sacrament of the Lord's Table. Wessel Gansfort of the Brethren, who did not deny transubstantiation, had yet so little concern for the physical as to say that Christ is present in his divinity and full humanity with any who call upon his name, even apart from the Eucharist.[20]

The New Testament itself inculcates a religion of the spirit and the many supporting texts are open to a Neoplatonic slant. The contrast is frequent in Paul between the spirit and the flesh,[21] though the flesh for him is not the corporeal component of man, but whatever is contrary to the mind of Christ, such as pride, envy, and anger. Yet there are texts in Paul susceptible of a Platonic interpretation, as for example when he says, "Though

our outward nature is wasting away, our inward nature
is being renewed."[22] In a single verse he combined the
contrast between the visible and the invisible, the
ephemeral and the abiding: "For the things that are seen
are transient, but the things that are unseen are eternal."[23]
Again he contrasts the spirit and the letter: "The written
code kills, but the Spirit gives life."[24] A verse in John's
gospel lends itself even more readily to a Platonic
dualism. It occurs in connection with the account of the
miracle of the loaves, where the bread is treated as
signifying the Eucharist. First comes the statement:
"Unless you eat the flesh of the Son of man and drink his
blood you have no life in you." Then the sense is
spiritualized: "It is the spirit that gives life. The flesh is
of no avail."[25] Again there is the word of Jesus: "Do you
not see that whatever goes into a man from outside
cannot defile him, since it enters not his heart but his
stomach. . . . From within, out of the heart come evil
thoughts. . . . All things evil come from within."[26] On
the basis of such texts in the New Testament Erasmus
might have elaborated his entire position, but at times he
Platonized the New Testament.

Are we to assume a still more decisive effect of the
English visit upon Erasmus? Some have thought that
Colet changed the whole course of his career, turning
him from the secular to the sacred.[27] This judgment rests
upon the reply which Erasmus made to an urgent plea
from Colet to lecture at Oxford on Genesis or Isaiah.
Erasmus answered that his unwillingness was not due to
a preference for poetry and rhetoric, "which, having
served their purpose [what purpose? diction, or tutoring
fees?], no longer interest me, but because I am not competent, I must return to Paris. When I have acquired
proficiency I will turn to theology. In the meantime

nothing would better please me than to discuss with you sacred subjects, whether by letter or in person."[28] This statement does not indicate any veering in the course of Erasmus. Three years earlier he had declined to take on students because he must prepare himself for a doctorate in theology[29] and a year later he had informed his bishop that he was wholly immersed in theological pursuits.[30] He had already been entranced by Jerome and Augustine and had lectured on the Scriptures at Paris. Nor did Erasmus afterwards ever give up secular studies. On the second visit to England he was to be engaged with More in translating Lucian and subsequently brought out renderings of Euripides, Plutarch, Aristotle, Ptolemy, and Galen. From the beginning to the end of his career he was dedicated to the dissemination of the classical Christian heritage. If Colet brought about any change it may have been to turn him from patristic to biblical studies and above all Colet's regret that he did not himself know Greek convinced Erasmus the more that the mastery of this tool was next on the docket. And this goal, he believed, could be achieved not so well in England as in Paris which had some native Greeks.

To Paris, then, he would return and also to see through the press the first edition of his *Adagia*.[31] He started out with a goodly purse which he had brought with him into England from France. His English friends assured him that he would have no difficulty in getting the money out of the country. They were poorly informed. The extortionate Henry VII laid hold of whatever he could for the royal exchequer and decreed that only a very small amount of currency could be taken from the realm. At Dover Erasmus was stripped and arrived in France close to penury.[32] He had to resort again to flattering encomia to stimulate patronage. His *Panegyric* on the Archduke

Philip was a most distasteful composition,[33] though it could be justified as holding before the young prince the image of what he ought to be in the guise of what he ostensibly was. Precarious years were tided over for Erasmus by the good offices of the indefatigable Batt and the generosity of the Bishop of Cambrai, of the Archduke Philip, and, in diminishing measure, of the Lady Anne of Veere. The plague made Erasmus more than ever a migrant. He fled from Paris for some six months to Orleans and then again took up his residence in various places in the Low Countries.[34]

During this period he describes himself repeatedly as wholly immersed in Greek.[35] At Orleans he borrowed a copy of Homer.[36] He had started to work on an edition of St. Jerome and needed Greek to check him against his sources. Presumably Erasmus received instruction from a native Greek, Hermonymus of Sparta.[37] Note by the way that at the same time Erasmus was editing Cicero's *De Officiis*.[38] The sacred and the secular persisted side by side.

The residence in the Low Countries lasted from the early summer of 1501 until late in the year 1505. This period is notable, apart from continual progress in Greek, on three counts. Erasmus encountered a friend, discovered a manuscript, and wrote a book.

The friend was Jean Vitrier, warden of the Observant Franciscan House, who, disillusioned by Scotist subtleties, had returned with delight to Ambrose, Cyprian, and Jerome and was especially fond of Origen. "When I asked him," said Erasmus, "how he could so delight in a heretic, he answered, 'the Holy Spirit cannot but reside in the breast of one whose books are so learned and fervent.'[39] He knew the letters of Paul by heart, and when I asked him how he prepared for preaching he replied that he would sink himself in Paul till his heart took flame. In preaching he used no theatrical gestures or shouting. He eschewed conspicuous mortifications such as going barefoot, sleeping on the ground, living on bread and water."[40] He would even disregard the Franciscan rule of travelling only on foot and would ride a mule, permitted to priests, or even a horse permitted only to laymen, if thereby he could engage a travelling companion in edifying conversation. He scorned indulgences and would not be silenced by an offer of a hundred florin towards the building of his church. His attempts to reform a dissolute nunnery led to his dismissal as warden and transfer to an obscure post. "In Colet," said Erasmus, "I have at times noticed a touch of the human, but never in Vitrier."[41] And now Colet has his place in all the histories of Tudor England, but Vitrier has passed into oblivion. He was for Erasmus the perfect exemplification of the *philosophia Christi*.

The manuscript discovered by Erasmus was a work of Lorenzo Valla. We have already noted his vogue in the Low Countries. Rummaging in the library of the Premonstratensians at Parc near Louvain, Erasmus came upon Valla's annotations on the New Testament and published them.[42] They contain nothing especially exciting. They are just philological notes, whether, for example, the name Mary in Latin should be spelled *Mariam*, like *Abraam*, or as *Maria*, and in that case declined. But that the New Testament should be subjected to the same sort of philological scrutiny as any other book may well have stimulated Erasmus to undertake his own translation and annotations. The preface to his edition of Valla is significant. St. Jerome, said Erasmus, emended the earlier translations. Now his translation is in need of emendation. Would any one say that in the Old Testament the Greek translation is superior to the original Hebrew or in the New Testament the Latin translation of Jerome superior to the Greek? If that were so why would Clement V have decreed that the ancient languages be studied? The reference is to the decree of the Council of Vienne in 1311–12 which called for the teaching of Hebrew, Aramaic, and Arabic at some of the great universities. The object then was the preparation of missionaries. Erasmus and his circle repeatedly invoked this decree in order to promote the acquisition of the linguistic skills requisite for Biblical scholarship.[43]

The book which Erasmus wrote was the *Enchiridion Militis Christiani*, which more than any other of his works was to make him the mouthpiece of the liberal Catholic reform, the counsellor of popes, and the mentor of Europe. The treatise is programmatic, for here in outline are those themes which Erasmus was to reiterate throughout his entire life. Though this little work did not at first attract great attention, perhaps because tucked in between other works in the initial edition, a decade later its vogue began, marked by a freshet of editions and translations.

The title has a double entendre. The word *enchiridion* comes from two Greek words meaning "in the hand," and was applied to a small weapon, a dagger, or to a small book, a handbook. In this instance the translation "dagger" is to be preferred because of the nature of the occasion which brought it into being. While Erasmus was staying with his friend Batt at Tournheim, he was requested by a distraught wife to attempt the reform of her wayward husband. He was a German of Nürnberg, by name Johann Poppenruyter, a manufacturer of armaments, who from the Netherlands as a base supplied

the tools of war to the emperor or his rivals. Johann was
a jolly boon companion, loose with the ladies, harsh to
his wife, and death to all theologians, except Erasmus,
who for that reason was urged to try to reclaim the
miscreant without disclosing the hand of his wife.
Erasmus, having completed the *Dagger of the Christian
Soldier*, presented it to the manufacturer of armaments.
He reciprocated by presenting Erasmus with his own
dagger. Neither made any use of the weapon of the
other.[44]

One can understand why the *Enchiridion* would not
altogether speak to the condition of a Poppenruyter, for
it advised him to study especially Origen, Ambrose,
Jerome, and Augustine for a better understanding of the
Scriptures. Nor would Johann have grasped the point
when told not to excuse himself by manipulation of
terminology, turning vices into virtues by redefinition, so
that gloominess becomes gravity, harshness severity,
odium zeal, sordidness frugality, adulation sociability,
scurrility urbanity. This list, modelled on a sermon of
St. Bernard, was altogether too sophisticated to move a
Poppenruyter. Erasmus was really addressing two
persons. The first was the wayward Johann. The second
was himself.

The opening of the treatise, to be sure, befits equally
the soldier and the scholar. It is a resolute call to action
in the Christian warfare. The lecherous Johann should
brace himself to renounce his amours. The timorous
Erasmus should overcome his timidity, shake off his
lethargy, dispel his pusillanimity. The feeling of in-
adequacy, which had plagued him in the monastery,
evidently persisted. He uses again the word *pusillanimitas*.
Let the Christian soldier, then, rise to meet the enemy,
who is wily, astute, unprincipled, using fiery darts and

poisoned arrows. He permits of no rest, and against him
the warfare must be unremitting.

But victory is assured. The merchant who encompasses
land and sea cannot count on the success of his enterprise,
but the Christian warrior cannot fail, for God is his ally.
"If God is for us who can be against us?"[45] The outcome
rests not with Fortune but with the Father in heaven.
That man only has failed to conquer who has not wished
to conquer. Aid is ever at hand. Christ will fight for you.
Every victory comes from him who overcame the
tyranny of sin. "Be of good cheer. I have overcome the
world."[46] But you must do your part, not relying supinely
on divine grace, nor with panic losing your head and
throwing away your arms.

All of this sounds very much as if for Erasmus the
assailant was the Devil, but Satan was for him largely a
metaphor. He did not, like Luther, think of the Devil as
a personalized foe with whom he could even engage in a
dialogue. The Christian warfare takes place within the
breast of each individual. This means, then, that there are
two selves. Yet the dualism of these two within does not
preclude the dualism of the inward and the outward. If
the warfare is not primarily with the devil, all the more is
it a conflict with the world and the flesh, from which in
this life man cannot escape, not even in a monastery. He
must live with them both, yet is to be subject to neither.
They are to be used in the spirit of Paul's phrase, "having
as not having."[47] This attitude affects not only food,
drink, and all material possessions, but also the externals
of worship: images, pilgrimages, relics, spoken prayers,
and the very structure of the Church, the grades of the
clergy, the outward aspects of the monastic life, and even
the Mass where Christ was believed to be corporeally
present upon the altar. Erasmus spiritualized all of these

to such a degree that he was accused of reducing Christianity to an attitude. He protested that the outward aids are useful to babes in Christ and may be retained by the mature out of consideration for the weak. Nevertheless the thrust, despite all disclaimers, made for rendering the outward apparatus of religion superfluous. This was basically why the Reformation and the Counter-Reformation saw in Erasmus a subversive influence.

Another theme, at times reinforcing, at times cutting athwart the first, is the imitation of Christ. He is to be imitated in the spirit, but at the same time his ethical precepts are to be kept quite literally without any attenuating glosses. As with à Kempis and the Brethren, the stress is laid upon the exemplification of the gentler virtues: humility, meekness, self-effacement, tenderness, compassion, yielding rather than asserting one's due, forgiveness, love of enemies, overcoming evil with good. All of these spring from an inner heartfelt faith, but they must find expression in concrete behaviour. A new urgency was thereby given to the critique of all of the outward forms and ceremonies of the Church. Insofar as they are merely outward they are not harmful in themselves, but if their observance impedes love and service to the neighbour, then they become an abomination. And the imitation of Christ demands not merely detachment from the world of sense, but also a conflict with the world of men addicted to the things of sense. Any one who refuses to share in their waywardness will be derided as a fool, a fool in Christ. Wherefore the insignia of the Christian are the cross, the crown of thorns, the nails, the lance, and the wounds.

And this is true for all Christians. The distinction is discarded between the precepts binding upon every Christian and the counsels such as poverty, chastity,

obedience, and non-resistance, voluntarily embraced by
the few who aspire to perfection and expect reward for
their extra goodness, called works of supererogation.
Erasmus hears a layman excusing himself by saying, "I
am not a priest, I am not a monk." "Yes," comes the
retort, "but are you not a Christian?" "Monasticism is not
a way of piety. It is a way of living" – suited to some but
not to others. And poverty is incumbent not upon monks
only but upon all Christians, not in the sense that they
should possess absolutely nothing, but in the sense that
they should have as if not having, counting not their
wealth as their own when another is in need. Here is a
wealthy man who says, "I came by my money honestly.
I inherited it. Why can't I do with it what I like?" And
when he hears of a poor girl who to keep alive sells her
body, he says, "And what is that to me?" To be sure
there are different codes of behaviour for different
occupations, but all have the same rigorous demand. The
magistrate should be ready to give his life for justice.
The titles of Pope and Abbot (both meaning father, the
one from Greek, the other from Hebrew) refer to love
not power.

Erasmus holds throughout to the military figure and
discusses the arms of the Christian warrior. Every one of
his weapons can be so blunted as to become an encum-
brance. The first weapon is prayer. Moses throughout the
battle kept his arms aloft in supplication. But there is no
merit in babbling long prayers, for even the silent
aspiration of the heart is heard by God. When Moses had
not yet so much as opened his mouth God said to him,
"Why are you crying unto me?"[48]

A mighty armament in the Christian warfare is the
Scripture, but not according to the literal sense, at any
rate not in many passages of the Old Testament, which

unless spiritualized by allegory are less edifying than Livy, for example the incest of Lot's daughters, the adultery of David, the concubinage of Solomon. Sometimes Erasmus sought to find some palliation for their behaviour. The daughters of Lot lay with their father to ensure the continuance of the race. David repented of his sin. But one could not do much with the concubines of Solomon save to allegorize them into so many virtues. And naturally Erasmus, like Origen, understood all the wars of Jehovah against the Canaanites as directed against the vices.

Prayers to the saints were not altogether discouraged by Erasmus who believed that St. Geneviève had saved him from the fever in his Paris days. Criticism is directed rather to the character of the petitions for material benefits, for the trivial and the unworthy. One beseeches St. Roche to save him from the plague, St. Apollonia from the toothache, and Job from boils, and enlists St. Hiero for the recovery of lost goods. "You pray to be saved from sudden death, and not rather to be of a better mind that you may not be unprepared wherever death may overtake you. Without giving thought to the improvement of your life you pray not to die. What then are you asking for if not that you may sin as long as possible? You think that I condemn the cult of the saints? Not at all. I condemn superstition. I will commend you for asking St. Roche to give you health if you will dedicate it to Christ. The cult of relics is mere superstition unless it serve to evoke remembrance and imitation of the saints. The colour of monastic habits, the wearing of girdles and sandals are all inconsequential. Better far to be reconciled with your adversary than to go dashing off to Rome or Compostella."

The themes delineated above receive no systematic

Qui sacra
uisut loca

presentation in Erasmus. Such a topical arrangement
would have blunted his eloquence. Let us then abridge a
passage directly from the *Enchiridion*. The sacraments, we
learn, are without value apart from the spirit.

Of what use is it to be sprinkled on the outside by holy
water if filthy within? No devotion better pleases Mary than
the imitation of her humility. Would you please Peter and
Paul? Then emulate the faith of the one and the charity of the
other. Thereby you will do better than if you make ten
pilgrimages to Rome. Would you imitate St. Francis? As it is
you are arrogant, avaricious, and contentious. Control your
temper, despise lucre. Overcome evil with good. You think it
important to be buried in the cowl of a Franciscan? To put on
his habit after you are dead will profit you nothing if you have
not put on his deportment while alive.

I do not condemn you for revering the ashes of Paul, but if you venerate mute, lifeless ashes while neglecting his living image, speaking, and as it were breathing in his letters, is not your devotion preposterous? You make much of a fragment of his body encased in glass but do you admire the whole mind of Paul shining through his epistles? You honour a statue of Christ in wood or stone and adorned with colours. You would do better to honour the image of his mind which through the Holy Spirit is expressed in the gospels. Are you excited over the seamless robe and the napkin of Christ and yet doze over the oracles of his law? Far better that you should believe than that you should treasure at home a piece of the wood of the cross. Otherwise you are no better than Judas, who with his lips touched the divine mouth. The physical presence of Christ is useless for salvation. Did not Paul say, "If I have known Christ after the flesh I will know him so no longer?"[49] When I talk in this fashion I am supposed to be recommending the abolition of all external ceremonies, all devotions of the simple, especially those approved by the authority of the Church. No. They are sometimes aids to piety and practically necessary for babes in Christ, but if the salt has lost its savour what good is it? I am ashamed to speak of all the superstitions attached to these ceremonies.

If you walk in the spirit, where are the fruits of the spirit? where is love? where is joy? where peace toward all? where patience, long suffering, goodness, kindness, compassion, faith, modesty, continence, and chastity? Where is the image of Christ in your behaviour? You say, "I am not an adulterer, a thief, a blasphemer. I keep my vows." What is that other than to say, "I am not as other men, extortioners, adulterers. I fast twice in the week."[50] The humble publican in Christ's parable, I tell you, and again I tell you, is better than those who recount their good deeds. Paul says "there is no condemnation to those that are in Christ Jesus, who walk not according to the flesh."[51] May you then in kindness correct the erring, teach the ignorant, raise the fallen, console the despondent, aid the toiling, relieve the needy. In a word, let all your possessions, all your concern, all your care be directed towards the imitation of Christ, who was not born for himself, lived not to himself, died not to himself, but for our sakes.

Do you think you will move God by the blood of a bull or by incense? "The sacrifices of God are a broken spirit."[52] You venerate the wood of the cross and have no regard for the mystery of the cross. You fast, refraining from that which does not defile, but you do not refrain from obscene conversation. You adorn a temple of stone, but of what use is this if the temple of the heart is full of abominations? With the mouth you bless, with the heart you curse. You enclose your body in a cell, while your mind wanders over the earth.

Creep not upon the earth, my brother, like an animal. Put on those wings which Plato says are caused to grow on the soul by the ardour of love. Rise above the body to the spirit, from the visible to the invisible, from the letter to the mystical meaning, from the sensible to the intelligible, from the involved to the simple. Rise as by rungs until you scale the ladder of Jacob. As you draw nigh to the Lord, He will draw nigh unto you. If with all your might you strive to rise above the cloud and clamour of the senses He will descend from light inaccessible and that silence which passes understanding in which not only the tumult of the senses is still, but the images of all intelligible things keep silence.

This conclusion, more than anything else in the writings of Erasmus, discloses the influence of the Platonic encounter. There are manifest echoes of the *Phaedrus* of Plato and of Pico *On the Dignity of Man*. The point that man should rise from the involved to the simple, that is from plurality to unity, is Neoplatonic, and a prominent theme in Colet. But when all this is said, the burden of the *Enchiridion* is that of the *Imitatio Christi* of Thomas à Kempis and the Christian ideal portrayed is fashioned in the images of Colet, More, and Vitrier.

After the seizure of his coins at Dover, Erasmus had

left England in an aggrieved, though not a rancorous
mood. At the end of the year 1505 we find him there
again. He told his prior that the reasons for the move
would take too long to explain, though adding that he
had been entreated by Lord Mountjoy and that England
had five or six scholars as well versed in Greek as any in
Italy.[53] There are hints that the hope of emoluments was
decisive. At any rate he stayed in England for a year and
a half, centering on London and lodging with various
friends. The old connections were renewed, for example
with Colet, and new friendships were formed. Grocyn
paddled Erasmus down the Thames to Lambeth to meet
William Warham, the Archbishop of Canterbury,
Chancellor of the realm, and keeper of the great seal.
Erasmus presented to him in manuscript a translation of
Euripides' *Hecuba*, completed earlier while at Louvain.
The archbishop, who avoided conspicuous benefactions,
took the author aside and handed him a monetary token of
appreciation. On the way back, Grocyn, not deceived by
the secrecy, inquired as to the amount. "A huge sum,"
replied Erasmus with gravity. Grocyn mildly snorted.
"And what's the meaning of that sardonic cackle?"
demanded Erasmus. "Don't you think he's rich enough,
or generous enough, or do you think I don't deserve
it?" "I've a hunch," confided Grocyn, "that he suspects
you fellows of dedicating the same manuscript to more
than one person." Stung by that insinuation, Erasmus, on
his return to Paris, published the translation together with
another of the *Iphigenia*, both dedicated to Warham,
without any thought then of returning to England or of
ever seeing him again.[54] This vindication of his integrity
was in later years to be richly rewarded.

Whereas on the first visit the friend with whom Erasmus was most intimately associated was Colet, on the

HECVBA, *& Iphigenia in Aulide Euripidis*
tragoediæ in latinum tralatæ Erasmo
Roterodamo interprete.

EIVSDEM *Ode de laudibus Britanniæ, Regisq̃*
Henrici septimi, ac regiorum liberorum eius.

EIVSDEM *Ode de senectutis incommodis.*

AL   DVS

The title page of Erasmus' translation of Euripides, dedicated to
Warham, and of the Ode in honour of England and King Henry
VII and his family.

second it was More. He was a barrister in London, who
despite his youth had served in the last parliament of
Henry VII and had incurred the royal displeasure by
persuading the Commons to whittle down the king's
financial demands. Whether More in consequence felt
insecure is debated, but at any rate he was not encumbered with public duties at the time of Erasmus'
arrival. He may well have been more involved in domestic
cares. He had just married Jane Colt, a daughter of the
gentry, a lass of seventeen, whom he instructed in letters

and music, so that she might have been to him a lifelong
partner of delight had not death claimed her after the
birth of several children.[55] Withal More did have time for
literary pursuits, not only with Jane, but also with
Erasmus. The two embarked upon a series of translations
of the dialogues of Lucian. What an enterprise was this
for a scholar dedicated wholly to sacred studies! Erasmus
answered that no better method was at hand for learning
Greek. Hermonymus of Sparta, his tutor at Paris, was
only a babbler. Consequently Erasmus must teach himself.[56] But still, he might have worked on Plutarch, as he
did later, rather than Lucian. Thomas More probably
determined the choice. Erasmus said of him that not even
an enemy could withstand his persuasiveness. "If he were
to lay it upon me that I join in a rope dance I would
readily comply."[57] A modern author has ventured the
surmise that if More and Erasmus had not translated
Lucian there would have been no *Utopia* and no *Praise of
Folly*. This is saying rather too much. After all, Erasmus
was working on St. Jerome who was no mean satirist and
was well versed in the satire of antiquity.[58] In any case
Erasmus had satire in his marrow. His description of
Lucian is a description of himself. "What grace had he in
speaking, what felicity of imagination, what charm in
jesting, what vinegar in castigating! How he titillates
with allusions, how he mingles seriousness with trifles
and trifles with the serious, how laughingly he speaks of
truth! He so depicts the behaviour of men with the brush
of a miniaturist that you seem not to read but to see the
scene before your eyes. No comedy, no satire is to be
compared with these dialogues, whether you are seeking
pleasure or profit."[59] Some of the Lucianic techniques
Erasmus was able to utilize directly. The contradictory
prayers by which Jove was plagued, to give rain for one

E.   D

CHAPTER FOUR

Italy: The Praise of Folly

*

THE trip to Italy, so long desired, was made possible
because the Italian physician of Henry VII, Dr. Boerio,
was sending his two sons to study at Bologna with an
Englishman as tutor and Erasmus as supervisor of
studies.[1] Why did Erasmus now wish to go to Italy if it
were true, as he said, that England had five or six scholars
who knew Greek as well as any in Italy and if his own
Greek was adequate for his purposes? As a matter of
fact neither statement was true. The Greek scholars in
England were Englishmen, those in Italy were Greeks.
Some had stayed on in Italy after the Council of Ferrara
and Florence. Some, after the fall of Constantinople in
1453, had come directly, or via Crete, to Italy. Greeks
teaching Greek were to be found at Florence, Padua, and
Rome, but nowhere so plentifully as at Venice because of
her proximity and commercial relations with the Byzantine empire. In Venice the great house of Aldus was
printing Greek works in exquisite type for consumption
in the Latin West.[2] And Erasmus had not yet the proficiency which would make his work outstanding in the
editing of the classics, the Church fathers, and the Bible.
In retrospect he summed up very soundly his reasons for
going. "This was the only trip I ever made entirely of my
own volition. I went partly that once in my life I might
see the sacred sites, partly that I might visit libraries and
enjoy the fellowship of scholars."[3]

The party delayed a couple of months in Paris to enable Erasmus to supervise the publication of his works, then continued by way of Orleans, Lyons, and the pass of Mt. Cenis. Gazing upon majestic peaks and verdant valleys Erasmus was not enraptured like Petrarch with the glories of nature, but instead composed a poem on old age. He was approaching his fortieth year. Lest any one in our day smile, be it remembered that in his day the average length of life was twenty-five years. Abridged and translated the poem reads:[4]

> How shortly ago was Erasmus
> Like to an opening flower.
> Now the signs of his aging
> Presage the ominous hour.
> Phoebus has scarce driven forty
> Rounds with his steeds since he came,
> And now the white hairs in his whiskers
> Prove that he is not the same.
>
> How quickly my days have been speeding
> Since I played with nuts as a lad,
> Wrangled with sophists and rhetors
> And read all the poets to be had,
> Painted tenuous fancies,
> Sucked every book like a bee,
> To know the Greek and the Latin,
> Encompassed the land and the sea!
>
> And now I scale snow buried passes
> To find new friends of the Muse.
> But O, the years that have vanished
> Where and how did I lose?
>
> O come, come now Erasmus!
> Do not give way to regret.
> You have no way of knowing
> How much is left to you yet.

> But take hold, be it great, be it little,
> Casting everything other aside.
> Your honour, your glory, your study
> Is this, that Christ be your guide.

Arrived on the Italian plain the party went first to Turin where Erasmus received the doctorate in theology, perhaps through the good offices of a friendly cardinal.[5] One wonders why he did not take it at Paris where he had worked so long rather than at Turin where he had not worked at all. He may have thought the Italian degree would carry greater prestige. He wrote to his northern friends rather apologetically for having taken it, but at any rate he deserved it. The next stop on which he commented was Pavia. Here he visited the temple constructed wholly within and without from top to bottom of white marble including altars, columns, and tombs. "How much sense is there," demanded Erasmus, "in squandering so much money in order that a few lone monks may chant in a marble church, which is to them more of a burden than a benefit in view of the inundation of tourists who come to gape at a church of white stone?"[6] This passage has led some to conclude that Erasmus had no interest in art. His stricture applied, however, only to ostentation.

The party then moved on towards Bologna, but turned aside to Florence on hearing that Pope Julius, *Giuliano il terribile*, was besieging Bologna in pursuance of his resolve to recover the estates of the Church which Caesar Borgia had been seizing for himself and secularizing. Death took care of the Borgia. Then Bologna asserted her independence, and Venice extended her tutelage over portions of the one-time patrimony of St. Peter. Julius set out to subdue Bologna by expelling the ruling Bentivogli. Erasmus and his party, hearing that the city was actually in the possession of the pope, continued their journey and arrived in time to witness the papal triumph. The procession was led by horsemen and then infantry in glistening armour, followed by the papal standard bearers and the pope's ten white palfreys with golden bridles, then the foreign envoys, next forty of the clergy with lighted candles, the cardinals preceding the pope in a palanquin and clad in a purple cope shot through with threads of gold and on his head a mitre sparkling with pearls and jewels. Patriarchs followed, archbishops and bishops, ecclesiastics, generals of the monastic orders, and at the end the papal guard.[7] Erasmus viewed the spectacle *magno cum gemitu*, "with a mighty groan."[8] Was Pope Julius the successor of Jesus Christ, he asked, or of Julius Caesar?

During the course of the following year Erasmus had occasion to observe papal taxation in the newly acquired territory. "When I went through the countryside I saw the poverty of the peasants whose entire fortune consisted in two cows, and who were scarcely able to maintain an entire family, I saw them mulcted by the papal collectors of a ducat each."[9] The year at Bologna was not too profitable for Erasmus except that he lodged with the professor of Greek, Paolo Bombasio, with whom he formed a lasting friendship. But Bombasio was not a Greek.[10]

After thirteen months Erasmus was bold enough to address himself to the great Venetian publisher Aldus Manutius. There was a touch of presumption in the approach. Erasmus, though forty, was not yet a scholar of great reputation. The *Enchiridion* had not attained its enormous vogue and the first edition of the *Adagia* was slight. The *Hecuba* and the *Iphigenia* were no more than

Venice in 1503.

translations, however adroit. Erasmus sounded out Aldus as to the publication of the *Adagia*, on which further work had been done during the year at Bologna. Aldus agreed to take it on, though he had not been doing well of late.[11] To see the work through the press Erasmus betook himself to Venice. His obligation to the Boerio lads terminated with the year and he was free to enter into a partnership with Aldus in which in the sequel each was to confer celebrity on the other. On arrival Erasmus was kept waiting for an audience with the great publisher who was busy with his printers and supposed the caller to be some casual visitor. Learning that he was Erasmus, Aldus promptly made him a member of his household.[12]

A household indeed it was, of over thirty members who worked together, ate together, slept together, and spoke together in Greek on pain of a fine for a lapse into the vernacular. Erasmus roomed with Jerome Aleander, destined to be the great opponent of Luther at the Diet of Worms and later to be a cardinal. At the time he was twenty-four years old and already a prodigy of learning, an accomplished Latin poet, proficient in Greek and Hebrew, progressing in Aramaic and Arabic, versed in music, mathematics, and the liberal arts.[13] Erasmus took to him as he had done to More, and later recommended him for a post which he secured as professor of Greek at Paris. Thereafter contacts diminished. Aleander wrote lamenting the lack of correspondence. "We are both to blame," he said, "but you the more, unless you have not received my letters. When I heard that you were in Paris [Aleander was away at the moment], I dropped important matters simply that I might see you, embrace you, joke with you, and enjoy your charming company, that we might renew the fellowship we had as roommates, for nothing in my life was ever so delightful. But it was not to be. Four days before my arrival you had left."[14]

The eating arrangements in the household of Aldus no more suited Erasmus than those in the monastery at Steyn or at the *Collegia Pauperum* at Paris. There was no breakfast. Lunch was at one and supper not until ten in the evening. The wine was poor, and Erasmus believed that the kidney stone which plagued him for the rest of his life was due to the vile beverage. The diet was meagre. The amount one eats, said Erasmus, is a matter of habit. The Italians are healthy on their fare, but a northerner needs more. Erasmus withdrew from the common table and was served in his room.[15]

He deprived himself thereby of the mealtime conversation in Greek with such distinguished scholars as Musurus and Lascaris, though he did not withdraw from their discussions which sometimes continued until cock crow on how ancient Greek was to be pronounced. These scholars had a feeling for language and a sense of history. They were aware that full appreciation of any tongue requires the ear as well as the eye and they knew full well that language changes. Several scholars observed, prior to Erasmus, that the pronunciation of ancient Greek could not have been that of the modern. What they noticed as a matter of antiquarian interest Erasmus made into a programme of educational reform. In pursuance of these discussions he later wrote a book on the pronunciation of both Greek and Latin.[16] Each of these languages afforded a clue to the pronunciation of the other in antiquity by way of transliterations. When Cicero was spelled in Greek as *Kikero*, it was certainly not pronounced as *Sissero*, and when *Paulos* in Greek was transliterated into Latin as Paulus, the pronunciation was not *Pafflos* or *Pavlos*, as in modern Greek. Other clues were to be found in spelling and diacritical marks. Ancient Greek had five vowel combinations which in the modern tongue all have the sound of *e* in eel. Erasmus believed that they must have been differentiated in speech. Because of the diacritical marks he insisted that ancient Greek was to be pronounced according to accent rather than according to vowel quantity like Latin. All of these points in the case of Greek were not of vast significance. Erasmus desired indeed a uniform pronunciation among those able to use Greek, but in the West they were not numerous. The pronunciation of Latin was more crucial because this was the language of Christendom. Its universalism would be forfeit if the pronunciation were so affected by the vernaculars that spoken Latin sounded like Spanish, Portuguese, Italian, or what not. Norms of pronunciation needed to be established and these should

be in terms of classical usage. The Erasmian pronunciation was eventually adopted in the schools of Europe and
America, both for Greek and for Latin, save that Holland
and England held to vowel quantity rather than accent
for Greek. The entire question has come to be a matter of
only antiquarian interest since Latin has ceased to be the
lingua franca of Europe.[17]

The Greek scholars were prodigiously obliging to
Erasmus and inundated him with manuscripts from which
he extracted new adages and fed them to the printers
right in the shop amid the clanking of the presses. The
Adagia of 1508 was enlarged from the 838 maxims of the
first edition till it came to number 3260. Greek sources
were this time copiously exploited and the practice was
commenced of writing essays with the proverbs as
texts. Under the rubric "a Batavian ear," meaning a dull
fellow, Erasmus introduced a defence of his fellow
Batavians, and the passage earlier quoted in praise of
Holland is from this essay. The saying "The labours of
Hercules" gave an opportunity to expatiate on the
Herculean task of digging out the adages.[18] The proverb
Festina lente, "Make haste slowly," was used to explain the
printer's mark of Aldus, the dolphin entwined about the
anchor. Aldus had taken it from a coin of Titus where it
was a nautical symbol. Erasmus interpreted it to mean
"Make haste slowly" because the dolphin is swift and the
anchor retards. The saying has, however, been attached
to more than one symbol.[19]

Among the essays on the adages, three in particular
enshrined favourite Erasmian themes. The *Dulce bellum
inexpertis*,[20] "Sweet is war to him who has no taste of it,"
carries further the indictment of war first voiced in the
monastic days. The *Scarabeus aquilam quaerit*,[21] "The
beetle seeks the eagle," plays upon the theme that God

uses the weak things of the world to confound the mighty. The Greek legend was that the beetle interceded with the eagle to spare a rabbit that had fled into the beetle's hole, but the eagle tore the rabbit apart. The beetle then sought successive nests of the eagle and cast out the eggs till Zeus imposed a truce. The story itself is not so much the point for Erasmus as that the ruthless eagle appears on the escutcheons of rulers equally brutal; whereas the beetle is despised, though his back has a brilliant sheen, his patience in rolling burdens is incredible, his cleanliness in the midst of filth is remarkable, and the annual renewal of his youth is inspiring. The dung-descended insect is more admirable than the ferocious bird.

The adage *Sileni Alcibiadis* "The Sileni of Alcibiades," is similar. Alcibiades said of Socrates that he looked like Silenus with a bovine, peasant face and a snub nose always dripping, but when one looked inside this Silenus, behold rather a god than a man, superior to all the jostling of mortals, transcending insults, and drinking the hemlock as cheerfully as if it were wine. "Is not the most extraordinary Silenus," commented Erasmus, "to be found in Christ himself, of whom the prophet spake saying, 'He has no form nor comeliness and when we behold him there is no beauty that we should desire him. He is despised and rejected of men'? He came not from the palaces of kings, from the seats of the Pharisees, from the schools of the philosophers, but from the tables of the tax gatherers and the nets of fishermen. But if we regard him from within what an ineffable treasure, what a pearl without price, in such humility what sublimity, in such ignominy what glory, in such labours what utter rest, and in so bitter a death what a perennial fount of eternal life!"[22]

ERASMI ROTERODAMI ADAGIORVM
CHILIADES TRES, AC CENTV-
RIAE FERE TOTIDEM.

ALD·STVDIOSIS·S·

Qv̈is nihil aliud cupio,q̈ prodeſſe uobis Studioſi.Cum ueniſſet in manus meas Eraſmi Roterodā
mi,hominis undecunq̈ doctiss.hoc adagiorũ opus eruditum.uarium. plenũ bonæ frugis,
& quod poſſit uel cum ipſa antiquitate certare,intermiſſis antiquis autorib. quos pa
raueram excudendos, illud curauimus imprimendum,tati profuturum uobis
& multitudine ipſa adagiorũ,quæ ex plurimis autorb.tam latinis , quàm
græcis ſtudioſe collegit ſummis certe laborib.ſummis uigiliis ,&
multis locis apud utriuſq̈ linguæ autores obiter uel correctis
acute, uel expoſitis erudite·Docet præterea quot modis .
ex hiſce adagiis capere utilitatem liceat,puta quē
admodum ad uarios uſus accõmodari poſ
ſint. Adde,q̈ circiter decē millia uer
ſuum ex Homero·Euripide, & cæ
teris Græcis eodē metro in
hoc opere fideliter, &
docte tralata ha
bētur,præ
ter pla
rima
ex Pla
tone, De-
moſthene, & id
genus ali
is·An
antem uenus ſim,
Ἰδὼ ῥόδῳ, Ἰδὼ καὶ τὸ πλόϛμα·
Nam,quod dicitur, αὐτὸς μύϛος αὐλῶ·

Præponitur hiſce adagiis duplex index·Alter ſecundum literas
alphabeti noſtri·nam quæ græca ſunt, latinâ quoq̈
habentur·Alter per capita rerum.

The mark of Aldus Manutius on the title page of the *Adages* of
Erasmus, published at Venice in 1508.

The Aldine edition of the *Adagia* was so bulky that
when Aldus offered Erasmus several hundred copies he
answered that he could accept only if he were given also
a horse.[23] The work completed, Erasmus moved on to
Padua, itself a second Venice, where now Musurus was
teaching Greek. At this point the financial resources of
Erasmus must have been depleted because he took on the
tutoring of Alexander Stewart, a natural son of the King

The printer's mark of Aldus, which Erasmus took to mean *Festina lente*, was taken by Aldus from a coin of Titus (see Pl. 3), where it was a nautical symbol. Aldus reversed the direction of the dolphin's head. One wonders whether he might have been influenced by an early Christian seal (see above), which as it stands has the same direction, but when stamped would be like the coin. The seal has the word *ichthys* (the sacred fish), cut in mirror script, referring to the dolphin. The anchor signified the cross.
(On the anchor as the cross see: Leo Eizenhöfer, "Die Siegelvorschläge des Clemens von Alexandrien und die älteste Literatur," *Jahrbuch für Antike und Christentum*, III (1960), 51–70.)

of Scotland, a youth of eighteen, already the Archbishop of St. Andrews. Erasmus described him as a lad of most engaging disposition of whom he became extremely fond.[24] From Padua they moved on to Siena, presumably on their way to Rome. There ill health detained Erasmus a couple of months. He worked on further translations from Lucian while Alexander composed the essays assigned to him on varied themes. The boy enjoyed a prank and one day brought to Erasmus a manuscript annotated in his own hand. Erasmus acknowledged the writing but declared that he had never laid eyes on the manuscript. "You must have done," insisted the boy.

"It is your handwriting." Then he laughed and confessed that he had imitated the penmanship. "I see," said Erasmus, "that you'll make an expert forger." Together they made a trip via Rome to Naples and visited the cave of the Cumean Sibyl.[25]

When the boy was called by his father to return to Scotland, in taking leave he presented Erasmus with an old Roman gem bearing the image of the god Terminus, the god of bounds.[26] Erasmus adopted it as his device with the motto *Concedo Nulli*! "I yield to no one." When reproached for arrogance, he replied that the words were not his own but those of the god Terminus, the ineluctable terminus of this mortal life.[27] Erasmus in his youth, as we observed, was tormented by the thought of death and throughout his life laboured breathlessly to complete his mission and prepare his spirit for the ultimate transition. Four years after the leavetaking came a poignant reminder that *Concedo nulli* is the motto of *Mors*. In the year 1513 the King of Scots, though married to Margaret Tudor, invaded England. At his side stood the young Archbishop of St. Andrews. On the field of Flodden the king fell and on the field of Flodden fell also that lad so beloved of Erasmus, Alexander Stewart. "Oh, I know he loved his country," said Erasmus, "I know he loved his father. But what a fool was his father ever to have invaded England!"[28]

Erasmus spent a period at Rome. His reputation was spreading. He was received as an honoured colleague by some half-dozen erudite cardinals, among whom the most intimate were the future Leo X, as well as Riario, the nephew of Pope Julius, and the learned Grimani.[29] Because of such contacts Erasmus always looked back on Rome with insuppressible nostalgia.[30]

But other impressions were less favourable. Even in the

ER · ROT

TERMINVS

Pallas Apelleam nuper mirata tabellam,
Hanc ait, æternùm Bibliotheca colat.
Dædaleam monstrat Musis Holbeinnius artem,
Et summi Ingenii Magnus Erasmus opes.

The god Terminus and Erasmus by Holbein in 1535.

papal circle he sensed a paganism in more than mere terminology. "When I was in Rome," he recalled, "I was urgently invited to attend a Good Friday service. Pope Julius was present, though usually for reasons of health he stayed away. There was a large concourse of cardinals and bishops, and besides the rabble, many scholars. I will spare the name of the orator. His introduction and conclusion were longer than the oration itself and were wholly taken up with the praise of Julius, who was hailed as Jupiter Optimus Maximus, brandishing in his right hand the trident and the inevitable lightning and with a nod achieving whatever he would. Everything important in recent years in France, Germany, Spain, Portugal, Africa, and Greece had been brought about at his behest. . . . But what has all this to do with the Julius who is head of the Christian religion, the vice regent of Christ, the successor of Peter and Paul? Then the orator went on to make the cross of Christ triumphal, plausible and glorious by comparisons with the martyrdoms of Socrates, Epaminondas, Scipio, and Aristides. What could be more utterly frigid and banal?"[31]

Cruelty in Rome shocked Erasmus. "I was dragged by friends to see a bull fight in the palace of Julius II. I have never been pleased with these cruel games, relics of pagan antiquity. But in the interlude between the killing and dragging off of the bull came a diverting pantomime. A man comes in with a cape wrapped around his left arm and a sword in the right. Then he imitates all the movements of the bull fight. First he comes in gingerly, then, as if seen by the bull, retreats. To divert the bull's charge he throws away his cape. Then, as if the bull were retreating, he very timidly retrieves it. Sometimes as if in fear he brandishes his sword, then leaps to the safety area in the centre of the arena. Next he races the bull and when the animal is breathless leaps on his back and crows in triumph. I enjoyed this pantomime much more than the gory sport."[32] That is Erasmus.

The superstitions of the people revolted him. "Do you think we do not know," he wrote to an Italian, "what the

Bullfight in St. Peter's Square in Rome at the Jubilee of 1500.

common people are like in Italy? They would be pious enough if the priests did their duty. We have seen too much of this neglect with our own eyes. Temples are silent. Rarely is Mass said, not to speak of the manner of living. Look at the tithes, indulgences, annates, confirmations, etc. I do not begrudge priests a modest living, but let them consider the needs of the people and not defend their authority with threats and punishments."[33]

But by nothing was Erasmus so outraged as by the sight of a pope leading his troops to the capture of a Christian city. Cardinal Riario at the instance of Pope Julius asked Erasmus to write essays pro and con on the pope's right to make war on Venice.[34] Erasmus complied. The essays are lost. He said that the case against the war was made overwhelmingly stronger than the case in favour, but the cardinal used only the latter. Despite the loss we have elsewhere an outline of what was to be said against the enterprise. The argument is a crescendo of ifs. A priest should not fight, said Erasmus, but if he may he should not fight for territory. If a priest may fight the pope should not, because he is closer to Christ. If some other pope may fight, Julius should not because he is old, clement, and hitherto pacific. In any case the supreme pontiff, whose arms are prayers and tears, should not deluge the world with blood for the sake of mundane territory. The peace of the Church should mean more to him than a few paltry fortresses. Besides, the outcome of even a just war is unpredictable. Better to arbitrate.[35]

Whither now Erasmus? The work on the *Adagia* was over and the tutoring of Alexander Stewart. With feelings so mixed about the papacy, Rome, and Italy, should Erasmus remain for the sake of the libraries and the company of scholars? And if so, on what then should he live? While he cogitated, letters came from England. Mountjoy wrote: "Our prince has become Henry VIII. You are not only acquainted with him but intimate, for he has written you letters. [He had sent two in his own hand to Erasmus in Italy.] If you knew how wisely he governs, how he loves the just and good, how he favours the learned, I venture to swear on my life that even without wings you would fly over. O my Erasmus, if you could see all the people rejoice over such a prince, you could not hold back tears of joy. The air smiles, the earth exults, the land flows with milk, honey, and nectar. Our king desires not gold or gems, but virtue, glory, immortality. I will give you a taste. A few days ago, when he expressed regret to me that he was not more learned, I said, 'That is not what we ask of you, but that you favour scholars.' He replied, 'How could I not, seeing that I can scarcely live without them...?' The Archbishop of Canterbury promises you a benefice if you will return and has given me £5 to send you to defray the expenses of your journey."[36] Archbishop Warham sent a confirmatory note.[37]

Erasmus went to take his leave of Cardinal Grimani who received him with the utmost deference, chatted with him for more than two hours and begged him to stay at Rome where the climate was salubrious and his library magnificent. "When I said to him that I had been invited by the king of England [a slight exaggeration] reluctantly he let me go."[38]

What did the three years in Italy add up to? The expansion of the *Adagia* from a slight collection of Latin proverbs largely into a panorama of the ancient world, the employment of some of the proverbs as texts for essays, a vastly increased command of Greek, and a host of new friends, so much so that when the German humanist, Ulrich von Hutten, later traversed the same ground he was everywhere received with exceeding hospitality because commended by Erasmus.[39]

After a few years Erasmus began to wonder whether he might not have done better to have stayed. At the time the move appeared wise. The long trek to England on horseback gave him abundant opportunity for reflection. On the descent into Italy he had queried the utility of scholarship of which there is never an end. On the way from Italy he was musing on the apparent futility of all human endeavour. Arrived in England and staying in the home of Thomas More, he cast his reflections into an essay, whimsical, facetious, ironic, tinged with melancholy, titled by a pun, for in Greek the *Encomium Moriae* might be taken to mean the praise of More or the praise of Folly.[40]

In this little jeu d'esprit Folly herself enters and like a professor mounts the rostrum to deliver a discourse to a classroom of scholars. She declares that she will speak extempore without regard to rules and then constructs her discourse with all the divisions and subdivisions of the rhetoricians. Since Aristotle declares that an encomium should commence with a genealogy, she begins her laudation of herself by announcing that she is the daughter of Pluto and the goddess of youth, born in the Fortunate Isles, and nursed by drunkenness and ignorance. But this is not at all the genealogy of Erasmus' *Stultitia*. Among her ancestors was the court fool, sometimes an imbecile, who instead of being placed in an institution, was cared for in the household of a prince, while the courtiers, half with malice, half with compassion, derived amusement from his infantilism. But then again, he was sometimes a clever rogue who lodged barbed darts of irony and with impunity because he wore the cap and bells. Yet again the fools of Erasmus were those pilloried by the medieval preachers and moralists such as Geiler of Kaisersberg and Sebastian Brandt, who filled his *Ship of Fools* with all those whom he meant to berate. The anomaly of Erasmus' Folly is that she herself berates the fools. Then at last she turns out to be the fool in Christ, who appears to be a fool to all those who in their folly esteem themselves as wise.

Our Folly is a very disconcerting dame. She is like

mankind, whom Erasmus, following Lucian and anti-
cipating Shakespeare, describes as actors on the stage of
life wearing as in the ancient drama now one mask and
now another. But the Erasmian Folly does not go
behind the wings to change her masks, but by sleight of
hand effects the shifts and thus tricks the reader into
thinking she is still in the same role. Is he regarding her

as a sot? then of a sudden she becomes a sage, and when
he gives credulity to her sagacity she turns into a satyr or
a sot. The change occurs again and again for Folly
prestidigitates from role to role.

She announces that it is she who keeps the human race
extant. "For what man would ever put his neck into the
halter of matrimony if, like the sages, he weighed the
inconveniences, or what woman would ever give herself
to a man if she took account of the perilous pangs of
childbirth and the trouble of bringing up children? Or
having done so once, would ever think of doing so again
unless attended by Lethe, the goddess of forgetfulness?"

Folly is spontaneity, a certain recklessness, an uncalculating readiness to take risks. She overrides prudence, yet is the highest prudence. For she delivers men alike from fear and shame and thus frees them to embark on great enterprises. Without her what cities, what empires would ever have been built?

Again Folly is the inhibition of that brutal candour which makes social intercourse insufferable. A little humbug is the lubricant of life. One can never get along with folk by utter truthfulness. A measure of dissembling, a touch of flattery smooths the path of friendship. All men are actors, deceived by their own masks, thinking themselves to be the very characters they impersonate. Shall we then pluck off the masks? Nay, rather let men play their parts, and happier perchance are we, too, if we do not perceive their masks. Illusion is the balm of life and a worse calamity than to be deceived is not to be deceived. If a man sincerely thinks his commonplace wife is a Penelope, all the better for their wedded bliss. Happier they who sit in Plato's cave, viewing the shadows, than those who come out into the light and see things as they really are.

The ignorance of the simple is a boon. How blessed were those pristine men of the golden age, who lived in accordance with nature, knowing nothing of grammar, rhetoric, or law, nor bothering their heads as to what lay beyond the sky! How happy flies and birds! And look at morons. They play, sing, and laugh and bring others pleasure with their childishness. Compare the moron with the scholar "who squanders his youth in mastering the disciplines, wastes the sweetest of his years in worry, sweat, and vigils, always frugal, poor, lugubrious, gloomy, unjust, and harsh to himself, grating and grievous to others, lean, frail, bleary-eyed, old before his time."

The reader asks himself at this point just which mask Folly now is wearing. Erasmus himself was dedicated to his scholarly vigils and continued his indefatigable labours to the very end. Is Folly now really foolishness, who in her blindness is asking the scholar what good will come of it all? Or is she that prudent imprudence which drives a man to go on, even if he cannot foresee whether any fruit will come from his sowing? She is ambiguous because changing again her role. Speedily she becomes unmistakably the foolishness which Erasmus derides – the foolishness of those who leave slaughtering to the lower classes, but consider carving up a beast felled in the hunt to be fit work for gentlemen, the foolishness of inordinate builders, of gamblers, of those who call upon the saints to cure the toothache, of the thief who, saved from the gallows by the intervention of a saint, feels himself commissioned to relieve men again of their wealth, the foolishness of those who mock him who tells them the way to die well is to live well. Again the foolishness of those who at a funeral act as if the dead would be embarrassed to return and find a paucity of candles and hired pallbearers, the foolishness of chauvinists whether French, English, Scottish, Italian, Turkish, or whatever you please.

Then again Erasmus excoriates the folly of merchants who impose on the public by a display of gold rings, of grammarians who deem it the highest achievement of twenty years' labour to be able to distinguish eight parts of speech, of lawyers who roll the stone of Sisyphus by emitting six hundred laws in one breath, of theologians who debate how in the Eucharist accidents can subsist without substance and who conjure up sophisticated inanities about quiddities and entities. Why not send the brawling Scotists, the adamant Occamists, the invincible

Albertists to fight the Turks? And the monks, who will
not touch money but are not so fastidious as to wine and
women. At the judgment day one of them will boast that
in sixty years he has never handled money save with
gloves. Another will present himself with a cowl so dirty
and greasy that no sailor would put it on. Another will
display a voice grown hoarse with chanting. Christ will
interrupt them saying, "Whence this new race of Jews?"
[that is, of legalists].

Opprobrium is thrown on kings who leave the care of
their subjects to the gods, fleece their people, and squan-
der their substance on feeding fine horses; ladies who
think the longer the trains they trail the nearer they are to
the gods; popes and cardinals who delegate to Christ the
care of their sheep; supreme pontiffs who, if there is any
work to be done, turn it over to Peter and Paul; popes
who think miracles outdated, instruction of the people
irksome, explanations of Scripture pedantry, prayer a
waste of time, who consider poverty to be sordid, defeat
in war dishonourable, and to die on the cross a disgrace.
They send men to hell with their excommunications and

shed Christian blood to defend the papal patrimony. Whereas the Christian Church was founded on blood, strengthened by blood, increased by blood, Christ's cause today is advanced by war too cruel to befit men or beasts.

Then comes a jibe at scholars who throw a smog of annotations over the works of others, "like that Erasmus." What an incredibly trivial conclusion to such a catalogue of enormities! By including himself was Erasmus throwing a sop to those whose gorge was rising?

After this startling interjection he takes one more fling at theologians who stretch Scripture like a sheepskin to justify the wars of Christians on the ground that Christ said "Let him who has no sword sell his mantle and buy one." (Luke 22: 36). "As if Christ, who taught nothing but patience and meekness, meant the sword used by bandits and murderers rather than the sword of the Spirit. Our exegete thinks that Christ equipped the apostles with lances, crossbows, slings, and muskets."

At this point Dame Folly makes her final metamorphosis. Now she becomes the foolishness of the cross. For:

no morons so play the fool as those who are obsessed with the ardour of Christian piety to the point that they distribute their goods, overlook injuries, suffer themselves to be deceived, make no distinction between friends and enemies, eschew pleasure, glut themselves with hunger, vigils, tears, toils, and reproaches, who disdain life, who crave only death, who seem utterly to contemn all common sense, as if the soul lived elsewhere and not in the body. What is this if not insanity? No wonder that the apostles appeared to be drunk with new wine and Paul seemed to Festus to be mad. Christ himself became a fool when he was found in fashion as a man that he might bring healing by the foolishness of the cross.

'For God has chosen the foolish things of the world to confound the wise, and the weak things of the world to confound
the mighty.'

The *Moria* like the *Enchiridion* ends with the Platonic
madness of ecstatic rapture, when the spirit rises above
the things of sense and man is utterly beside himself, not
knowing whether he is in the body or out of the body,
for he experiences that which "eye hath not seen and ear
hath not heard and neither hath it entered into the heart
of man." He has already known a foretaste and a glow of
that ineffable blessedness which shall be his when this
mortal shall have put on immortality.

Then Folly leaves the rostrum saying, "Adieu, clap,
live, drink, you celebrated devotees of *Moria*." And now
once more she is the goddess of the cap and bells.

One interpreter has suggested that the *Praise of Folly*
is the final attempt of the Renaissance to reduce all life to
rational order, art to perspective, business to bookkeep-
ing, war to strategy, statecraft to diplomacy. Now by
Erasmus the irrational is shown to be the rational. Yes,
but the irrational is shown to be the rational only because
the rational is shown to be the irrational and all those

disciplines so neatly reduced by men to order are but striving after wind.[41]

Another interpreter also suggests an influence of the Renaissance, the Italian Renaissance, for in Italy Erasmus had tasted of the amenities of gracious living, and had come to distrust the fevered fury of those who inhabit the northern lands.[42] But Erasmus had long since tasted the amenities of life in the north while kissing nymphs at Mountjoy's estate, whereas in Italy's sunny clime he had laboured like a veritable Hercules. The point of the *Moria* is not to bask in the *dolce far niente*. It is not a moralistic denunciation as in Brandt's *Ship of Fools*. It is not buffoonery. It is not the *gaudeamus igitur* of the goliards. Erasmus himself said that the point was precisely the same as that of the *Enchiridion*. What there he had said seriously he said now in the guise of jest.

One may the better understand both the *Enchiridion* and the *Moria* by comparing them with another passage where Erasmus was commenting on the text, "All is vanity."

Whence comes such vanity in the lives of Christians who enjoy the truth of the Gospel? With what tumults everywhere our lives are filled! We do business, we sail the seas, we engage in wars, we make treaties and we break them, we beget children, enroll heirs, buy fields and sell, cement friendships, erect buildings and tear them down. We are tonsured, anointed, vestured in cowls. We are exercised in various arts, sweat and become doctors of laws and theology. Some prefer the mitre and the crozier. With such cares we torture ourselves. In this we wax old. In this we let slip so many years and lose that precious treasure which alone is of worth. Then will come the last tribunal where only truth can stand. Too late we shall perceive that all these vanities were but shadows and we have squandered our lives in the delusion of a dream.

Some one will say "Shall a Christian, then, have nothing to do with all of these vanities?" No, not that, but we shall participate only with detachment, being ready to forsake all for the sake of the one thing needful, as Paul said, "Having a wife as if not having," weeping as if not weeping, rejoicing as if not rejoicing, selling as possessing nothing, using the world as if not using, for the fashion of this world passes away. Use then the world but delight not in it.[42]

Observe that the list of vanities here enumerated corresponds to those pilloried in the *Praise of Folly*, which, in the light of such similarity, may be described as an ironic version of the *contemptus mundi*, the contempt of the world. To say that it is ironic means, however, that it is not the medieval contempt of the world. Erasmus would not be willing, like Jerome and Colet, to see propagation cease that earth might be emptied and heaven filled. A more significant difference is the blending, everywhere to be found in Erasmus, of the Christian and classical themes. The Stoics distinguished the wise men and the fools, who because not governed by reason were both sots and knaves. The Neoplatonists deplored the servitude of man to the carnal. The first stage towards emancipation and self-mastery was self-knowledge – "Know thyself." The fool in the period of the Renaissance is consequently often portrayed eyeing himself quizzically in a mirror. He thus perceives that "everyman" is a fool including himself. His very existence depends on that *élan vital* which is not amenable to reason. This insight enables him to smile at himself as Erasmus does on more than one occasion.[44] The smile is not a laugh of scorn so much as of pity and of hope. For man, enthralled by the senses and spending himself for ephemeral goals, can be emancipated by Folly of another sort, that divine rapture of Plato transcending reason, and the divine self-emptying of the Christian, who pursues his earthly pilgrimage with fidelity and detachment, following in the footsteps of him who trod the *via dolorosa*.

The *Praise of Folly* was hailed by Huizinga as the work of Erasmus alone destined to be immortal.[45] "For only when humour illuminated that mind did it become truly profound." By that token some of the *Colloquies* would qualify. But one may question whether Erasmus was profound only when witty. The *Moria* is a diverting fantasy. Yet the work of Erasmus which most profoundly shaped the mind of the Western world was one which today is consulted only by a handful of historical specialists, his edition of the New Testament in Greek, which served as the basis for the great vernacular translations.

CHAPTER FIVE

The Scourge of Princes and Prelates

*

ON arriving again in England Erasmus stayed naturally
for a time with the man who had so ardently invited him.
Then for a period he roomed in London with an Italian,
whom he had met previously, but with whom he now
grew intimate, the secretary of Henry VIII, by name
Andrea Ammonio, learned, delightful, a poet and *molto
simpatico*.[1] Next came a lengthy stay in the household of
Thomas More, who had recently lost his first wife and,
having four little children, married within a month Dame
Alice, a widow with a daughter of her own.[2] Erasmus
had thus an opportunity to share in the life of More's
charming domestic circle. Dame Alice grew cool towards
him, however. One can understand that with two families
to integrate she did not relish the complication of an
outsider, particularly one who could not speak English.
Erasmus went then to Cambridge, where he was domiciled
at Queens' college. Since the promised emoluments were
slow in materializing he was driven to assume lectures on
Greek and sacred studies, but that he held the Lady
Margaret professorship cannot be established. The
Cambridge years were quiet years. Erasmus worked like
a mole save that his surface eruptions became evident
only at a later time. He was strenuously engaged in
building up still further the *Adagia*, translating more of
Lucian, editing Seneca and Cato, translating Plutarch and
St. Basil, and above all editing the letters of St. Jerome,

thus once more combining the classical and the Christian concerns. His most significant activity was the commencement of the translation of the New Testament directly from the Greek and diverging from the Vulgate.[3]

Contacts with old friends were naturally renewed and notably with Colet, who, having received a legacy from his father, used it to establish a school named St. Paul's for his favourite apostle. Colet would have been pleased to have had as its first preceptor Erasmus himself, who was, however, of no mind to abandon his programme of education. He did take a lively interest in the school and composed for the boys a declamation about the boy Jesus, concluding:

Who in all history, is like to Jesus, ineffably, inconceivably God of God, born before all times, eternal and fully equal to his eternal and loftiest parent? Does not his human birth easily overshadow that of all kings? By the will of the Father and the breath of the Spirit he was born a Virgin, a man in time and still God, unsullied by our corruption. Who is richer than he who gives all things and is not diminished? Who more illustrious as the splendour of the glory of the Father, enlightening every man that comes into the world? Who more powerful than he to whom the Father has given power in heaven and on earth? Who more mighty by whose nod the universe was established? at whose nod the sea is calm, species changed, diseases flee, armed men fall on their faces, devils are expelled, rocks rent, the dead raised, sinners repent, and all things are made new? Who is more august whom angels adore and before whom devils tremble? Who more invincible than he who has conquered death and cast down Satan from heaven? Who more triumphant than he who has harrowed hell and brought souls to heaven where he sits at the right hand of God the Father? Who is more wise than he who founded and governs the universe in harmony? Whose authority is greater than his of whom the Father said, "This is my beloved Son.

Hear ye him.""? Who is more to be feared than he who can cast body and soul into hell? Who more fair than he whom to behold is perfect joy? Who is more ancient than he who has no beginning and will have no end? But perhaps boys may better think of him as a boy, lying in swaddling clothes in a manger, while angels sang, shepherds adored, the animals knew him, the star stood over where he lay, Herod trembled, Simeon embraced, Hanna prophesied. O humble simplicity! O sublime humility! How can thoughts conceive or words suffice to express his greatness? Better to adore than to seek to explain. What then shall we do, if John the Baptist said he was unworthy to unloose the latchet of his shoes? Strive, my dear boys, to sit at the feet of Jesus the teacher.[4]

This is the heart of Erasmian piety. Much of the lyricism is reminiscent of the *Imitatio Christi*. Here, too, there is barely an allusion to the passion of Christ. The stress is all on glory, power, majesty, humility, and condescension by reason of which Jesus is the perfect teacher.

Two of the years spent by Erasmus at Cambridge present a riddle. From December 1508 to April 1511 we have not a single letter from his pen, whereas in the year 1501 there were twenty-five and in the year 1511 there were twenty. On the other hand the gap is not altogether unparalleled because for the years 1507 and 1508 there were only three per year. Still, that a man with so many friends should have written no letters at all for two and a half years is odd. One suggestion is that he was in poor health, another that he suppressed the correspondence because it contained virulent references to the warrior pope Julius II.[5] But if such letters were actually sent one marvels that they could have been so completely retrieved. We are left to conjecture.

This is plain, that Erasmus was rancorous towards Pope Julius but chary of alienating him, because only popes can grant dispensations from certain canonical regulations and Erasmus stood in need of dispensations. He had already obtained one while still in Italy, excusing him from wearing the habit of the Augustinians. While strolling around Bologna in this garb, he had nearly been mobbed by those who mistook him for a physician assigned to the plague victims and wandering outside of the quarantined area. Was this dispensation valid also for England? Then another dispensation was necessary to relieve him from the obligation of residence at the monastery at Steyn. His prior was endeavouring to recall him, but Erasmus was of no mind to relinquish his liberty to travel wherever books, scholars, and printers were to be found. At long last Archbishop Warham handsomely supplemented other patronage by a pension of twenty pounds from the living of Aldington in Kent. The Archbishop explained that he was not in the habit of encumbering a parish with a levy for an enterprise beyond its bounds, but in this instance he had made an exception because "the consummate scholar Erasmus was the star of his age, who, though he might have lived opulently in France, Germany, or Italy, had chosen to finish his days among his English friends. Besides he could not serve the parish since he did not know English."[6] Was Erasmus qualified, however, to hold any sort of a benefice? Was he indeed in a position to be a priest at all, seeing that he was a bastard? While in Italy in 1506 he had secured from Julius a dispensation also for this disability, but again was it valid for England? Erasmus evidently had some doubt, because later on he secured a more comprehensive dispensation from Leo X. In any case to emit a virulent blast against the reigning pope was not the part of discretion.[7]

Yet privately he composed a scathing epigram, com-

paring Pope Julius with Julius Caesar, greatly to the disadvantage of the pope. Only one point is lacking to make
the analogy complete, says the poem, namely another
Brutus. The authenticity of the epigram was long doubted
until recently a manuscript of the poem was discovered
in Erasmus' own hand. The paper comes from the neigh-
bourhood of Paris between the years 1503 and 1513.
Erasmus made a brief trip to Paris in 1511. The reverse of
the manuscript has the word *Russo,* a pseudonym of
Thomas More, to whom apparently Erasmus presented
the epigram on his return to England.[8]

In the year 1512 Erasmus had even greater reason for
resentment against Julius, for, having humbled Venice
with the aid of the French, he then turned on the French
and made an alliance with Venice. This alliance was
joined by Henry VIII who prepared an expedition to
invade France. The troops were to sail at Easter. Colet
preached the Good Friday sermon before the court and in
the presence of the king and queen exhorted his hearers
to fight under the banner of Christ the King. "Scarcely,"
said he, "is brotherly love, without which none can see
God, scarcely is it compatible with plunging a sword into
the bowels of a brother. A Christian prince would do
better to imitate Christ rather than the Juliuses and the
Alexanders."[9] King Henry took Colet aside and told him
he feared such talk would undermine the morale of his
soldiers. The king was mollified, by what words we do
not know.

Erasmus wrote to Cardinal Riario saying, "I came to
England expecting the age of gold, literally mountains of
gold, beyond the wealth of Midas, and now the trumpet
of Julius has thrown the whole world into war."[10]
Ammonio informed him of the League of the Pope,
Venice, and England.[11] Erasmus replied, "Suppose the

French are expelled from Italy. Would you rather have the Spaniards as lords? . . .[12] How truly is Julius playing the part of Julius!"[13] A subsequent pope had reason to rue the failure to envisage such a contingency when the troops of the king of Spain sacked Rome. Ammonio accompanied the English troops to France and kept Erasmus abreast of the progress of the war.[14]

To the abbot Anthony of Bergen in the Low Countries Erasmus wrote exploring the possibility of a stipend from Prince Charles which would make it possible to carry on his labours in his native land. "It is not that I am dissatisfied with Britain or with my Maecenases. Neither a brother nor a father could have been kinder to me than the Archbishop of Canterbury, but war has suddenly changed the whole climate of this island. How can men give of their bounty when their ranks are so thinned? For the lack of good wine I am nearly dead from the stone. May God allay this tempest of all Christendom! . . . Julius started this war. Will Leo be able to stop it?"[15]

The reference to Leo indicates that Julius was dead. The new pope was elected on March 11, 1513. During the course of the next year a dialogue was circulating in manuscript which described the arrival of Pope Julius in armour together with some of his soldiers, at the gate of heaven, where admission was refused by Saint Peter.[16] The dialogue may be summarized as follows:

Interlocutors: Pope Julius, St. Peter, and a spirit.

JULIUS. What the devil is up? The gates not open? Some one has monkeyed with the lock.

SPIRIT. Maybe you have the wrong key. You've got the key of power.

JULIUS. It's the only one I ever had. I'll bang. Hey, porter, are you asleep or drunk?

PETER. Immortal God, what a stench! I'll peek through this crack till I know what's up. Who are you?

JULIUS. Can't you see this key, the triple crown, and the pallium sparkling with gems?

PETER. It doesn't look like the key Christ gave me. How should I know the crown which no barbarian tyrant ever dared to wear? As for the gems and the jewels I trample them under my feet.

JULIUS. Come on now. I am Julius the Ligurian and I suppose you know these two letters (pointing to his chest) P.M., if you can read.

PETER. *Pestis Maxima.*

JULIUS. *Pontifex Maximus.*

PETER. I don't care if you're Mercury Trismegistus, unless your life is saintly.

JULIUS. Saintly! For centuries you have been only a saint and I have been most saintly, *sanctissimus*, with six thousand bulls to prove it.

PETER. You are called *sanctissimus* but are you *sanctus?* You don't look it: cassock over armour, eyes savage, mouth insolent, forehead brazen, eyebrows arrogant, body poxed by debauchery, reeking with drink, a shambles of a man.

SPIRIT. Graphic!

PETER. I suspect you're Julian the Apostate back from hell.

JULIUS. Come on now. If you don't open I'll strike you with the lightning of excommunication. The bull is ready.

PETER. Bull? I never heard anything like that from Christ. What authority have you to excommunicate me?

JULIUS. Why, you are a mere priest, if even that.

PETER. Show your merits. No entry without merits. Have you taught true doctrine?

JULIUS. Too busy fighting. The friars look after that.

PETER. Have you won souls by holiness to Christ?

SPIRIT. He has sent plenty to hell.

PETER. Have you worked miracles?

JULIUS. They're out of date.

PETER. Have you prayed and fasted?

Title page of a German translation of the *Julius Exclusus* (1522–1523).

SPIRIT. This is getting nowhere.

JULIUS. To defer to Peter, a fisherman and almost a beggar, is beneath the invincible Julius. But I'll tell you. I'm a Ligurian and not a Jew like you. I was nephew to Pope Sixtus. By industry I gained wealth and by wealth became a cardinal. I had the French pox but I never lost hope. You were terrified by a servant girl. A gypsy promised me the triple crown and I got it, partly through French help, partly by incredible bribery with sums borrowed at usury. I made it and the Church of Christ in all centuries has never owed so much to any one as to me.

PETER. What did you do?

JULIUS. Revamped the finances, increased the revenue, annexed Bologna, beat Venice, harassed Ferrara, expelled the French, and would have expelled the Spaniards if I hadn't come up here. I killed some thousands of the French, broke treaties, celebrated gorgeous triumphs, built sumptuous edifices, and left 500,000 ducats in the treasury. All this I did not by my birth – I don't know who was my father – not by my learning – I had none – not by my popularity – I was hated – not by my clemency – I was tough. At Rome I was regarded as more a god than a man.

PETER. Well now, what is this rabble along with you?

JULIUS. Soldiers who died fighting for me. I promised them heaven if they did.

PETER. So these are the ones who tried to crash the gate a while ago?

JULIUS. And you didn't let them in?

PETER. I admit only those who clothe the naked, feed the hungry, give drink to the thirsty, visit the sick and those in prison. Incidentally, why do you call yourself a Ligurian? Does the family of Christ's vicar make any difference?

JULIUS. I want my country to have the credit of me.

PETER. You know, I'm surprised the papacy is so sought after. In my day it was hard to get even priests and deacons.

JULIUS. Of course. You had only fasts, vigils, and perhaps death. Today bishops are lords.

PETER. Tell me now. Why did you attack Bologna? Was it heretical?

JULIUS. No.

PETER. Was Bentivoglio a tyrant?

JULIUS. No.

PETER. Why then?

JULIUS. I needed the revenue!

PETER. Why did you harass Ferrara?

JULIUS. I needed it for my son!

PETER. What? Popes with wives and sons!

JULIUS. No, sons, not wives.

PETER. Is it possible to get rid of a pope, say for murder, parricide, fornication, incest, simony, sacrilege or blasphemy?

JULIUS. Add six hundred more and the answer is still no. He can be deposed only for heresy and he determines what is heresy.

PETER. So! Well then, the only recourse seems to be that the people should rise up with stones and bash this pest of the world. Another question, why did you suppress the Council of Pisa?

JULIUS. I shudder to answer. They wanted to reduce the opulent church to the penury of the apostles.

PETER. Tell me again, what have you done for the Church?

JULIUS. I found the Church poor. I made her splendid with regal palaces, splendid horses and mules, troops of servants, armies, and officers.

SPIRIT. And glamorous prostitutes and obsequious pimps.

PETER. But how now? The Church was not like this when founded by Christ.

JULIUS. You're thinking of the old days when you nearly starved as pope. Times have changed. The Roman pontiff is vastly different than when you merely had the name. Now you should see the splendid palaces, thousands of priests, bishops in arms, purpled cardinals with legions of attendants, horses more than regal, mules decked in gold and gems and shod with gold and silver. You should see the pope carried in a golden chair by his soldiers with the crowds adoring as he waves his hand. Hear the boom of the cannons, the notes of the bugle, the beating of the drums. See the engines of war, the flames of the torches. Hear the acclaim of the populace, see the loftiest princes kissing the blessed feet of the pope. Behold the Roman pontiff placing the golden crown on the head of the emperor, the king of kings (though only a shadow). What would you say if you saw all of this? If you could but have witnessed my triumph at Bologna and Rome. What spectacles! chariots, horses, troops, comely boys, torches flaring, dishes steaming, pomp of bishops, pride of cardinals, trophies, booty, shouts rending the heavens, trumpets blaring, coins tossed to the crowds, and me as well nigh a god, the author and head of it all. You would say the Scipios and Augusti were squalid compared to me.

PETER. Paul did not speak of the cities he had stormed, the princes he had slaughtered, the kings he had incited to war. He spoke of shipwrecks, chains, dangers, plots. These are the glories of the Christian general. I beseech you, the chief pastor of the Church, have you never thought how the Church began, increased, and was established? Was it by wars, was it by wealth, was it by horses? No indeed. It was by patience, the blood of the martyrs including mine, by prisons and by stripes. You say the Church is increased when the priests have thrown the world into tumult. You consider it flourishing when drunk with debauchery, tranquil when enjoying vices without reproof, and when the grand robberies and furious conflicts are justified by the princes and doctors as the "defence of the Church."

Julius, refused admittance, says that when more of his soldiers arrive he will knock down the gates of heaven.

This satire was anonymous. The first dated edition appeared in 1518. Erasmus was promptly suspected as the author. Was the surmise valid? Erasmus did not say, "I did not write it." but assumed rather the air of "How could any one suppose I would do such a thing?" He had good reason to evade responsibility because the lampoon is not a photographic portrait of Pope Julius but rather a conflation of the Renaissance popes, and the new Pope Leo, though he had no love for his predecessor and did relish a joke – he chuckled over the *Praise of Folly*[17] – might yet feel that he, too, would not emerge unscathed from a dialogue with St. Peter. There was also a more fundamental consideration. Reform admits of two strategies. The one is to slug, the other to reason. He who slugs can scarcely then say, "Come now, let us reason together." Someone else will have to do that. Erasmus was combining the two methods, by not letting his right hand know what the left was doing. This may be inferred from the quality of his denials which were so phrased as to apply strictly only to the publication and not to the composition of the satire. There are strong indications that he was the author. A manuscript was extant in his own hand. He might, of course, have simply copied it, but at that time of his life he employed a secretary to transcribe his own work. The content was no more stinging than that of the poem now believed to have come from his pen. Thomas More, who did know the circumstances, sought to exculpate his friend first by pointing out the unlikelihood that he would have done it and then by saying, "But suppose he did. The blame rests not on the author but on the publisher." Would More ever have made the supposition if he had known quite definitely that Erasmus had not written it? There are also many other minor clues.

The chief obstacle to the assumption of the Erasmian authorship is that an edition appeared with the initials *F.A.F. Poete Regij Libellus*, that is, Fausto Andrelini of Forli, Poet Laureate to the King. This was that gay blade, the old friend of Erasmus in Paris. The date of this edition was 1518 when Fausto was dead. But the edition without the initials appears to have been earlier than the one carrying them because the edition with the initials corrects a mistake. The solution may lie in collaboration between Erasmus and Fausto, like that between Erasmus and More on the *Utopia*. Erasmus and Fausto were together in Paris in 1511 and Fausto may have supplied the many details about Julius' dealings with the French which we omitted from the above abridgment. The probability is very high that Erasmus was the author.[18]

In any case England's involvement in the war of Julius drove Erasmus back to the continent. For the next seven years the base of his operations was to be in the Netherlands, from August 1514 until November 1521, when he transferred to Basel. Many places in the Low Countries display the room occupied by Erasmus and with complete authenticity. His letters were written from Louvain, Antwerp, Brussels, Bruges, Anderlecht, and St. Omer. There were a few excursions. He was back in England very briefly in May 1515, in August 1516, and in April 1517 to negotiate and receive a final dispensation from all of his disabilities at the hand of Ammonio, acting as the pope's representative. Erasmus made repeated trips to Basel to supervise the printing of his works: in August 1514, March 1515, August 1515, September 1516, May 1518, and December 1518. He said himself that if Ulysses was the wisest man in Greece because he had visited so many cities Erasmus' horse was the wisest in Europe because he had attended so many universities.[19] When criticized as a gadabout Erasmus inquired how Paul could have converted the Mediterranean world by staying in Tarsus.[20] But Erasmus did have a base. It was the Netherlands and his longest residence was at Louvain.

Busleiden's mansion.

His financial condition was very precarious. In September 1516 he was compelled to sell his two horses to buy winter clothing. "I cannot ride naked," he wrote, "but I cannot afford both to ride and to be clad."[21] Already in 1515 there was an intimation that he would be appointed as a councillor to Charles, who had succeeded his father Philip as lord of the Netherlands. Erasmus entered upon this office in January 1516, but by Pentecost of 1517 the stipend attending the office was a year and a half in arrears. Le Sauvage, the chancellor of Charles, bestowed on Erasmus the canonry of Courtrai in July 1516.[22] By October so little had evidently been paid that Erasmus could write to More, "Being well clad, I fear I shall die of hunger."[23] Obviously he did survive. Friends helped. And despite privations his spirit of independence did not flag. "I hear," he wrote, "that the Christian King will make me a bishop in Sicily. I am glad he thinks of me, but I would not give up my freedom to study for the most splendid of bishoprics."[24]

Among the friends who did help was Jerome Busleiden, a statesman in the councils of the Archduke Philip, a learned man who delighted to collect books, the builder of a mansion which inspired that of Thomas More at Chelsea and which is to this day the architectural gem of the town of Mechlin. The interior decoration combined local pride, Old Testament themes, and classical mythology. On one wall was a fresco of Belshazzar's feast where plainly the queen was Margaret of Austria. Daniel wore a scarlet mantle fringed with ermine and the heavy gold chain of the councillors of Mechlin. But on another fresco were the gods of Olympus. The greatest ornament was an organ built by a craftsman from Nürnberg, but nothing could equal the library with manuscripts richly bound in silk, with choice illuminations clasped by silver. There were books in Latin, Greek, and Hebrew, codices of the Latin classics, besides a collection of the coins and medals of antiquity. Erasmus was a frequent visitor.[25]

Busleiden conceived a great admiration for him and Erasmus reciprocated not only by dedicating to him a further translation of Lucian but also by inserting a warm encomium in the *Panegyric* of the Archduke Philip.[26]

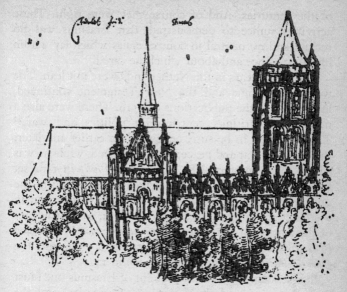

The Church at Anderlecht.

One might have supposed that Erasmus would have played upon the intimacy with Busleiden to secure for himself an endowment for life. Instead he induced his friend to bequeath his fortune to the establishment of a college at Louvain for the teaching of the three languages Latin, Greek, and Hebrew. When Busleiden died in 1517, on the way to Spain in the service of Charles, the role of organizing the *Collegium Trilingue* fell to Erasmus. His task was to assess the candidates for the three chairs time after time and to defend the college against the attacks of the conservatives who feared that its purpose was to displace the Vulgate as the authoritative translation of the Scripture on which rested the dogmatic pronouncements

of the centuries. And of course they were right. These
activities suffice to demonstrate that Erasmus was no
recluse and no neutral in controversies which lay within
his competence and about which he cared.

The seven years in the Netherlands were not lean. The
work on Jerome and the New Testament continued,
leading up to the publications of 1516. There were also a
number of writings centring on politics and war.[27]
These themes, to be sure, engaged him earlier and later;
the theme of war and peace, as we observed, while he was
still in the monastery. The *Panegyric of Philip* in 1504 set
forth the image of what the prince ought to be in the
guise of what he allegedly was. Politics and war recur in
the letter to Anthony of Bergen in 1514, in four adages
of the edition of 1515, in the *Institutio Principis Christiani*
(*The Education of the Christian Prince*) in 1516 and the
Querela Pacis (*The Complaint of Peace*) in 1517.

In assessing the political thought of Erasmus one must
again bear in mind the fusion of the classical and the
Christian. On the classical side several concepts run
through his thinking. The first is *Concordia*.[28] For the
Stoics concord was cosmic, the immanent rationalism
which holds in harmony dissident elements, a concordant
disharmony, a harmonious discord. It could be discerned
in the harmonies of music, in the movements of the
heavenly bodies, in the behaviour of the animals. As
Dion of Prusa put it, "The sun graciously gives way at
night to the weaker stars and moon, and even by day
suffers himself to be eclipsed or shrouded by cloud and
mist. The stars in turn show each other consideration and
preserve their orbits without collision. Likewise in the
lower world the birds nest beside the birds, the ants
assist the ants, and the bees do not quarrel over the same
flower."[29] Men, of all creatures, being endowed with

reason, with speech, with laughter, and with tears, are best able to perceive the harmony of the universe and to resolve their own differences in reasonable ways. Alas, how far do they so often fall from their true naturel Concord in the political realm tended to be a conservative principle, opposed to revolution which disrupts society. The Gracchi were blamed by the pillars of the established order as the disrupters of concord.

Another concept is *Humanitas*,[30] already mentioned in connection with Erasmus' educational ideal. When applied to political relations, *humanitas* excludes the lust for vengeance and inculcates instead magnanimity, that greatness of soul which does not resent a slight nor harbour a grudge. To the offender it extends clemency. Man endowed with these qualities has dignity and man is sacred to man.

The third concept is cosmopolitanism.[31] It emerged gradually in the ancient world. One stage was the breakdown of the distinction between the Hellene and the barbarian. Another was the attempt of Alexander to marry and mingle the peoples and the cultures of the Greeks and of the Near East. The Stoics preached the unity of mankind, embracing not only all peoples but also all classes, slaves as well as free.

On the Christian side also we have the concern for unity. The Apostle Paul said, "Live in harmony with one another."[32] "Let there be no dissensions among you but be united in the same mind."[33] "The body does not consist of one member but many, and the eye cannot say to the hand, 'I have no need of you.' "[34] The Christian goes beyond magnanimity and clemency to forgiveness and compassion, beyond courtesy to readiness to lay down one's life for another. National, ethnic, and social distinctions are overcome not simply because of the unity of mankind, but because all are sons of God, redeemed by Christ, strangers in every fatherland, pilgrims with no abiding place on earth. Never are they to seek power for the sake of power, for he who offered to Christ the kingdoms of the world was Satan. "You know," said Jesus, "that the rulers of the Gentiles lord it over them. . . . It shall not be so among you."[35] At the same time the state is necessary and rulers are ordained of God to protect the good and punish the bad. Rulers are to be obeyed.[36]

Erasmus himself was a cosmopolitan,[37] in the sense that he loved every country and belonged to none. He would praise all and criticize all. For his native heath he had a real affection, though he might describe his countrymen as boors. He could speak of "my France" and "our Germany." England was a second home. He could never dispel a nostalgia for Rome, "the freedom, the light, those exhilarating strolls and conversations with men of learning."[38] When twice invited to become a citizen of Zürich, he answered, "I wish to be a citizen of the world, not of a single city."[39] He was surprised and annoyed when innocent remarks on his part touched off nationalistic resentments. The French were incensed because he dedicated a book to Henry VIII as king of England *and France*. Erasmus thought it only a formal courtesy to call a king what he called himself.[40] Again the French were outraged when Erasmus translated the ejaculation of St. Paul, "O foolish Galatians!" as "O foolish Gauls!" The Galatians were, of course, Gauls, but in Latin the French were called *Galli*.[41] The Spaniards were enraged when he said that Naples was *occupied* by the Spaniards, as if they were not there as of right.[42] Such nationalist touchiness appeared to Erasmus to be incredibly silly. He would reiterate, "The whole universe is my fatherland."[43] Concretely he had a sense of belonging to only two societies, both European in scope. The first was the republic of letters. "I am so devoted to the humanities," said he, "that wherever I find men dedicated and versed in these disciplines there I recognize my kinsmen."[44] The other society was the Christian Church.

A concept from the classical world inescapable for Christian social concern was that of law: natural law, statute law, and the application of law. With Erasmus all of these concepts were brought to the bar of the mind of Christ, the *philosophia Christi*. The two most fundamental tenets of natural law were that man, together with the animals, has the right to propagate and defend his life. Erasmus heartily endorsed the first, seeing that the precepts of Christ do not abrogate the law of nature.[45] The right to propagate served his polemic against the requirement of celibacy for churchmen and church-women, but he severely circumscribed the right of self-defence, couched in the formula that force may be repelled by force, *vim vi repellere*. Only magistrates may bear the sword and that not in their own defence but only on behalf of the aggrieved. Ecclesiastics are not to defend themselves. Erasmus then describes the erosion of the restriction in Christian history. First the law of the Church permitted the use of weapons of defence – shields and greaves – then the pope came to have a guard and bishops to travel with thirty armed retainers.[46]

Statute law and its implementation brought into play the principle called in Greek *epieikeia*, in Latin *aequitas*, meaning that which is equitable, fair, and just. With Aristotle this meant extending the intent of the lawgiver to cover unforeseen contingencies, which might require an historical investigation into the mind of the legislator. For Erasmus this meant to seek the mind of Christ. For the Romans *aequitas* meant loose interpretation of the law to make it fit what the executor of the law deemed to be just, and justice was interpreted as giving to each his due, primarily with reference to life and property. Erasmus was much more concerned for persons than for property. Like Thomas More he criticized the law which inflicted the penalty of death for theft but treated adultery lightly.[47] The medieval theologians took *aequitas* to mean leniency in the infliction of penalties. Erasmus was so fully in accord that he would not shift the penalty of death from theft to adultery.[48] Besides, if the Old Testament penalty of stoning for adultery were revived, a mountain would not suffice for the missiles.[49] For Erasmus, Christ himself was a lawgiver, though his precepts were not to be treated legalistically, but with an eye to circumstance. The oath, for example, has no place among Christians, but in a society where men are not believed unless they swear, some accommodation is necessary, just as Moses allowed divorce, not as ideal, but "because of the hardness of men's hearts."[50]

With these assumptions Erasmus approached the problems of politics and power, and focused them, as did Machiavelli, on the person of the prince. This was not because Erasmus identified the state with the prince. There can be a state without a prince, though not a prince without a state.[51] The two most distinctively political tracts of Erasmus could not disregard the person of the prince, because addressed to princes. The first was the *Panegyric of Philip of Burgundy*, the second, *The Education of the Christian Prince*,[52] addressed to Charles, later to be the emperor. These two works appear at first to be little more than a catena of maxims drawn from the wisdom of antiquity, but there are differences and there are contemporary applications. Whatever Erasmus appropriated

VICTORIA

Charles V.

from the classical world was passed through the Christian alembic. With Plato and Cicero he affirmed that he only is fit to be a ruler who has no desire to rule.[53] Kingship as an onerous responsibility was then brought by Erasmus under the rubric of the *Imitatio Christi*. Rulership is a form of cross-bearing, seeing that the ruler must forgo pleasure, assume cares, labour long, curtail sleep in order that his subjects may rest securely. He must be ready to endure ingratitude and reviling, and if he cannot rule without injustice must be ready to resign.[54] The prince

is subject to grave temptations. Peter denied his Lord
when he was in the courtyard of the high priest, and the
courts of pontiffs and princes are the very places where
Christ is most readily denied.[55]

Nevertheless the Christian must run the risks and assume
the responsibilities. Nor should the Christian prince neglect
his proper tasks in order to engage in pious exercises. Let him
not spend so many hours rattling off prayers that he leaves
undone that for want of which the state may gravely suffer.
Compare the prince, if you will, to Martha and the priest to
Mary. Grant that to pray, meditate, and sacrifice is more
perfect than to care for the state, but still this is the prince's
task. Grant that the work of the priest is of a higher order
than that of the prince, even when his vigilance averts war.
Nevertheless, the prince, under the circumstances, achieves a
greater good because so many evils are entailed in war. Nor
has one the right to say that the prince does not pray. He may
plead with God more effectually in a very few words. If he
stills the tempest of war, defends the liberty of the people,
staves off famine, appoints incorruptible magistrates, he
pleases God better than by saying six whole years of prayers.
Not that I disapprove of prayers. But they are not the prince's
job.[56] [What Erasmus here says sounds very much like
Luther's doctrine of the calling.]

But not only must the prince be devoted to his vocation.
He must also be noble, generous, compassionate, magnanimous, and above all wise, in a word, Plato's philosopher
king.[57] But how is he to be obtained?

One would suppose that Erasmus would have favoured
popular election since he repeatedly averred that government rests upon the consent of the governed, but he
made no suggestions as to how consent should be
ascertained. He would utilize the one advantage of the
hereditary system that the prince is known from birth
and his education can begin in infancy. Great care should

be exercised in the choice of his tutor, whose responsibility is perchance even heavier than his own.[58] The tutor should be no flatterer. In fact, the ideal tutor would be a horse because he does not know the difference between a prince and a pauper.[59] The programme of education for the prince recommended by Erasmus does not follow the model of Castiglione's *Cortegiano*. The prince is not to be taught how to dance, dice, and dine.[60]

With regard to specific tasks Erasmus would have the prince give the greatest attention to domestic and the least to foreign affairs. Although an internationalist, Erasmus was in many respects a political isolationist. He did not wish to see the restoration of the ancient Roman empire, nor even of its shadow, the Holy Roman Empire, to which Charles of Spain would bring greater power and prestige by his election as emperor than he would derive from the office.[61] Universal monarchy, in any case, has the disadvantage that the prince cannot be personally acquainted with all parts of his domains.

If his capital should be at Constantinople how could he tell what was going in Ethiopia or on the Ganges, and if he knew, what could he do about it? Besides, the discovery of new lands not yet explored makes it appear that the earth is of immense vastness.[62] The prince does better to confine himself to his own domain and should travel very little to any other. Woe to the land whose prince is always on leave of absence![63] Princes should eschew foreign alliances and especially marriages beyond their borders. What sense is there in an arrangement whereby a marriage suddenly turns an Irishman into a ruler of the Indies or makes a Syrian into the king of Italy?[64] Actually royal marriages do not ensure peace. England made a matrimonial alliance with Scotland, but James of Scotland nevertheless invaded England.[65] Even treaties are to be avoided, for they do not cement friendship, but serve rather as pretexts for accusations of bad faith.[66]

But if there is not a universal state how then is peace to be preserved? Not, as Dante supposed, through a world monarchy. Great states, as a matter of fact, have never been brought into being save by great slaughter. [67] Peace is to be achieved by concord among small independent political units. This concord is the more fitting and should be the more attainable in a society whose unity is cemented by the Christian bond, where the universal monarch is Christ himself. [68]

Within his own realm the prince is the *pater patriae*. He is of course to use the sword to repress the bad and protect the good. But the coercive power is to be used with the utmost restraint. The death penalty should be exacted only as an ultimate recourse. The prince should rule not by intimidation but by persuasion and consent. He is to look after the economic needs of the land, to regulate weights and measures, suppress monopolies, build dykes to keep out the sea [written plainly by a Hollander]. He is to restrain luxury by sumptuary legislation, abolish public mendicancy by compelling the able to work and caring for the infirm. [69]

There is scarcely a single social reform advocated in More's *Utopia* for which a parallel is not to be found in the works of Erasmus. [70]

One of the most imperative duties of the prince is to keep the peace within and without his land. On no subject did Erasmus speak so often and with such passion. We have already looked at his youthful essay on the theme. To review all of his utterances on peace would be tedious. We may raise again the question of his sincerity, seeing that his most famous tract, the *Querela Pacis* (*The Complaint of Peace*), was composed at the instance of the Chancellor Jean Sauvage [71] at a moment when the pamphlet could serve the Hapsburg propaganda. We are here to bear in mind that not only the youthful tract but also the adage *Dulce Bellum* were earlier in date and without political prompting. Another interpretation is that Erasmus sincerely advocated peace but for a reason of very limited validity, since the prosperity of Holland depended upon peace between the great powers.[72] Here be it recalled that his earliest protest was directed against wars between feudal families within the Netherlands.

One may inquire whether his propaganda for peace contained anything novel, since, for the most part, he drew from earlier sources. But at some points Erasmus went beyond his predecessors in that he punctured the theory of the just war. It had been built up first in classical times by stages culminating in the formulation by Cicero. A war to be just, said he, must have as its object the vindication of justice and the restoration of peace. It may be waged only under the auspices of the state. The code requires a formal declaration, respect for treaties, the sparing of the innocent, and the humane treatment of hostages and prisoners. Augustine christened the code by adding that the motive must be love and that justice can be on one side only because a just war requires an unjust war. The entire theory rests on the analogy between war and the administration of justice within the civil state, and this is precisely the point which Erasmus demolishes. The civil state, he reminds us, has juridical machinery whereby impartial judges can appraise a dispute and determine where justice lies. In wars between states there is no such juridical body. Each side adjudges its own cause to be just. But, as a matter of fact, in disputes over territory, justice is impossible. What strip of territory is there which has not been held at divers times now by one state and now by another? On the ground of one-time ownership the Romans might expect to hold Spain or Africa, and Padua might try to recover the site of ancient Troy because, according to Virgil, the founder of Padua was a Trojan. A dispute as to who should own a piece of land cannot be resolved by an appeal to previous possession.[73] It can only be resolved by mutual accommodation. Nothing so penetrating as this had previously been said and nothing wiser has ever been said.

The proper way to settle disputes, according to Erasmus, is the way of arbitration, and the preferred arbitrators to his mind were churchmen. "Are there not bishops?" he demands. "Are there not abbots and scholars, are there not irreproachable magistrates?"[74] In suggesting arbitration Erasmus was in no sense an innovator. The Greek city states had practised arbitration extensively, though never sufficiently to prevent devouring one another. Close to the time of Erasmus widespread examples were available from the whole of Europe, from the Baltic to the Balkans, from Scandinavia to Spain. Such instances, rare in the twelfth century, increased to their peak in the first half of the fifteenth and then dropped off, presumably because of nationalism. The arbitrators in the above instances were normally laymen, seeing that the Church was sometimes a litigant and at all times might inject her own interest. Erasmus was anachronistic in assuming that the Church could ever again become as much of an arbitrator as she had been in the days of Innocent III,[75] though again he was realistic when he declined to advise Pope Leo to mediate because certainly kings would not listen.[76]

An analysis of the Erasmian arguments conveys nothing of the passionate flow of his eloquence. This may best be suggested by an abridgement of *The Complaint of Peace*. Its continued appeal lies in its universalism. There are few direct references, though there are some allusions to contemporary events. At that juncture of Europe's history Erasmus had reason to believe that his plea might

be heard. A new set of rulers had emerged devoted to the
new learning. Henry became king of England in 1509,
Leo X was elected pope in 1513, Francis succeeded to the
throne of France in 1515, and Charles the next year
became king of Spain. All bore titles indicating their
devotion to the Prince of Peace. Francis was the *Most
Christian King of France*, Charles *His Most Catholic Majesty*
of Spain, Henry was called *The Defender of the Faith*, and
Leo, of course, the *Vicar of Christ*. Their conduct already
belied too sanguine a hope. Henry, for his campaign
against France in 1513, had cast twelve great guns, each
named for one of the apostles, who were to belch fire
against the Most Christian King. Erasmus' observation
that the expense entailed in besieging a city was enough
to build another was well illustrated by the expedition for
which Wolsey supplied forty thousand knocked down
wooden huts to house the English troops during the
siege of Tournai. The city surrendered at once. The
English went home, leaving the huts which served as
summer houses for the inhabitants of Tournai.[77] The
reference to preachers who endangered their lives by
protesting against war may be an allusion to Colet's
sermon. The picture of princes fawning upon each other
while plotting mutual destruction was spelled out in all
the gorgeous pageantry on the meeting between Francis
and Henry at the Cloth of Gold, where excessive civility
masked duplicity. As for the royal marriages, one example
will suffice. Louis XI of France betrothed his son Charles
to the daughter of Edward IV of England, then broke
the agreement and affianced him to Margaret of Austria,
aged two. She stayed with her intended husband's family
until she was thirteen, when it appeared expedient to send
her back (without repaying the dowry) that Charles
might marry Anne of Brittany.[78]

In Erasmus' *Complaint of Peace* Peace speaks in her own person, for was she not in antiquity a goddess? Here in brief is her plea:

Surely men are mad to reject me since I am the fount of every blessing and war the greatest bane. I could the better bear rejection were it by stupid brutes and not by creatures endowed with reason, responsive to the divine mind, born for benevolence and concord. The celestial bodies in diverse orbits keep for aeons a constant covenant. The very elements in the midst of discord maintain the equilibrium of eternal peace. The irrational animals, the swine and the sheep, the grackles and the storks, the ants and the bees congregate together and the very plants intertwine. Among the wild beasts what boar strikes his tusk into another boar? What serpent injects venom into another serpent? and the concord of wolves is proverbial. If animals do fight it is only to assuage their hunger. But what can reconcile man to man? He who has reason, he who has speech, he who has tears which dispel the cloud of rancour with a shower. Man depends for his very existence upon co-operation. He comes into the world physically helpless and cannot survive without assistance. Why then should man prey upon man?

When I hear the name of man and Christian I expect to be received. I approach hopefully a city begirt with walls and governed by laws, but only to discover factions. I turn from the common rout to kings and find them embracing with obsequious flattery while conniving at mutual destruction. The learned men, the philosophers, are little better with their wrangling schools. Nor even are the religious orders superior, though they bear the name of brother, dress in white, and carry the cross, for they are continually contentious. The home is indeed better, yet not without discord, and even in the breast of a single individual the passions are at war with the reason.

All this is the more amazing when one considers the precepts of the Christian religion. In the Old Testament the prophet Isaiah predicted the coming of the Prince of Peace, and when he came, I beg you, was his birth heralded with trumpets? Did the angels sing of victories, triumphs, and trophies? And when he was grown did he not say, "My peace I give unto you. Love one another as I have loved you. Father, I pray that they may all be one."? Does not the Lord's Prayer teach concord? How can you say *Our* Father if you plunge steel into the guts of your brother? Christ compared himself to a hen: Christians behave like hawks. Christ was a shepherd of sheep: Christians tear each other like wolves. Christians have the same supper of the Lord, the same heavenly Jerusalem, but they are less peaceful than the Jews who fight only with foreigners and the Turks who keep the peace among themselves. Look at the last ten years. What land has not been irrigated by Christian blood? What sea or stream has not been incarnadined?

And who is responsible for all this? Not the common people, but kings who, on the strength of some musty parchment lay claim to neighbouring territory or, because of the infringement of one point in a treaty of a hundred articles, embark on war. Not the young, but the greybeards. Not the laity, but the bishops. The very cross is painted on their banners and cannons are christened and engraved with the names of the apostles, so that Paul, the preacher of peace, is made to hurl a cannon ball at the heads of Christians. In the recent war between England and France the clergy mutually fulminated and, were I to name the few who protested, their lives might now be endangered.

Consider the wickedness of it all, the breakdown of laws which are ever silent amid the clangour of arms. Debauchery, rape, incest, and the foulest crimes are let loose in war. Men who would go to the gallows in peace are of prime use in war, the burglar to rob, the assassin to disembowel, the incendiary to fire an enemy city, the pirate to sink his vessels.

Consider the cost of it all. In order to prevent the enemy from leaving his town one must sleep for months outside of one's own. New walls could be built for less than is required to

batter down old ones. When all the damage is taken into account, the most brilliant success is not worth the trouble.

How then is peace to be secured? Not by royal marriages, but by cleansing the human heart. Why should one born in the bogs of Ireland seek by some alliance to rule over the East Indies? Let a king recall that to improve his realm is better than to increase his territory. Let him buy peace. The cheapest war would be more expensive. Let him invite the arbitration of learned men, abbots, and bishops. Let the clergy absent themselves from silly parades and refuse Christian burial to those who die in battle. If we must fight, why not go against the common enemy, the Turk? But wait. Is not the Turk also a man and a brother?

Above all else let peace be sincerely desired. The populace is now incited to war by insinuations and propaganda, by claims that the Englishman is the natural enemy of the

Frenchman and the like. Why should an Englishman as an Englishman bear ill will to a Frenchman and not rather good will as a man to a man and a Christian to a Christian? How can anything so frivolous as a name outweigh the ties of nature and the bonds of Christianity? The Rhine separates the French from the German but it cannot divide the Christian from the Christian. The Pyrenees lie between the French and the Spaniards but cannot break the indissoluble bond of the communion of the church. A little strip of sea cuts off the English from the French, but though the Atlantic rolls between it could not severe those joined by nature and still more indissolubly cemented by grace. In private life one will bear with something in a brother-in-law only because he is a brother-in-law, and cannot one then bear anything in another because he is a brother in Christ? If nothing else will move your majesties, not the sense of nature, not respect for religion, not such frightful calamity, let the power of the Christian name bring you to concord. How much of the world is Christian? In the midst of the non-Christian world Christians are as a city set upon a hill to give light, but how will they move the heathen to embrace the faith when they so contend among themselves? If we would bring the Turks to Christianity we must first be Christians.

This mortal life is beset with calamities which concord can alleviate and with joys which harmony can enhance. But how trivial are the objects of our strife! Death is ever at hand, for kings as well as for commoners. What tumults a little animalcule incites who will himself soon be wafted away like a whiff of vapour! At the door is eternity. Why rack ourselves to be possessed of shadows, as if life would last forever! How miserable are those who neither believe nor hope for the blessedness of the godly, but how impious those who think blessedness can be attained by war, seeing that blessedness consists in the ineffable communion of souls. Let us then repent and be wise, declare an amnesty to all past errors and misfortunes, and bind up discord in adamantine chains which can never be sundered till time shall be no more.

CHAPTER SIX

The Eloquence of God: Basel: The Bible

*

THE political writings just reviewed were composed mainly during the years Erasmus spent in the Low Countries from 1514 to 1522. Coincidently he was working on patristic and Biblical studies to be published by Froben at Basel. For that reason Erasmus had repeatedly to journey up and down the Rhine. The first of these excursions took place in September of 1514. On the way Erasmus paused at Strasbourg and there received an ovation from the literary circle which included the venerable Wimpheling, a Christian humanist who had been the rector of the University of Heidelberg; Jacob Sturm, later of great political influence as a member of the city council; Sebastian Brandt, author of *The Ship of Fools*, and others of less enduring renown. Erasmus was overwhelmed by their cordiality. To Wimpheling he wrote that no glory could so please him as the approbation of such distinguished men. "How fortunate Agamemnon would have been could he have had ten such Nestors!" as those of the Strasbourg circle. The city itself, said Erasmus, had the orderliness of Rome, the wisdom of Athens, the discipline of Sparta, and should be called not the silver city (*Argentoratum*), but the golden. Not only here, but elsewhere as well, "my Germany" abounds in learned men.[1]

For Erasmus this reception was a tangible token of the reality of the fraternity of scholars. He had met them in the Low Countries. He had met them in France, in England, in Italy, and now Germany was no whit behind. But why did the Strasbourg circle so adulate Erasmus? Thus far he had published two editions of the *Adagia*, some translations, the *Enchiridion* in two editions, and the *Praise of Folly*. With respect to meticulous scholarship in the ancient tongues he was not unsurpassed. Was it then the *Praise of Folly* which had brought him such renown? Scarcely! Brandt of the *Ship of Fools* was hardly equal to the subtle ambiguities of Erasmus' disarming *Stultitia*. Certainly this group did not take Erasmus for a scoffing Lucian. Rather, he was for them the exponent of the fusion of the Christian man and the cultivated man, the foe of the barbarians, of the logic choppers, of the stolid legalists. He was the prophet of simplicity, urbanity, and piety. And although he spoke of "my Germany" they did not demand of him that perfervid patriotism which marked their devotion to *Germania*.[2]

From Strasbourg he went on to Basel and there presented himself to Froben, saying that he came with letters from his intimate friend Erasmus, who would confirm anything which he concluded with regard to the publication of his works. "We so resemble each other," he continued, "that he who sees me sees Erasmus." Froben then tumbled to his identity. Promptly Froben's father-in-law raced to the inn, paid the bill, and brought the bags and horses to the house of Froben. There were horses because Erasmus commonly travelled with an amanuensis. The celebrity was thereupon wined, dined, and introduced to distinguished men of the city including the rector of the university, Ludwig Bär, called in Latin Ursus; William Cop, a physician, "the Hippocrates of our age"; Gerard Lister, a medical humanist versed in Latin,

Erasmus with an amanuensis, artist unknown.

Greek, and Hebrew; Bruno Amerbach of the family
outstanding in jurisprudence and printing; Henry Loriti,
called Glareanus,[3] then assisting Froben (Erasmus later
secured for him an advantageous post in Paris); and
Ulrich Zasius, an eminent jurist, with whom in his last
days Erasmus was to be intimately associated.[4] A new
world of friends had been assembled through the
printing press.

Erasmus plunged into work, scarcely taking time to
eat. Seneca, Jerome, and the New Testament were on the
docket. The Jerome appeared in 1516 in nine volumes, of
which only the first four comprising the letters were
edited by Erasmus, on the basis of a text differing from
that of six earlier editions.[5] The work was prefaced by a

E.

F

life of Jerome, which has been hailed "as a new departure in the field of Christian biography."[6] One might better say "Christian hagiography," for Erasmus was of no mind to recount prodigious feats of asceticism. His biographical writing has been characterized as static,[7] seeing that he had no concept of development in character. The reason here assigned is not correct. Erasmus complained of deterioration of character in Luther, Hutten, and Aleander. The materials available on Jerome scarcely provided documentation for the unfolding of a personality. Yet the judgment is sound to this degree that Erasmus was less interested in chronological sequence than in seizing the essence of a man in a vignette, like those admirable sketches which he did of More, Colet, and Vitrier. The life of Jerome is not precisely detached biography, because it is at the same time another tract against "the barbarians." The famous dream of Jerome played into their hands, the dream in which an angel accused him of being a Ciceronian rather than a Christian. "Does this mean," interrogated Erasmus, "that the saint never thereafter read a secular book? You say he was no theologian because he did not syllogize. If Jerome is not to be enrolled in the senate of the theologians how about Peter and Paul? O pitiable Christianity which has not enjoyed a theologian for over a thousand years!"[8]

In editing the letters of Jerome Erasmus strove to improve the text and to distinguish the genuine from the spurious writings. He provided scholarly notes called *scholia* and sometimes also an *antidotus* in which he frankly took issue with the saint. Ordinarily, however, the comments exalted the patristic period as the ideal to which the Church should return after her grievous fall, but then would come the concession that perhaps after all a full restoration was not possible or even desirable, since the Church must accommodate herself to the increasing hardness of men's hearts. And then once more, despite disclaimers, Erasmus would upbraid the Church of his day for defection from the patristic ideal.

Here are two excerpts from his comments:

In this epistle Jerome does not exhort, but enjoins clerics, elders, and priests to embrace poverty. Come now, most holy Jerome, are you saying that clerics should not have gold in their chests, silver in their purses, nor furniture in their houses? What would you say today of prince bishops whose wealth makes them the envy of secular princes? What would you say of supreme pontiffs who fight for goods and spoils? We assume that the spirit of Christ resides in their breasts and take no umbrage at palaces reared to heaven, at the multitude of their servants, the armed retainers, troops of horses, resplendent with gems of gold and purple. All of this we say belongs to the dignity of the Church. I think, though others may not agree, that Jerome meant his injunction to be a counsel rather than a precept, that is, advice rather than a command. In the next section Jerome does not condemn all wealth, but only the pursuit of wealth. Of course we today must make a distinction between the Church of his time and our own. Then the Church, being devoid of riches, relied solely on the riches of Christ. Presently wealth increased and led to temporal power. Whether this comports with the philosophy of Christ I will let others decide. I am writing footnotes, not a treatise on doctrine.

Again Erasmus comments:

Let not any one be offended if Jerome does not lay upon monks the rules required by us today. He does not forbid living with a mother or a sister and does not separate the sexes save to avoid dangerous intimacy. He says nothing about the monastic habit, its shape or colour. He never mentions the three solemn vows. He does not forbid all private possessions. I wonder if it would not be better if we had fewer monasteries and those few with the same liturgy, prayers, and rule, and the very minimum of ceremonies, which savour more of Judaism than of Christianity.

Some may be offended because Jerome reproves the adorning of churches, seeing that in our day there are princes who make up for a lifetime of war, murder, and crime by building a sacred edifice. Some think it an unforgivable sin to take money donated for a church and use it to save those dying of hunger. To do so, they say, is to despoil Christ and the Virgin Mary. Jerome does not condemn all adornment, but he would rather adorn living temples, that is, Christ's poor.[9]

Far more significant than the editing of Jerome was the printing for the first time of the New Testament in Greek. This was a landmark in the history of Biblical scholarship. The achievement has been disparaged because the work was hastily done, "precipitated rather than edited,"[10] as Erasmus himself said. He hurried, presumably under pressure from Froben, who may well have wished to anticipate the publication by Cardinal Ximenes of the New Testament portion of the great *Complutensian Polyglot*. This New Testament was already in print in Greek in 1514, but publication was withheld supposedly to obtain papal permission which was not forthcoming until 1520.[11] By bringing out the Erasmian version in 1516 Froben had a lead of four years. Erasmus was disappointed by the paucity and late date of the manuscripts available to him at Basel, only four for his first edition and nothing earlier than the eleventh century. The great Vaticanus was unfortunately at Rome. With what he had, Erasmus worked furiously for six months, but in that time could not expend the same care which he had devoted to his Jerome on which he had worked for fifteen years. The fresh translation of the

Greek into Latin, commenced at Cambridge, was now completed. Erasmus was far from satisfied with the entire production and devoted the remainder of his life among other labours to the improvement of this edition. Before his death there were in all five editions, in 1516, 1519, 1522, 1527, and 1535. For the fourth he was able to collate seven manuscripts in all and to take advantage of better readings in the *Complutensian Polyglot*, especially for the Book of Revelation. The editing of this book was the most unsatisfactory of the entire production. Erasmus had but one manuscript with interlinear comments in Greek. The text had, therefore, to be extracted and copied freshly for the printer. Erasmus committed this task to an assistant, who made errors in transcription, which Erasmus did not take time to check for the first edition, nor adequately at any time. The manuscript lacked the last five verses of Revelation which Erasmus himself translated from the Latin back into Greek.[12] He was promptly and properly criticized for this procedure.

Despite all of the defects the magnitude of his achievement is not to be depreciated. The mere fact alone that the New Testament in Greek was available in book form, whatever the text, was of immense significance, because thereby the task of collation was expedited. Manuscripts could not be transported from country to country without grave risk. Printed copies could be sent to the manuscripts and variant readings recorded in the margins. Then the books could be gathered and the evidence assembled. If in the process a book were lost it was not irreplaceable.

At the same time we are not to exaggerate the significance of mere publication, because if Erasmus had not accomplished it, Ximenes would have done so very shortly. The contribution of Erasmus to Biblical studies lies even more in the questions which he raised, the controversies which he precipitated, and the awareness which he created as to the problems of text, translation, and interpretation. Ximenes would have left these questions comparatively untouched. Erasmus covered the text of Scripture, a fresh translation and exegesis by way of critical annotation and popular exposition. His methodology was set forth in three prefaces to the first edition of his New Testament. These were later expanded, consolidated, and printed separately. Thereafter they began to drop out of the continuing editions of the text.[13] The annotations still remained, however, and were often enlarged into veritable essays some of which also came out separately. Quite independently the *Paraphrases* elucidated the meaning of the New Testament in simple terms with Erasmian nuances.

After the very first publication, attacks came from many quarters and persons: in Germany from John Eck, Luther's famous opponent; in England from Edward Lee, later the Archbishop of York; in Spain from Jacob Zuniga (Stunica); and in the Netherlands, even before publication, from Martin Dorp. Some of these men were old friends, who unfortunately went beyond scholarly criticism to personal invective, accusing Erasmus not merely of faulty erudition but also of deficient orthodoxy. The first charge touched his pride, the second his very existence as a member of the Christian community. He was hypersensitive and frequently replied with a prolixity far exceeding the scope of the publications attacked. Personal relations were at times highly strained. Much of this polemic is desultory reading, but it did serve to awaken the contemporary world of scholarship to important issues.

An appraisal of the contribution of Erasmus to Biblical

studies involves the points above mentioned: the text; the new Latin translation; the exegesis; and the popular exposition. First came the recovery and printing of the Greek text, and only afterwards, of course, the translation. The very rumour that he was about to undertake this assignment elicited an attack. Dorp, a friend and colleague at Louvain, had earlier been distressed by what he took to be the tone of levity in the *Praise of Folly*. Placated on that score by the assurances of Erasmus and of More that the intent was serious,[14] Dorp was shocked and outraged to hear that Erasmus proposed to publish the New Testament in Greek and accompanied by a new translation. To be sure Ambrose and Augustine had not depended upon Jerome's translation, but after he had castigated all of the errors his renderings had become standard as the basis for the decrees of councils. "What councils?" demanded Erasmus, "There were Greek councils which did not know Latin at all." "Don't listen to the Greeks," said Dorp. "They were heretics." "But," rejoined Erasmus, "Aristotle was even a pagan. Will you not read him? If you claim that the Vulgate is inspired equally with the original Greek and Hebrew and that to touch it is heresy and blasphemy what will you say about Bede, Rhabanus, Thomas Aquinas, and Nicolas of Lyra, not to mention others who undertook to make improvements? You must distinguish between Scripture, the translation of Scripture, and the transmission of both. What will you do with the errors of copyists?"[15] Dorp was eventually persuaded and Erasmus was thereby confirmed in his judgment that courtesy rather than invective is the better way to win over an opponent. A sharper antagonist was Sutor, once of the Sorbonne, later a Carthusian who asserted that "if in one point the Vulgate were in error the entire authority of Holy Scripture would collapse, love and faith would be extinguished, heresies and schisms would abound, blasphemy would be committed against the Holy Spirit, the authority of theologians would be shaken, and indeed the Catholic Church would collapse from the foundations." Erasmus pointed out that prior to Jerome the early Church had not used the Vulgate and had not collapsed.[16] To all who cried, "Jerome is good enough for me," he replied, "You cry out that it is a crime to correct the gospels. This is a speech worthier of a coachman than of a theologian. You think it is all very well if a clumsy scribe makes a mistake in transcription and then you deem it a crime to put it right. The only way to determine the true text is to examine the early codices."[17]

Erasmus did recognize, however, that in addition to the manuscripts of the New Testament, translations like the Vulgate have value as witnesses to the text employed by the translator, provided, of course, that the text of the translation is correct. The same observation applies to quotations from the Scripture in the works of the Church Fathers who wrote centuries earlier than any manuscript available to Erasmus.

At several points Erasmus threw doubt upon passages in the Vulgate. They were not omitted from the text but the annotations pointed out their dubious authenticity. One was the conclusion of Mark's gospel following verse 16: 8. Erasmus noted that according to Jerome the Greek manuscripts of his day gave it as an appendix and some Christians in that day did not accept it.[18] The other passage was the story of the woman taken in adultery of which Augustine and Chrysostom make no mention.

Two outright omissions blew up a storm. The most serious was that of the verse traditionally used to support the doctrine of the Trinity. The verse is I John 5: 7:

"For there are three that bear witness in heaven, the Father, the Word and the Holy Spirit: and these three are one," followed by the verse "And there are three that bear witness on earth, spirit, water, and blood: and these three are one." The Greek manuscripts accessible to Erasmus lacked verse seven and gave verse eight in the form: "There are three witnesses, the Spirit, the water and the blood; and these three agree." This was the form printed by Erasmus which immediately drew fire.

The most vehement assailant was the Englishman Edward Lee, later the Archbishop of York, a close friend of Thomas More. When in his first edition Erasmus had said that he would welcome corrections, Lee had supplied a few which Erasmus had treated disdainfully. Resenting the slight, Lee let it be known that he had further objections which, though urged, he would not show to Erasmus and eventually published. The omission of the Trinitarian verse, said he, was the proof that Erasmus had lapsed into the heresy of the Arians who denied that the Son was of one essence with the Father. Lee predicted that in consequence "the world would again be racked by heresy, schism, faction, tumults, brawls, and tempests." Erasmus replied, "My New Testament has been out now for three years. Where are the heresies, schisms, tempests, tumults, brawls, hurricanes, devastations, shipwrecks, floods, general disasters, and anything worse you can think of?"[19] "As a matter of fact, if the verse had been left in," said Erasmus, "it would not have refuted the Arians, because it does not say that the three heavenly witnesses are of one substance, but only that they are of one mind."[20]

Rashly Erasmus promised to restore the verse if it could be found in a single manuscript.[21] One was produced – manufactured in England, as we now know and as Erasmus suspected. Another was discovered in Spain and he surmised that this one had been copied from the one in England. True nevertheless to his promise, Erasmus made the restoration in his third edition of 1522, while at the same time increasing doubt as to the authenticity by mentioning in his annotations the discovery at Antwerp of a Greek manuscript in which the words had been written on the margin in a recent hand. In the edition of 1527 Erasmus reported that his friend Bombasius, in Rome, had checked the Vaticanus and had discovered the words to be lacking. With all of this evidence against the reading why did Erasmus suffer himself to be pressured into restoration? Was his motive simply to quell the storm? His own defence was that the verse was in the Vulgate and must therefore have been in the Greek text used by Jerome. Since it was not known to Cyril in the East and Bede in the West there must have been discrepant readings as early as the fourth century. How then could a modern editor decide? "In the meantime," said Erasmus, "it should be no crime to seek the truth without contention."[22] The weak point in the argument of Erasmus was ignorance as to the transmission of the text of the Vulgate in which this verse is not to be found prior to A.D. 800.[23] The quarrel with Lee on the personal side was eventually appeased through the mediation of More.[24] The attack of Stunica, though captious and persistent, need not detain us. He objected to the same points as Lee, with the addition of many minor corrections which were not infrequently right.

A second omission was due to the text of the Vulgate which lacked the doxology at the end of the Lord's Prayer in Matthew 6: 13, "For thine is the kingdom and the power and the glory, forever. Amen." It was in the

Greek manuscripts in the hands of Erasmus. It could not have been in the Greek manuscripts accessible to Jerome, who would never have been guilty of a deliberate omission. The doxology, surmised Erasmus, probably crept into the Greek through the influence of the liturgy. In this surmise Erasmus has been sustained by modern scholarship.[25]

A dispute with regard to the reading of a word precipitated the most distressing personal controversy with Jacques Lefevre,[26] the noted French Biblical scholar, with whom, while in Paris, Erasmus had had a most amiable and admiring encounter.

Lefevre proposed to diverge from the Vulgate on theological grounds. The dispute was as to the reading of Hebrews 2: 7. Should it be, "Thou hast made him a little lower than the angels," or "a little lower than God"? The reference was to Christ. The verse was a quotation from the eighth Psalm where the Hebrew does mean God. But the author of the Epistle to the Hebrews did not use the Hebrew, but rather the Greek translation, called the Septuagint, which had, instead, "angels." Both Jerome and Erasmus insisted that the text of Hebrews must be faithfully reproduced even though it contained an error. Lefevre objected that in fact Christ could not be lower than the angels. This remark was made prior to the appearance of the work of Erasmus who in a note in the first edition of 1516 took issue with him. Lefevre replied that to make Christ lower than the angels was "audacious and impious." Erasmus then, in the edition of 1519, expanded his note to fifty-six numbered paragraphs. The charge of incompetence he could endure, but not the charge of impiety. "To tax a friend with impiety is odious. Yet I will not forswear friendship." In addition to the note Erasmus published also an *Apologia*.[27] A mutual friend sought to compose "the lamentable contention." William Budé it was, an eminent jurist, a learned antiquarian who wrote a notable work on Roman numismatics, a Hellenist who delighted to compose long letters to Erasmus in Greek. "You had reason," he wrote to Erasmus, "to be offended when Lefevre accused you of impiety, but your reputation will not suffer if you are silent, whereas if you score a victory you will increase enmity."[28] Erasmus took his counsel and sent Lefevre a gracious bid for reconciliation.[29] No reply came for a year and Erasmus was worried that rancour smouldered beneath the silence of contempt.[30] Finally the response came: "Most gracious Erasmus, all the world holds you in esteem. You will forgive my silence. I didn't know where you were. I heard you were in England. I heard you were in Holland. I heard you were in Basel. Although your letters are most precious to me I will not take it amiss if you do not write, so long as you love me."[31] When later persecution flared in France against the evangelical movement and Lefevre was in exile at Strasbourg, Erasmus wrote on his behalf to Bishop Giberti.[32]

After the text came the translation. Erasmus felt that the Vulgate was in a number of respects inaccurate. Jerome, for all his learning, made mistakes,[33] and a new translation was in order. Erasmus was of no mind to displace the Vulgate in the schools, in the liturgy, or even in debate. "But I venture to think that any one who reads my translation at home will profit thereby."[34] The first task of the translator is, of course, the understanding of the language to be translated. At this point Erasmus noted that Greek was not the mother tongue of the evangelists and their use of it was affected by their native idioms. They did not write the Greek of Demosthenes.

"Do you mean to say," demanded John Eck in Germany, "that the best Greek was not written by the apostles on whom the Holy Spirit conferred the gift of tongues?" "My dear fellow," answered Erasmus, "if you will look at the list of languages of which the Holy Spirit gave command to the apostles on the day of Pentecost you will discover that Greek was not one of them. Besides the gift lasted for only one day."[35]

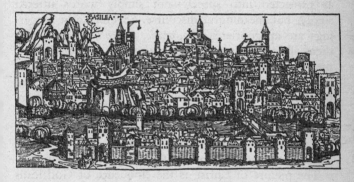

Basel in 1493. Note that one tower of the Münster is under construction.

Some of the translations of Erasmus created a furore. One was of Matthew 4: 17, where Jesus says, "Repent, for the kingdom of heaven is at hand." The Vulgate has *poenitentiam agite*, which was taken to mean "do penance." Erasmus in 1516 translated it *poeniteat vos*, "be penitent," and thereafter *resipiscite*, "change your mind," thereby removing any possible philological connection with the sacrament of penance. Luther made good use of this version.

The other rendering to create a stir was of John 1: 1, "In the beginning was the Word." The Vulgate rendering

for "Word" was *verbum*. Beginning with the edition of
1519 Erasmus translated it as *sermo*. He was accused of
complete innovation and suspected of demeaning the
incarnation. He proved that he was no innovator by
citations from the Fathers, but regardless of the tradition,
sermo, said he, is a better translation.[36] The word it
renders from the Greek is *logos*, which in antiquity meant
both the reason immanent in the universe and also reason
as projected into speech—not simply words uttered
singly, but meaningful discourse. Several Latin renderings are appropriate: *ratio, oratio, sapientia*. Superior to
them all is the circumlocution *eloquentia vera theologica*,[37]
the divine eloquence, the persuasiveness of God. In his
treatise on the training of preachers Erasmus affirmed
that the title *sermo* is bestowed only on Christ. Men are
sometimes called sons of God and even gods, but never
the Word of God. Christ was the *sermo*. We are to preach
the sermons.[38] This was the Christian version of that
eloquence to which Erasmus trusted to renew his world.

The picture of Christ as the eloquence of God leads
Erasmus into a homily.

Do we desire to learn, is there then any authority better
than Christ? We read and reread the works of a friend, but
there are thousands of Christians who have never read the
gospels and the epistles in all their lives. The Mohammedans
study the Koran, the Jews peruse Moses. Why do we not the
same for Christ? He is our only doctor. On him the Spirit
descended and a voice said, "Hear ye him!" What will you
find in Thomas, what in Scotus to compare with his teaching?
But as there are school masters who by their severity make
boys hate learning, so there are Christians so morose as to
instil distaste for the philosophy of Christ, which could not
be more agreeable. Happy is he whom death overtakes
meditating thereon. Let us then thirst for it, embrace it, steep
ourselves in it, die in it, be transformed thereby. If any one

shows us the footprints of Christ we Christians fall down and
adore. If his robe is placed on exhibition do we not traverse
the earth to kiss it? A wooden or a stone image of Christ is
bedecked with jewels and should we not place gold gems and
whatever may be more precious on the gospels which bring
Christ closer to us than any paltry image? In them we have
Christ speaking, healing, dying and rising and more genuinely
present than were we to view him with the eyes of the flesh.[39]

After the text and the translation came the elucidation of
Scripture, the popularization of the Bible for the masses.
Vernacular versions were in order of which Erasmus
highly approved, though he did not himself produce a
version in Dutch. Simple explanation was likewise in
order and this he did undertake in the form of *Paraphrases
of the New Testament*. He said that he would like to see the
sacred word in the hands of "the farmer, the tailor, the
traveller, and the Turk."[40] In the case of his *Paraphrases*
he expanded the list to include "the farmer, the tailor, the
mason, prostitutes, pimps, and Turks."[41] The inclusion
of the disreputables was directed at those who feared that
if the Bible were rendered easily accessible it would find
its way into unsavoury places. "Do you think," retorted
Erasmus, "that the Scriptures are fit only for the per-
fumed?"[42] The *Paraphrases* were written in Latin and
obviously could not circulate as widely as he wished save
in the vernaculars. They were speedily translated into
French, German, Bohemian, and English. During the
reign of Edward VI in England the *Paraphrases of the
Gospels* were to be set up in all of the churches. The project
of translation was sparked by Katherine Parr, the widow
of Henry VIII, supervised by the dramatist Nicholas
Udall, and the Princess Mary would have rendered the
paraphrase of John's gospel had not ill health impeded.
Erasmus commenced with the epistles and only after-

wards went on to the gospels. He evidently had done some work on Romans by the summer of 1514. He described to a friend how he and his groom had started on horses from Ghent to Basel in late August. About six miles underway Erasmus' horse shied and so wrenched his back that he could not even dismount. His groom helped him down. Then he could not remount and could not think of walking back the six miles to Ghent. He addressed himself to the Apostle Paul, promising that if delivered from this extremity, he would complete the *Paraphrase* of Romans. Erasmus was then able to remount and return to Ghent, where after speedy recovery he gave thanks to God and the apostle.[43] One suspects that if Paul had known what Erasmus would do with the Epistle to the Romans he would have made him walk. The doctrine of predestination was emasculated.

In his interpretation of the Scriptures Erasmus followed the traditional methodology, which saw in every verse of Scripture, the plain historical sense, of course, but in many passages also three other meanings, the tropological of moral obligation, the analogical of comforting assurance, and the allegorical of the spiritual significance beneath appearances. Erasmus criticized the scheme only at the point of paucity. Scripture is so rich that it may carry more than four meanings. The same man may not be aware of them all, for, as St. Gregory said, "Scripture is a stream in which an elephant can swim and a lamb can wade."[44] In the quest for meaning one must begin, said Erasmus, with the historical circumstance and examine diligently a saying to learn how it happened to have been said, by whom, to whom, under what circumstances, after what, and before what, and then go on to other meanings.

The differentiation of meanings originated in the early

Church largely in order to explain the relation of Christianity to Judaism by way of both continuity and discontinuity. The great divine drama of redemption embraced the two religions as forerunner and culmination. In the beginning God created the world and man and saw that they were good. Adam fell and his posterity so far deteriorated that God wiped out the race save for a remnant in Noah's ark. Then came three covenants: with Noah that the waters should no more return upon the earth; with Abraham that his seed should possess the land of promise; and with Moses and Israel to whom God swore that he would be their God and they should keep His law. The ensuing history was marked by fallings and risings with recurrent foreshadowings of Christianity. The prophecies of a coming redeemer and of all peoples going up to Mount Zion were referred to Christ and the Church. In addition there was a variety of allegory called typology whereby certain persons or deeds were viewed as types of the dispensation yet to come. In the New Testament itself we find examples of this mode of treating the Old. The serpent lifted up in the wilderness by Moses was a type of Christ lifted up upon the cross, and the passing of the Israelites through the Red Sea was a type of baptism. Erasmus diverged in no significant manner from this traditional way of discovering continuity between Judaism and Christianity.

Then came the problem of discontinuity. The Church was rejected by the synagogue. Should the synagogue be rejected by the Church? How could Christians retain the Old Testament which enjoined the keeping of the law, seeing that Christians did not keep the law? St. Paul offered an historical explanation that the law was a preparation for Christ and with his advent was abrogated. Much more serious than the law were the deviations from

the Christian moral code on the part of the Old Testament
worthies in response to divine command, or at any rate
without divine disapproval. How explain the polygamy
of the patriarchs, the lie of Abraham, the incest of Lot's
daughters, the despoiling of the Egyptians by theft, the
suicide of Samson, the tyrannicide of Judith, and the
unprovoked war of aggression of the Israelites against the
Canaanites? One solution was to suggest extenuating
circumstances, as that polygamy was then necessary to
replenish the earth. Another was the blank statement that
whatever God did was right because God did it.[45] Here
again was the problem of the limits of omnipotence.
Erasmus would rather curtail omnipotence than undercut
the religious foundation of the Christian ethic. In the
early Church Marcion had rejected the Old Testament
altogether because of these considerations. Erasmus
would not have found it difficult to be a Marcionite.
When an overly zealous Jewish convert to Christianity
wished to destroy the Jewish books Erasmus said that so
long as the New Testament was secure he would prefer
to let him have the Old rather than disturb the peace of
Christendom.[46] In marked contrast to Luther, Erasmus
wrote very little by way of commentary on the Old
Testament, only on a handful of Psalms, and one of those
he chose because of a pun. The first Psalm begins in
Latin *Beatus vir* (Blessed is the man) and could thus
appropriately be dedicated to Beatus Rhenanus. Erasmus
did, however, keep the Old Testament and, like his
favourite Church Father, Origen, solved the difficulties
by allegory. The concubines of Solomon were so many
virtues and the Canaanites to be exterminated by the
Israelites were so many vices.[47]

The mode of allegory which Erasmus preferred was the
transfer of the physical to the spiritual. We find this

approach in the New Testament itself where water is the water of life and bread the bread of life. This mode of exegesis was reinforced for Erasmus by the Platonic disparagement of the corporeal and the endeavour to go beyond the body to the spirit, beyond the visible to the invisible, beyond the temporal to the eternal.[48]

Erasmus asked why our Lord, who can raise those who have been dead for a thousand years, should have waited four days to raise Lazarus. The answer was that the Master desired to point to the slowness of the resurrection of the soul.[49] In dealing with the miracle of the loaves Erasmus interpreted the bread not as the Lord's body but as the bread of the gospel. The Lord told the disciples how to feed the people with this bread. Erasmus admonishes:

Don't worry as to where this food is to come from and do not assume that you are a great doctor of whose wisdom the people should not be deprived. Just see what you have at home and bring that to the Lord. He will bless it and give it back to you to distribute. The people will then receive more benefit than if some superstitious Pharisee, some arrogant philosopher, some eloquent orator should come with a carefully prepared discourse. In addition to the loaves there were two small fishes. A very sparse diet indeed. Yet four thousand were fed. If some pompous doctor comes announcing that he has more to deliver than time will permit and mysteries to expound which will be over the heads of his audience, they will go away hungry. Just bring the two little fishes. Bring them to Jesus. Nothing which he has not touched will be of any avail. Have you then eloquence, have you philosophy, have you ability, have you knowledge of sacred Scripture, of laws and pontifical decrees, whatever you have, place it in the hands of Jesus. Let him bless and break it and give it to you. Then you will give it to the people, not as your own but as coming from him.[50]

Take again the instance of the blind man restored partially to sight. Here Erasmus both allegorized and amplified. "Those who have not fully received the light of the gospel," said he, "magnify what they see in the world. An opulent man appears to them to be a plane tree. A magistrate or a prince is an apple or a cypress. A bearded Stoic or a Pharisee with broad phylacteries are taken to be fig trees. But when the eyes are cleansed these prodigies are cut down to size."[51]

On occasion Erasmus utilized the simple historical narrative to make the point that the physical is without efficacy unless accompanied by the spiritual. Those who touched the hem of Jesus' garment were healed of their diseases, but observe that those who smote him, who scourged him, who nailed him to the cross made contact with his naked flesh, yet none of them was cured of anything. There is no profit in touching Jesus to one who has not first been touched by him. Physical contact without faith is vain.[52]

At times Erasmus took the plain gospel account and elaborated the details imaginatively as Luther was wont to do. Take the case of the man sick of the palsy, who was let down before Jesus through a hole in the roof.

What a saucy, shameless trick to rip the tiles off another man's roof and inject a repulsive spectacle into the throng! Those who would not make room for the poor fellow to come in through the door have him thrust upon them through the ceiling. What then is done by the gentle physician? He does not upbraid the impudence and importunity. He does not chide the interruption of his discourse by this loathsome sight. The friends who brought the paralytic stand on the roof and ask nothing. The man himself is not able to utter a word. Their speechlessness is all the more moving. No need for prayers. The sight itself awakes compassion. What the friends have done makes sufficiently plain what they expect of the Lord. And Jesus, touched by their confidence, does more than ever they have expected.[53]

The mental states of Mary and Martha were analysed.

The two sisters were equal in their love of the Lord but differed in temperament. Mary was ravished by the words of the Master. Martha was flitting about the house that nothing should be lacking to perfect hospitality. Martha, well knowing that her sister could never be detached from the feet of Jesus, did not chide her, but in a way remonstrated with Jesus for so charming her sister that she neglected to do what needed to be done. "Master," she said, "don't you care that my sister leaves me to do all of this alone? Tell her to help me. I know she won't leave you unless you tell her to, so entrancing are your words. But the dinner must be made ready and one pair of hands is not enough." Then the Lord, who was delighted with the devotion of both women, did not chide the attachment of Mary, nor did he blame the complaint of Martha, though he leaned to Mary. "Martha! Martha!" he said, "Don't be so worried about getting the dinner and all worked up about many things. Mary has chosen the better part, to forget the things of the body and to be concerned for the things of the soul. I am grateful to you for preparing the dinner for me and my disciples, but to save souls is my meat and drink. The things of the body will pass away when 'that which is perfect is come.' At the same time, those who do as you have done will not lose their reward. They feed the hungry, clothe the naked, visit the sick, and entertain strangers. Yet those who attend to the one thing needful do more. But let no one complain of another, for each serves according to the gift received from God."[54]

In the case of the parables there was no need to do anything other than to draw out what lay already to hand. No parable was more congenial to Erasmus than that of the prodigal son. He wrote:

When the prodigal came to himself he arose. Now to arise is the first step in salvation. "And while he was a great way off his father saw him." He who had the greater love did first espy the other. The father saw the lad who had departed so insolently, now ragged, famished, filthy and weeping. The father saw him and had compassion and ran. The boy had prepared a speech. He would say, "Father, I have sinned against heaven and before thee, and I am no longer worthy to be called thy son. Make me as one of thy hired servants." But before he had even started to speak his father fell on his neck and kissed him. Now in the natural love of this father for his son behold the goodness of God, who is far more clement to sinful man, if only he repent and despise himself, than any father towards his son, however tenderly he may love him.[55]

This is the essence of Erasmus.

In the year 1516, when the Jerome and the New Testament were issued, he was fifty and now the recognized leader of the liberal reform movement throughout Europe. He had reason to glow over his output: the *Adagia*, the *Enchiridion*, *The Praise of Folly*, the *Panegyric of Philip*, *The Education of the Christian Prince*, *The Complaint of Peace*, the Jerome, and the New Testament, not to mention translations and editions of classical authors. To be sure there had been blasts from the conservatives, but "Why should the nations rage and the peoples imagine

Leo X commends the New Testament of Erasmus. The New Testament of Erasmus, first published in 1516, received two years later this commendation from the Pope, reprinted at the head of all subsequent editions beginning with that of 1519. The decorative borders with virtues and vices would not have disquieted Erasmus, but he would scarcely have liked the depiction, at the top, of the victory of the German commander Arminius over the Roman general Varus, a theme popular with the German nationalists. Erasmus was devoid of national feeling.

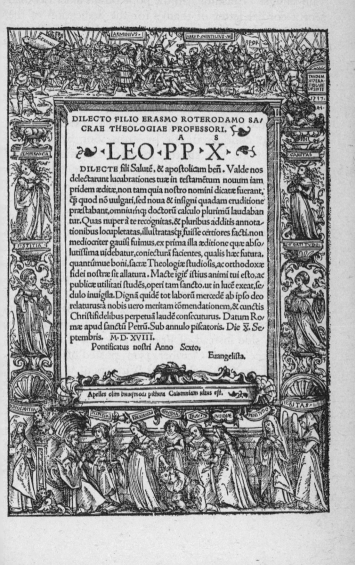

DILECTO FILIO ERASMO ROTERODAMO SA/
CRAE THEOLOGIAE PROFESSORI.

A S

❧ LEO·PP·X ❧

DILECTE fili Salutē, & apostolicam beñ. Valde nos
delectarunt lucubrationes tuæ in testamētum nouum iam
pridem æditæ,non tam quia nostro nomini dicatæ fuerant,
c̄q̄ quod nō uulgari,sed noua & insigni quadam eruditione
præstabant,omniumq̄; doctorū calculo plurimū laudaban
tur.Quas nuper à te recognitas,& pluribus additis annota
tionibus locupletatas,illustratasc̄q̄ fuisse cērtiores facti,non
mediocriter gauisi fuimus,ex prima illa æditione quæ abso
lutissima uidebatur,coniecturā facientes, qualis hæc futura,
quantūue boni,sacræ Theologiæ studiosis,ac orthodoxæ
fidei nostræ sit allatura. Macte igit̄ istius animi tui esto,ac
publicæ utilitati studēs,operi tam sancto,ut in lucē exeat,se
dulo inuigila.Digna quidē tot laborū mercedē ab ipso deo
relaturus:à nobis uero meritam c̄ōmendationem,& cunctis
Christifidelibus perpetuā laudē consecuturus. Datum Ro
mæ apud sanctū Petrū.Sub annulo piscatoris. Die X̄. Se
ptembris. M·D·XVIII.
Pontificatus nostri Anno Sexto.

Euangelista.

Apelles olim huiusmodi pictura Calumniam ultus est.

vain things?" Erasmus had the pope on his side. Leo had
sent a cordial letter of thanks for the dedication of the
New Testament. It was printed at the head of all subsequent editions. The political outlook was hopeful.
Erasmus looked with enthusiasm to the four rulers to
whom he was to dedicate his paraphrases of the four
gospels: Henry of England, Francis of France, Charles of
Spain, Ferdinand of Austria. And with what enthusiasm
he greeted the new Pope Leo, the disciple of the Prince of
Peace, who conquered not by arms, but by dying.[56]
This same pope was shortly to grant Erasmus a comprehensive dispensation relieving him from all of the
disabilities which might hamper his studies.

When in May 1516 Erasmus returned to the Netherlands to be near the court of Charles, whose councillor he
had become, he found there two letters awaiting him from
Pope Leo inviting him to Rome. "If only these had
reached me while I was at Basel," he replied, "no danger
could have deterred me from hastening to your blessed
feet."[57] As it was, he now felt obligated not to desert his
prince. One cannot but wonder what the blessed feet of
his Holiness might have done or left undone had Erasmus
been at his side instead of Prierias and Eck after Martin
Luther on the 31st of October, 1517, posted his *Theses* on
the door of the Castle church at Wittenberg.[58]

CHAPTER SEVEN

Under Fire: Luther

*

THE full import of Luther's posting of the theses was not at first appreciated by his generation. Pope Leo saw to begin with only a new squabble between the monastic orders when the Augustinian Luther attacked the preaching of the Dominican Tetzel, the vendor of the indulgences. To many, including both Luther and Erasmus, the case appeared to be a continuation of a controversy already well advanced between the humanists and the obscurantists over the question of freedom to pursue the study of Hebrew literature. The principals were John Reuchlin, an eminent jurist of Tübingen and a pioneer of Hebrew studies among the Christians, and John Pfefferkorn, a converted Jew, who, as we noted, demonstrated his zeal for his new-found faith by agitating for the destruction of Jewish books. The controversy came to the attention of the Emperor Maximilian who appointed a committee to render an opinion. Reuchlin, as one of the members, advised that nothing be done indiscriminately and that chairs for the study of Hebrew be founded in the universities in order that Christians might be competent to have a judgment. The Dominicans then rallied to the support of Pfefferkorn and brought the case before Jakob von Hochstraten, the Inquisitor for Heretical Pravity for the diocese of Cologne. He rendered a judgment adverse to Reuchlin. An appeal was made to the pope, who at first exonerated Reuchlin, but then, when the agitation continued, enjoined silence and saddled Reuchlin with the costs. But Reuchlin did not keep silence and did not pay the costs. A victory had been won for free investigation.

Erasmus became speedily involved because his educational programme was at stake and in particular his effort to promote the study of Hebrew through the *Collegium Trilingue* at Louvain. In May of 1515 he wrote to Cardinal Riario on behalf of Reuchlin, "a man venerable and venerated, of unsullied reputation, esteemed by the Emperor Maximilian, deserving of an abundant harvest from his noble studies in which he is pre-eminent in Germany."[1] At the same time Erasmus made it entirely plain that he was not endorsing Reuchlin's Cabalistic speculations which he regarded as sheer fantasy.[2] Pfefferkorn was excoriated for disturbing the peace of Christendom.[3] The course of Erasmus was clear. He would defend Reuchlin's freedom without endorsing everything for which he stood, and would strive, even at the price of sacrificing the Old Testament, to preserve the peace of the Church.

This course drew upon Erasmus distrust from both sides. Hochstraten could not be expected to be happy over the flouting of his verdict and might readily abet an attempt to suppress the *Collegium Trilingue* at Louvain. On the other side were some lusty young humanists who pilloried Hochstraten in one of the world's great satires, *The Letters of Obscure Men*,[4] in which simple-minded monks in racy dialogue with each other so defended Hochstraten in monstrous Latin as to make asses of themselves. Erasmus chuckled over the first instalment which was genial in tone.[5] Then came a continuation, witty, stinging, virulent, interspersed with personal references to Erasmus, described as "a man entirely on his own."[6] "I don't

Louvain in the sixteenth century.

think much of Erasmus," says one of the participants. "He is an enemy of the monks, says all they know how to do is to gourmandize, guzzle, and babble the Psalms. He is a good Latinist and that's all he knows. Our master Hochstraten has examined his edition of Jerome and finds it dreadful. Erasmus says that St. Jerome was not a cardinal. That is *lèse majesté*."[7] Erasmus let it be known that he did not like the invective and did not relish the personal reference.[8] The author of this second instalment took umbrage. He was that fulminating German poet and patriot, Ulrich von Hutten, who had been simply ecstatic when Erasmus had given him honourable mention in his edition of the New Testament[9] and was unreservedly grateful when commendation from Erasmus gave him a most cordial entrée among the humanists of Italy. Now he felt that the adored proclaimer of liberty was recoiling under pressure.[10]

Erasmus was following a straight line: to defend the man, though not all of his opinions, and to refrain from riling his opponents by invective. When Reuchlin died Erasmus composed a colloquy describing his reception in heaven, very different from that of Pope Julius. The tone of the *Apotheosis of Reuchlin* is set by the opening remark that some people are too conservative to change their shoes or their underwear or to eat fresh eggs. Then the narrator has a dream in which he sees Reuchlin wafted to heaven in a white robe, not a monastic habit. He is received by Jerome without a cardinal's hat or his pet lion and is made to sit down among the saints. "Among the saints!" ejaculates an interlocutor. "Do you not hesitate to make him a saint when he has not been canonized?" "And who, pray," comes the retort, "canonized St. Jerome, St. Paul, or the Virgin Mary?"[11] To publish this colloquy in 1522 was an act of courage because by that time the affair of Reuchlin had found its sequel in the affair of Luther.[12] The cause was the same: freedom to speak. The opponents were the same: the Dominicans. And the first university to condemn Luther's teaching was Cologne in the district of Jakob von Hochstraten.

The earliest intimation of Luther's existence to reach Erasmus was oblique. Spalatin, the chaplain of Frederick the Wise, wrote Erasmus in December 1516 that an unnamed Augustinian monk took issue with the Erasmian interpretation of the Epistle to the Romans, where the apostle was talking about original sin and rejecting the whole law of Moses and not simply the ceremonial portion.[13] Here already was the nub of the later controversy. Two and a half years later came the first letter of Luther to Erasmus. The tone was adulatory.[14] In the meantime Erasmus had become well aware of his identity, had seen the Ninety-Five Theses, and had sent a copy to More.[15] He had seen likewise the refutation of the Ninety-Five Theses composed at the behest of Pope Leo by the Dominican Prierias, the Master of the Sacred Palace, with endorsement of the jingle of Tetzel, "As soon as the coin in the coffer rings, the soul from purgatory springs." Prierias had asserted, moreover, that the Church consists virtually in the pope and that he who does not accept the doctrine of the Roman Church and of the Roman pontiff as the infallible rule of faith is a heretic and that he who dissents from what the Roman Church actually does in the matter of indulgences is a heretic.[16] Erasmus wrote to a sympathizer with Luther that the Ninety-Five Theses would be approved by all men save for a few points on purgatory. The reply by Prierias, he said, is utterly inept. "This monarchy of the Roman pontiff is the pest of Christendom before whom all the Dominicans fall down on their faces. I do not know whether this ulcer can be openly touched. This is a job for princes, but I am afraid that in collusion with the pontiff they will divide the spoils. I do not know what has possessed Eck that he should attack Luther."[17]

Every phrase in the above statement is fraught with weighty implication. Erasmus says only that the Theses will be approved by all. He does not say that he approves, but he implies as much. With respect to purgatory, just what he did not like or thought others would not like is not clear. Luther had said that the pope had no jurisdiction over purgatory and that if he did he should empty the place gratis. Erasmus may have thought this too strong but he pointed out that no papal bulls offered immediate release.[18] The tone of German belligerency against Italian chicanery would not kindle his cosmopolitan heart, but he would respond to the excoriation of extortion. "I do not condemn indulgences," said he, "but I think it is nonsense to suppose one can buy one's way to heaven. What a filthy traffic this is, designed to fill coffers rather than to stimulate piety!"[19]

But the financial aspect of indulgences was the smallest part of the offence. They were at first remissions of the penalties for sin, imposed by the Church on earth. Only at the end of the fifteenth century was their scope extended to cover penalties imposed by God in purgatory. Some bulls went even so far as to promise the remission of sins. The recipient of such favours was expected to make a contribution, and this way of raising money commended itself highly because voluntary and not productive of resentment like compulsory tithes collected on pain of excommunication. The ability of the pope to confer such benefits rested on the assumption that he was able to dispense from the treasury of the accumulated merits of the saints who were better than they needed to be for their own salvation and whose superfluous credits were stored in a treasury, the *thesaurus meritorum sanctorum* from which they could be transferred to the accounts of those who were in arrears. This entire theory Luther demolished by asserting that no one has enough merits to save himself. Even the saints are sinners. There is no such thing as a treasury of the merits of the saints. No one can be saved by merits on the part of any one but only by reliance in faith on the grace of Christ. Now, all this Erasmus said, too, and said it repeatedly.[20] He was entirely at one with Luther that salvation depends solely on grace. And as for the papal primacy, it is merely a matter of practical utility.[21] The power of the keys was conferred on Peter almost enigmatically and in any case intermittently. He was at first not fit to exercise the power.[22] Luther has spoken moderately, said Erasmus, about the power of the Roman pontiff. Alvaro Pelagio, Sylvester Prierias, and Cardinal Cajetan have spoken immoderately.[23]

In his writings of this period Erasmus introduced passages which might well appear to have been inserted in order to support Luther and some there were which went even beyond what Luther had said up to this point. The *Enchiridion* was reissued in 1518 with a new preface addressed to Volz. In it Erasmus excoriated contemporary monasticism in the name of Benedict, Augustine, and Francis. "At the outset," said Erasmus, "monasticism was a withdrawal from the world of pagan idolatry. The monks lived in evangelical liberty without vows and did not revile each other over matters of food and dress. They worked with their hands in order to give to the poor. The only contest among them was the contest of humility. This was the kind of monasticism approved by Basil, Chrysostom, and Jerome, but now. . . ." And then he took off.[24]

In the annotations on the New Testament in the edition of 1519 this passage was introduced: "By how many human regulations has the sacrament of penitence and confession been impeded? The bolt of excommunication is ever in readiness. The sacred authority of the Roman pontiff is so abused by absolutions, dispensations, and the like that the godly cannot see it without a sigh. Aristotle is so in vogue that there is scarcely time in the churches to interpret the gospel."[25]

The edition of the *Ratio* in 1519 had the assertion that Peter was the voice and representative of the entire

Christian people. Christ said to him, "Feed *my* sheep," not "*your* sheep!"[26] The edition of the following year made this insertion: "There are those who, not content with the observance of confession as a rite of the Church, superimpose the dogma that it was instituted not merely by the apostles but by Christ himself, nor will they suffer one sacrament to be added or subtracted from the number of the seven, although they are perfectly willing to commit to one man the power to abolish purgatory. Some assert that the universal body of the Church has been contracted into a single Roman pontiff who cannot err on faith and morals, thus ascribing to the pope more than he claims for himself, though they do not hesitate to dispute his judgment if he interferes with their purses or their prospects. Is not this to open the door to tyranny in case such power were wielded by an impious and pestilent man? The same may be said of vows, tithes, restitutions, remissions, and confessions, by which the simple and superstitious are beguiled."[27] In 1522 this was added: "We do not impugn the majesty of the Roman pontiff. Would that he had the qualities attributed to him, that he were not able to err in matters of piety, that he were able to deliver souls from purgatory."[28]

Erasmus went further and wrote letters on Luther's behalf which he knew perfectly well would be published. To Frederick the Wise, Luther's prince, he wrote on the 14th of April, 1519.[29] He began by saying that according to report Luther had been shamefully handled by Cardinal Cajetan. The reference was to the hearing at Augsburg when Catejan dismissed Luther with the blunt word that he should not return unless willing to recant. Erasmus continues:

Luther is entirely unknown to me. Hence I cannot be suspected of favouring him out of friendship. I cannot pass

Iber generationis IESV . A.

Christi filii Dauid filii

1. John Colet at prayer

Waramus Arch Bʳ Cant

2. Archbishop Warham by Hans Holbein

3. A coin of Titus

4. Thomas Moore: from the preliminary sketch for a portrait
by Hans Holbein

5. Frederick the Wise, Luther's prince

7. A medal of Pope Adrian VI showing a refined and somewhat ascetic face. He appears also to have had some mechanical skill for he is credited with having designed a swivel chair 8. enabling him to work at three desks. When he went as Pope to Rome he desired to have the chair shipped to him from Louvain. A friend instead sent the sketch below that a Roman craftsman might construct a duplicate

6. John Froben by Hans Holbein

7.

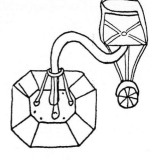

8.

9. Conrad Pellikan

10. Albrecht Dürer's Erasmus

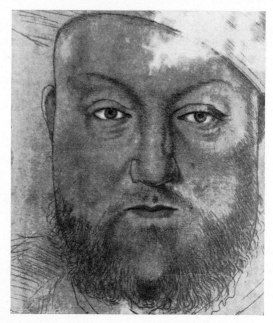

11. Henry VIII by Hans Holbein

12. Boniface Amerbach by Hans Holbein

on his opinions because I have barely leafed through his
books. I know of no one who does not commend his life. He
is free from avarice and ambition. . . . Yet no one admonishes
him, no one instructs, no one corrects. They simply cry
heresy. No author is free from error, whether ancient or
modern. If everything taught in the schools is an oracle why
do the schools disagree among themselves? The very doctors
of the Sorbonne agree only by collusion. The best part of
Christianity is a Christian life. He who accuses another of
heresy ought to exhibit charity in admonition, kindliness in
correcting, candour in judging, latitude in pronouncing. Why
do we prefer to conquer than to cure? Let him that is without
error not break a bruised reed, nor quench the smoking flax.
. . . Most illustrious prince, since your highness has the
responsibility of protecting the Christian religion, it is not
seemly to suffer an innocent man under the pretext of piety to
be subjected to impiety. Pope Leo does not wish this, for
nothing is dearer to him than the protection of the innocent.

A few weeks later Erasmus wrote in a similar vein to
Albert of Brandenburg, the Archbishop of Mainz, the
Primate of Germany, and an Elector of the Holy Roman
Empire.[30] He it was whose instructions to the vendors of
indulgences in his territories had touched off Luther's
Theses. This letter in large part repeats the one to
Frederick. Erasmus says: "I dare not judge of Luther's
spirit. But if I favour him as a good man, as accused, as
oppressed, this is the work of justice and humanity. If he
is innocent he should not be delivered to a faction. If he is
guilty he should be corrected. The detractors are condemning passages in the writings of Luther which are
deemed orthodox when they occur in the writings of
Augustine and Bernard."

The measure of support which Erasmus had given to
Luther and the obvious similarity between their pro-
grammes of reform led not unnaturally to the judgment

E.   G that Erasmus laid the egg which Luther hatched.[31] Erasmus did his best to dispel the imputation. In the case of Luther, as of Reuchlin, he was defending the man rather than his opinions. Nor would Erasmus admit that he was the source of Luther's opinions. If any one was the source it was the Apostle Paul.[32] Even more disconcerting was the charge that the revival of the humanities was responsible for the resurgence of heresy. The renaissance of humane letters, it was said, had tottered the pillars of Christendom and produced the rubble of Lutheranism. "As if," retorted Erasmus, "Luther had been nurtured upon humane letters rather than upon scholasticism."[33]

As Luther's language against the papists grew more violent, Erasmus grew more diffident in his support. If in one respect he saw in Luther the new Reuchlin, in another he came to regard him as the new Pfefferkorn, flinging the apple of discord. Erasmus remonstrated with him. "Why don't you cry out against bad popes rather than against all popes? Let us not be arrogant or factious, but rather devoid of ire and vaunting of oneself. Not that you are not devoid but that you may continue so to be. I have digested your commentary on the Psalms and am immensely pleased."[34] This was such a feeble rebuke as to augment the suspicion that Erasmus was abetting Luther, and while deploring the tumult Erasmus conceded that it might be needful if anything significant were to be achieved. To a well-wisher of Luther he wrote, "Better it is to instill the mind of Christ than to tilt with fellow Christians. But I don't see how we can until we are rid of the Roman See and its satellites, the Dominicans, Carmelites, and Franciscans, and I don't see how that can be attempted without grave tumult."[35] In a similar vein he wrote to Luther's young associate, the prodigy in

Greek studies, Philip Melanchthon, the grandnephew of Reuchlin who disowned him for favouring Luther. Young Philip was never disowned by Erasmus. He wrote: "I favour Luther as much as I can, even if my cause is everywhere linked with his. Those who favour him wish he would be more civil and less mordant. But to remonstrate is now too late. I see sedition under way. I hope it will turn out to the glory of Christ. Perhaps scandals have to come, but I don't want to be their author."[36] That is Erasmus. He could plot a steady course without assurance that it would be an effective strategy.

The pressures were intensified when the letters became public. His old friend Aleander showed them to the pope.[37] Aleander was on the way to becoming the spearhead of the conservative opposition. The first step against Luther emanated, however, from the circle of Jakob von Hochstraten and from the very university where Erasmus was in residence, Louvain. Its leaders, disturbed over the spread of Lutheran ideas,[38] sent a message to the University of Cologne for a judgment on a list of Luther's opinions. Cologne replied that Luther was guilty of gross error as to confession, indulgences, and the treasury of merits, and he had impudently attacked the authority of the Holy See. His books should be burned and he should be compelled to recant.[39] The person commissioned to deliver this response to the University of Louvain was none other than Jacob von Hochstraten, the Inquisitor of Heretical Pravity.[40] He was himself the more inflamed because he had seen the letter of Erasmus to Luther.[41] Louvain then issued a similar condemnation except that no mention was made of "the impudent attack on the Roman primacy," seeing that Louvain was not too fond of the Roman primacy. The document was prefaced by a letter from Adrian of Utrecht, another old friend of

Erasmus and later pope, who said that Luther was all the more manifestly in error because he declared himself ready to die for his opinions and asserted that to reject his opinions was heresy. Such pestiferous doctrines must not be suffered to seduce others. "But be careful," added Adrian, "that you quote Luther accurately."[42]

Erasmus wrote to Cardinal Wolsey in England that he deplored these condemnations.[43] Luther wrote a forthright rejoinder to the two universities and Erasmus applauded him in a letter to Melanchthon.[44] Then appeared an anonymous account of how the Louvain professors railroaded through a hasty and far from unanimous judgment, which, it was pointed out, did not agree entirely with that of Cologne. The professors were reminded that it would be much easier to take Luther out of the libraries than to eradicate him from the hearts of men.[45] Erasmus was promptly suspected of being the author of this document. He did not admit it. One passage makes one doubtful whether he could have written all of it.[46] There is a scathing treatment of Aleander against whom he scarcely felt so bitter at this juncture. And there was the statement that Aleander was of Jewish extraction. Aleander thought Erasmus started the rumour. If he did and considered it a reproach, it will have been because for him Judaism was a synonym for ceremonialism, legalism, and obscurantism.

On the 15th day of June 1520 the dilatory Pope Leo aroused himself to compose the bull *Exsurge*, "Arise O Lord. A wild boar has invaded thy vineyard. Arise O Peter! Arise O Paul!" The pope aroused all the saints as if without their aid the Lord Jesus would have been unable to clear the vineyard of the wild boar. Luther was given sixty days in which to make his submission. The time clock began to tick only when the bull was actually delivered to the person named and in this case so great was the obstruction even on the part of German bishops, that John Eck, commissioned to make the delivery, did not succeed until the tenth of October. This gave Luther until the tenth of December. His immediate response was to issue the tract entitled *Against the Execrable Bull of Antichrist*, in which he called the authenticity of the bull into question. So also did Erasmus because "this bull is appalling, breathing rather the savagery of the Mendicants than the spirit of the gentle Pope Leo."[47] When its genuineness became incontestable the only recourse was then to lay the blame on the pope's evil advisers.

Should Luther not submit, his fate was predictable. On the sixteenth of July Aleander was created nuntius and protonotary with commission to go to the court of the emperor at Brussels and there to call upon his Majesty as well as upon all princes, barons, and prelates to enforce the bull should Luther prove recalcitrant.[48] This meant, of course, that he would be sent to the stake. No such action could be taken, however, before his period of grace had expired. In the meantime his books should be burned. The bonfires began in the Low Countries. Here it was that the inquisitorial aspect of the Counter-Reformation had its inception. The primary reason was that the civil authority abetted rather than obstructed the suppression. In this area Charles ruled by hereditary right rather than simply as emperor and was under no obligation, therefore, to obtain the consent of any local prince. No Frederick the Wise stood here in his way. The mind of Charles had been formed by that Adrian of Utrecht, who regarded Luther's teaching as pestiferous. The first great *auto da fé* of Lutheran books took place at Louvain on October 8th. When the fire was merrily burning students threw in works of some of the scholastic theologians.[49] Erasmus tried to prevent a similar burning in England. This may appear anomalous seeing that Erasmus discouraged Froben from publishing any more of Luther's works.[50] He would halt the increase of combustible material but would not destroy that which was already out. His intervention in England was fruitless. The books were publicly burned at St. Paul's Cross and the sermon on the occasion was preached by an old friend of Erasmus, the utterly incorruptible and utterly orthodox Bishop of Rochester, John Fisher.[51]

Despite all disclaimers of complicity with Luther, Erasmus could not shake off the allegation. The rector of the University of Louvain, Nicolas Egmont, ascended the pulpit of the church of St. Peter to preach on charity, but speedily abandoned the theme to denounce Erasmus as a Lutheran.[52]

At this juncture who should pay a call on Erasmus if not that incendiary, more Lutheran than Luther, Ulrich von Hutten! Erasmus was fond of him, admired his genius, and had dedicated to him a charming portrayal of Thomas More. The touch of estrangement over the *Epistles of Obscure Men* was fleeting. Hutten had come both for a visit and also to request letters of introduction to notables at the imperial court. Although now in the service of Albert of Mainz, Hutten was on a mission of his own to enlist the support of the emperor and his brother Ferdinand for the grandiose scheme of welding Germany into a national state comparable to France, England, and Spain by converting the Holy Roman Empire into a Holy *Deutsches Reich*. That could not be done unless the hold of the Roman Church on the economic and political life of Germany were broken. This would require a war, a priests' war, a *Pfaffenkrieg*.[53] Hutten unfolded his plan to Erasmus who at first thought he was joking and played along. "And what will you do with the priests?" asked Erasmus. "They are Romanists," said Hutten. "And will you then hang Hochstraten?" "In short order." In his subsequent account Erasmus said anyone could have seen they were joking. But when Hutten kept on about his war on the Romanists Erasmus perceived that he was passionately in earnest and then remonstrated. How on earth did Hutten think he could dislodge the pope who was not only powerful in his own right but had many princes at his beck? Even if the enterprise were legitimate it was foolhardy, with no hope of success.[54]

Hutten met with no encouragement at Brussels and, leaving the service of Albert of Mainz, joined himself to Franz von Sickingen, the last great leader of the German knights, a condottiere who hired them out to the emperor or the king of France. At the same time Sickingen was something of a Don Quixote, capable of being enlisted for an ideal. He was willing to support Hutten in his *Pfaffenkrieg*. From Sickingen's fortress, the Ebenburg, Hutten wrote to Erasmus: "Do you think that you are secure now that Luther's books have been burned? Flee, Erasmus, flee! You first bestirred the minds of men for liberty. You cannot trust Aleander. If he is incensed against you when you have been extremely mild, what will it be when we have recourse to arms? They would have been used before now if Sickingen had not entertained hopes of help from Charles, which he might have given had it not been for that Slav [meaning Aleander]. Flee, come here to me. You say the attempt is difficult. Indeed, most difficult, but noble, and, if we fall, others will rise from our ashes. Arise you nobles, arise you peasants. Cast out your masters. Shake off base servitude. Break the yoke. Remember we are Germans who would

rather die than not be free. And Erasmus, remember that
if you are not openly threatened at Louvain, there is
secret poison. There is the dagger."[55]

Hutten may have supposed that he was merely exhorting Erasmus to be faithful to his own convictions.
Had Erasmus not said that the ulcer of indulgences could
be cured only by the princes? Presumably what Erasmus
meant was that only the princes could prevent the
exportation of gold from their lands to Rome. Certainly
he did not mean that the civil rulers should employ
violence. In telling Hutten that the pope could not be
dislodged because supported by so many princes Erasmus
was premature in his judgment. In a little less than a
decade the imperial troops were to sack Rome, not,
however, with the intent to convert the Holy Roman
Empire into a German national state. Regardless of
whether the political forecasts of Erasmus were acute or
obtuse he was not to be deflected from his own course.
Yet Hutten had instilled in his mind the suspicion of
poison.

In the meantime Martin Luther did not ease the path
of the pacifier. During the summer of 1520 he brought
out two of his most devastating tracts. The first was *The
Address to the Christian Nobility of the German Nation*, that
is to say, the ruling class in Germany, including the
emperor in whom Luther had not yet lost confidence.
The temporal arm should reform the spiritual arm of
Christendom. This programme was by no means un-
precedented. The temporal arm during the Middle Ages
had more than once expelled an unworthy pope or
bishop. But Luther's tract reverberated with the
grievances of the German nation and played upon the
theme dear to the Wycliffites and Hussites of the contrast
between Christ and Antichrist, the pope. Luther added

THE WAR AGAINST THE PAPISTS from the title page of a work by
Ulrich von Hutten. Above, God, like Jupiter, is about to launch his
thunderbolt, while David with his harp quotes Psalm 92:2: "Rise
up, O judge of the earth; render to the proud their deserts!" In the
middle of the right is Hutten and on our left Luther, who would
sanction the references to God and David above, but would emphatically disapprove of the war against the papists below.

also the contrast of Peter and the pope in a vein reminiscent of the *Julius Exclusus*. Luther's aim was to make the papacy a purely spiritual institution without temporal power and lordly possessions, a church in which every layman is a priest, and in consequence the superiority of the sacerdotal over the civil is demolished. The programme sounds like Hutten's except that Luther was not interested in a German national state and would have no violence. Much of Luther's programme would suit Erasmus, though he was not so inclined to elevate the layman.

The other tract was entitled *The Babylonian Captivity*, meaning that the sacraments of the Church had been taken captive by the traditions of men. To Luther's mind a rite must have been instituted by Christ if it were to be a sacrament. By this token he reduced the number of the sacraments from seven to two, namely baptism and the Lord's Supper, though in the case of penance he retained confession on a voluntary basis and not necessarily to a priest. He denied that the Mass is a sacrifice. It should not be celebrated for the dead, nor by the priest alone without participants. The wine should be given to the laity as with the Bohemians. Christ's body is physically present upon the altar because he said, "This is my body." How this can be we need not define. There is no transubstantiation wrought by the words of consecration, because actually the body of Christ is everywhere. His presence is peculiarly disclosed in the sacrament.

When Erasmus read this tract he ejaculated, "The malady is incurable." But he added "as it seems," implying presumably that the Church could never be expected to come to terms with such affirmations rather than that he himself regarded them as beyond discussion. At any rate he did not desist from his efforts at mediation.

DE CAPTIVITATE
BABYLONICA
ECCLESIAE,
Præludium Martini
Lutheri.

Vuittembergæ.

Title page of Luther's tract dealing with the sacraments.

And as a matter of fact there was nothing in Luther's programme which he could not endorse, save the indiscriminate reference to the popes as Antichrist.[56] As for the sacraments, we shall examine his position more fully later on. Suffice it to say for the moment that in his eyes no rite of the Church, no external framework of the Church was necessary for salvation, which depends rather on a heartfelt piety which can be cultivated apart from outward aids. This was a position actually more radical than that of Luther, and Melanchthon acutely observed that the views of Erasmus "with respect to the sacrament of the altar would have given rise to much graver tumults had not Luther arisen to channel the zeal of men in another direction."[57]

In November of 1520 the new emperor, Charles V, having been crowned at Aachen, passed through Cologne with his suite. Aleander was there to make sure that his Majesty did not waver in his resolution to crush Luther. Erasmus was there as an imperial councillor. Aleander invited him to dine. Erasmus, mindful of Hutten's suspicion of poison, ate first, and only afterwards came for a conference of five hours' duration. The old friends parted with the kiss of peace[58] which was as durable as a political treaty. Frederick the Wise was also there with his chaplain Spalatin. Frederick stood high in the graces of the emperor whose election he had ensured by declining to vote for himself. Aleander sought to induce Frederick to turn Luther, bound, over to the ecclesiastical authorities. Frederick desired guidance and sought it from Erasmus. At the interview Frederick talked German, Erasmus Latin, and Spalatin interpreted. "What sin had Luther committed?" asked Frederick. "Two," said Erasmus. "He has struck at the tiara of the pope and the bellies of the monks."[59] Spalatin asked Erasmus for a memorandum on how to deal with the Lutheran affair. He responded with the *Axiomata* in which he declared that the cruelty of the bull offended the right-minded and was unworthy of the gentle vicar of Christ. The universities have condemned but have not convicted Luther. His case should be referred to impartial judges. A much fuller and specific recommendation was issued under the

Jerome Aleander.

name of the liberal Dominican Johann Faber with the almost certain collaboration of Erasmus. The impartial judges should be the emperor and the kings of England and Hungary. Repeatedly the assertion is made that compulsion is the work of asses. Theologians should teach with gentleness. Burnings may empty libraries but not hearts. Frederick secured from the emperor the promise that Luther would not be condemned unheard, *nisi auditus*.[60] Erasmus returned to the Netherlands.

Luther again embarrassed the moderates when on the

tenth of December he burned the papal bull and the Decretals, making the malady appear all the more incurable. So said Erasmus. But when a new bull put Luther under the ban of the Church and the Edict of Worms put him under the ban of the empire, Erasmus called the bull ferocious and the edict even worse. Frederick the Wise spirited him away to hiding at the Wartburg. The rumour circulated that he had been assassinated. Albrecht Dürer, then himself in the Netherlands, recorded in his diary. "O God, if Luther is dead, who will so clearly teach us the gospel? O Erasmus of Rotterdam where are you staying? Ride forth, you knight of Christ. Defend the truth and win the martyr's crown."[61]

Erasmus was ready to ride forth as a knight of Christ but only in his own way. He would not die for the paradoxes of Luther. For a full four hundred years he has been accused of being unwilling to die for anything because he confided to a friend, "Not all have the strength for martyrdom. I am afraid if conflict should come I would imitate Peter."[62] But in passing judgment one should recall that he who mistrusts himself may be more courageous under test than one who like Peter boasts in advance. Elsewhere Erasmus said, "I would be happy to be a martyr for Christ, but I cannot be a martyr for Luther."[63] And again, "Would that with my little body I could allay this dissension. How gladly would I lay down my life."[64] He was quite clear in what sense he would be a knight of Christ. He would not leave the Church of Rome.[65] He would not desert the rock of Christ. He would not belong to a faction. He would not attack Luther.[66] Far be it from him to deprive the universities of that honour.[67] He would strive to compose this quarrel.[68]

He hoped that he could do so by continuing at

Louvain. But Aleander was at Brussels inciting the emperor to burn Luther's books and half a dozen Lutherans alive. Four hundred of the books were given to the flames at Antwerp in the presence of the public officials and a great concourse peering through all the windows. A bystander suggested that the books might better have been sold and the money sent to Rome to burn the pederasts. At Ghent a fiery preacher addressed fifty thousand, including the King of Denmark and the emperor, beaming with satisfaction over another conflagration. A baker suggested to a Franciscan that if the ashes of Luther's books got into his eyes he might see the better.[69]

Satirical pamphlets continued to appear. One bore the title *The Lamentations of Peter*. Actually it was lamentations of all the authors of the New Testament because their books were no longer read. Paul suggested that John's writings fared better than the others because he drew from Plato. "Nonsense," retorted Peter. "Do you suppose Zebedee taught Plato to his son?" James put the blame for the neglect on the monks to whom Luke had given a handle by writing, "Blessed are the Mendicants." "I wrote nothing of the sort," bristled Luke. "I said, 'blessed are the poor,' meaning the poor in spirit." Augustine and Jerome then join the company. Augustine says there is one good monk among his Augustinians. His name is Martin Luther. Augustine and Jerome pay him a call. Luther asks Augustine which is the best monastic order. "The Brethren of the Common Life," he answers. "Not your own, the Augustinians? They dress better." To this Augustine replies that dress is a trivial matter. Jerome exhorts Luther to attack the Sophists. Luther excuses himself because he is afraid of the pope. "Who's the pope?" asks Jerome. "I never heard of him."

"He's Leo," says Luther. "O yes," rejoins Jerome. "I do know him. He won't do you any harm."[70]

Aleander taxed Erasmus with the authorship of this skit.[71] The atmosphere was so surcharged that he said he would rather be caught "on the pikes of Swiss mercenaries than on the pens of his detractors."[72] As for the attitude of Luther, a preacher cried out, "If I could bury my teeth in Luther's gullet I would not hesitate to go with bloody mouth and receive the body of Christ."[73]

This was just too much. Erasmus left the Low Countries for Basel. He who only five years earlier had been warbling about the advent of the age of gold, now declared that his century was the very worst since the days of Jesus Christ.[74]

CHAPTER EIGHT

The Worst Century

*

ERASMUS declared that he had gone to Basel because at Louvain he would be unable to avoid entering the arena against Luther. His life in the Netherlands would have been intolerable were he not willing to become a hangman.[1] In Basel he could function as a mediator. The cordiality of his reception by Froben must have done much to soothe his lacerated spirit. The great publisher took him into his own ménage for ten months in the house *zum Sessel* in the *Todesgässlein* No. 3.[2] But the news from the world without confirmed the judgment that this was the worst of all centuries since Christ. Luther, of course, was not dead but in hiding at the Wartburg. During his absence the reforms at Wittenberg advanced to the point of disorder. Andreas Bodenstein von Carlstadt came to the fore and in plain clothes celebrated the Mass, largely in German, and gave the cup to the laity. The monks of the Augustinian order disbanded. Some married. Carlstadt, himself a priest, took to wife a girl of fifteen. Priests who obstructed the reform were intimidated. Images were removed or smashed. Some weavers arrived from Zwickau announcing communications from the Holy Ghost. Such was the confusion, reported an observer, that one could not tell who was the cook and who the waiter.[3] Erasmus had news of all this in February 1522. The town council invited Luther to return to Wittenberg that he might restore order. He

E.   H came in March. Somewhat later Erasmus had news of Anabaptists who "murmur anarchy." The letter containing this reference is dated by the editor in June 1523.[4] If the date is correct this is the earliest occurrence of the word "Anabaptist," which otherwise does not appear until 1525.[5] This makes one wonder whether the date of the letter should not be advanced by two years. However that may be, enough had happened to warrant Erasmus in saying that Luther was beginning to look almost orthodox in comparison with the extremists, and again to say that the Lutherans were worse than Luther.[6]

The news of the election of a new pope was both encouraging and ominous. The choice had fallen on Adrian of Utrecht, the old friend of Erasmus, an upright man who would strive to reform the curia. But how much could he do? He was old and the cardinals were only waiting for his demise. With respect to Luther he would not be mild, for this was the Adrian who had told the University of Louvain to burn Luther's books and force his recantation. But to Erasmus he was very favourable and twice invited him to take up his residence in Rome.[7] Erasmus answered:

I trust you will permit your little lamb to speak freely to its shepherd. Is it your thought that I should come to Rome in order not to be corrupted by the Lutherans? I assure you I am far enough away to obviate that danger. As for curing them, more can be done at close range. How can a patient be healed by a doctor who is not there? Besides, if I come to Rome the Lutherans will cry that I have been suborned and will refuse to read me. You will say that my letter thus far has been full of complaints and you wish counsel. Some would advise you to cure this malady by toughness. This course would be very imprudent and might end in frightful slaughter. The disease has gone too far for surgery. I realize that in England the

Lollards were driven under ground, but they were not extinguished and in any case what was done in England under a centralized government cannot be done in Germany in a multiplicity of small states. If the proper method is to eradicate this evil by prisons, floggings, confiscations, exiles, censures, and executions you have no need of my counsel. But this course is not consonant with your gentle nature. First you should try to discover how this evil arose. Offer immunity to those who were seduced by others. Better still offer a general amnesty. If God daily pardons the contrite should his vicar do anything else? The suppression of innovations by the magistrates leads not to piety but to sedition. I would like to see the publication of books restricted and scurrilous tracts suppressed. Then all will breathe the sweet air of liberty.[8]

At that juncture a visitor arrived in Basel with whom if Erasmus had had public dealings all hope of mediation with Rome would have been precluded. That person was Ulrich von Hutten. He had failed in his attempt to enlist Ferdinand and Charles in his war against the Romanists. The only quarter from which he received a favourable response was that of his own class, the knights, a waning force in Germany's political life, because superannuated by gunpowder, but still to be reckoned with so long as employed in the mercenary service of Franz von Sickingen, who, as we noted, had been enlisted for Hutten's quixotic adventure. The *Pfaffenkrieg* was launched against Richard von Greifenklau, the Archbishop of Trier. If he were dislodged the Rhine could be controlled and the grandiose dream of a German national state might perchance be realized. The campaign was a disaster. Von Sickingen, wounded, retired to his fortress on the Ebernburg, there to die, and Hutten fled to Basel, arriving on November 28, 1522.[9]

Through a friend he sent word that he would like to

see Erasmus, who replied that, since he could not endure
the heat of a German stove, and Hutten in his illness
could not do without one, they would be unable to find
common ground. Hutten would have preferred an outright refusal to such a palpable excuse. He was altogether
lacking in sensitivity not to perceive why Erasmus was
unwilling to see him. How unlike Melanchthon, who
when near Basel did not come to visit Erasmus lest he be
thereby compromised in Catholic eyes!¹⁰ Erasmus was
exceedingly sorry not to have seen him. To see Hutten,
fresh from an attack on an archbishop, was another
matter. Yet Erasmus was of no mind to forswear friendship and was loath to repulse a colleague in the service of
bonae literae.¹¹ As a token of continued friendship he
offered to let Hutten have some money.

As a matter of fact, the excuse about the stove was not
what set off the controversy. Hutten went to Mühlhausen
and from there the correspondence is known to have
continued, though the letters were lost when Hutten's
bag was rifled. What incensed him was the sight of a
letter written by Erasmus to a certain Laurinus at Bruges
which sounded like a capitulation to the papists. In this
letter Erasmus reviewed his situation.

Rumour has it that my old, if not very intimate friend,
Hochstraten, has burned my books in Brabant. A reliable man
at Rome reports that my books have been condemned by the
pope. I laughed. I have just had a cordial letter from the pope.
I am accused of grabbing perquisites. Never, though I have
accepted stipends. Rumour has it that the Lutherans have
come to Basel to consult me and even Luther himself. Would
that all the Lutherans and all the anti-Lutherans would come
to seek my advice! Hutten was here for a few days but we did
not see each other. Cronberg was here and we had several
pleasant chats. [This was Hartmuth von Cronberg, a German

knight who also had shared in the *Pfaffenkrieg*. One wonders why Erasmus was willing to see him, unless perchance because he was less belligerent.] I hate dissension, not only because of the precepts of Christ, but by a certain hidden force of nature, *occulta quadam naturae vi*. I do not know whether either side can be suppressed without grave fear of ruin. No one can deny that Luther calls for many reforms which brook of no delay. If only in my old age I could enjoy the fruits of my labours. But each side pushes me and each reproaches me. My silence against Luther is interpreted as consent, while the Lutherans charge that I have deserted the gospel out of timidity. Luther's abusiveness can be condoned only on the ground that perhaps our sins deserve to be beaten with scorpions. His reply to Henry VIII was outrageous, for no prince is more beloved by his people. The detractors say that the pope is Anti-Christ, that the bishops are seducers and the Roman See an abomination before God. If I should say this to a good pope I would be unfair and if to bad popes I would only rile them. I am said to misinterpret the ninth chapter of Paul's letter to the Romans on predestination. Has not this question been debated since the birth of Christ? I think it better not to be lost in an impenetrable abyss. I cannot be other than what I am. I cannot but execrate dissension. I cannot but love peace and concord. I see the obscurity in all things human. I see how much easier it is to start than to assuage a tumult. Those who raised this tumult claim to be impelled by the Spirit. This Spirit has never impelled me. When it does perhaps Erasmus will be Saul himself among the prophets.[12]

This letter it was which touched off Hutten to write an *Expostulatio*, which at first circulated in manuscript. Then he had to flee from Mühlhausen and was given an asylum by Zwingli at Zürich. Here very shortly he died and only recently has his grave stone been discovered on a little island in the Zürich lake. Some of Hutten's more militant friends then published the blast. In it he said:

I am stupefied and shaken to know what has happened that you who once joined with us to demote the pope, you who inveighed against the cesspool of Roman crimes, you who detested bulls of indulgence, who damned ceremonies, expelled the papal courtiers, execrated the canon law and the decretals, in a word you who denounced the universal hypocrisy, that you now turn completely around and join the enemy, that you now butter Hochstraten and Pope Adrian. Formerly you attacked the Dominicans, now you curry favour. You have been suborned by the lure of emoluments. What could be more impious and contrary to the spirit of Christ than to say, as you do, that the truth is not always to be proclaimed, the truth for which Christ wishes us to die? You render us invidious by saying that we are responsible for stirring up tumult and dissension. Did not Christ say there would be hate and dissension, wars and bloodshed on account of his teaching? The Romanists rage against Luther only because they cannot bear the gospel. Show us how truth can prevail and those who incite wars can be pacified. Lift up your voice. Cry out. You say that Luther throws the apple of discord. Any one who proclaims the gospel throws the apple of discord. Have you not said that if Luther goes under, evangelical truth and liberty will suffer a great loss? How can you then oppose? Don't you see what it will mean for your reputation if, right or wrong, you line up with the mighty? I would never have thought this of you. I would have sworn that you would stand to your post. I believed you would be unshakable for truth. I grieve over your defection.[12]

Erasmus was so stung that he could not refrain from a reply. He might have held it back had he known that Hutten was dead, but still his *Sponge to Wipe Away the Aspersions of Hutten* was addressed not so much to Hutten as to the entire Lutheran party. It begins with an address to Hutten:

You reproach me with having written a civil letter to Hochstraten. If he is curable, civility is in order. If he is not,

Title page of Hutten's *Expostulatio* with cut of Hutten.

modesty will damage his reputation more than invective.
How far do you think I would get if, seeking a benefice for a
good priest from a bad pope, were I to start out like this,
"Impious Antichrist, extinguisher of the gospel, oppressor of
liberty, flatterer of princes, bestower of benefices unworthily
on the unworthy, I petition you to give this good man a
benefice"? I do not deny that I seek peace wherever possible.
I believe in listening to both sides with open ears. I love
liberty. I will not, I cannot serve any faction. I have said that
all of Luther's teaching cannot be suppressed without
suppressing the gospel, but because I favoured Luther at first
I do not see that I am called upon to approve everything he
has said since. I have never called Luther a heretic. I have
complained of dissension and tumult. At the same time I have

always deplored tyranny and vice in the Church. But if the bad men at Rome make the Church to be no Church, then indeed we have no Church. I have not wholly condemned indulgences. When have I ever condemned the canon law and the decretals of the popes? I agree that originally the church at Rome had only Peter and Paul at the head, but why should this see not develop into a metropolitan church? I have never defended the power subsequently assumed. But even if the papal primacy did not originate with Christ, there is still need for a head.

Already the audience addressed in this apologia was shifting and Erasmus began to talk of Hutten in the third person.

He says one should be ready to die for the gospel. I would not refuse if the case called for it, but I am of no mind to die for the paradoxes of Luther. It is not a question of the articles of the faith but as to whether the Roman primacy was instituted by Christ, whether the order of the cardinals is a necessary member of the Church, whether confession was instituted by Christ, whether bishops by their constitutions can obligate any one to commit a mortal sin, whether free will contributes to salvation, whether any work of man can be called good, whether the Mass can be called a sacrifice, whether faith alone confers salvation. These are subjects for scholastic disputation. Over such matters I would not take away any man's life nor do I propose to lay down my own. I would hope to be a martyr for Christ if I have the strength. I am not willing to be a martyr for Luther.

Let us not devour each other like fish. Why upset the whole world over paradoxes, some unintelligible, some debatable, some unprofitable? The world is full of rage, hate, and wars. What will the end be if we employ only bulls and the stake? It is no great feat to burn a little man. It is a great achievement to persuade him.[14]

This last exhortation was obviously meant more for

Rome than for the Lutherans. Erasmus was fighting on two fronts. His *Sponge* scarcely mollified the Lutherans and gave Rome greater reason to suspect that he was secretly abetting them.

On all sides he was informed that if he would dispel this suspicion he must take up his pen in a tract specifically against Luther. Henry VIII proposed that the theme should be the freedom of the will.[15] Erasmus excused himself to Wolsey saying that although he had not written a book against Luther he had written some letters and as for a book he had something better to do.[16] Pope Adrian wrote, "Beloved son, you are a man of great learning. You are the one to refute the heresies of Martin Luther by which innumerable souls are being taken to damnation. Rise up to the defence of the Church. How much better that the Lutherans should be reclaimed by your eloquence than by our thunders to which, as you know, we are averse."[17] Erasmus replied, "Who am I to write? What understanding have I? I am said to be a Lutheran because I do not attack Luther, but I am reviled by the Lutherans. I once revelled in the fraternity of scholars. I'd rather die than renounce so many friendships. And I would die rather than join a faction. How often have I testified that I am not a Lutheran!"[18]

This conclusion was an indirect way of saying that he did not propose to bring out a book against Luther. To Zwingli Erasmus wrote: "I have received pleas from the pope, and the emperor, from kings and princes, from the most learned and dearest friends to write against Luther. But certainly either I shall not write or shall so write as not to please the Pharisees."[19] Duke George, the ruler of southern Saxony next to Bohemia, incensed against Luther after his endorsement of the Bohemian heretic John Hus, must have sent Erasmus a very urgent plea to judge by the response: "Most illustrious Duke, the Lutherans are worse than Luther. At first the question was as to indulgences. Luther wrote much that was offensive to pious ears, but also much that was good. Now that the heat is on, the good also is being condemned. The bull against him was ferocious and the imperial edict worse. Papal authority, indulgences, human constitutions, and scholastic discussions are all very well, but do not greatly aid evangelical fervour. They do not stir us up to despise the world and aspire to heaven. We are not to renounce the authority of the pope but above all we should glorify Christ. Would that this holy work could be done with gentleness. I am not equal to the task of writing against Luther, even if I had the time. I cannot read him in German. Better to treat this controversy with silence."[20] Duke George answered: "Most learned Erasmus, I see now why you will not write against Luther. You agree with him. He has just attacked me viciously and by name at that. But I will never again ask you to write against him. I suspect that your plea of inability to read his German books is a subterfuge."[21] [It was hardly that, though Erasmus was not wholly ignorant of German.]

The suspicions of Duke George were not altogether unwarranted and Erasmus did not allay them by diminishing his pleas for the sort of reformation in which he did believe. When his friend, the bishop of Basel, asked his opinion about dietary regulations, saints' days, and the celibacy of the clergy he gave a straightforward reply:

Fasting may be wholesome for those whose constitutions are used to it and who wish to subject themselves to perpetual mortification in order to avert the wrath of God. But to require it of the young, the aged, and the infirm is to pass a sentence of death. To require the eating of fish where fish is scarce is to decree a famine. Such regulations discriminate against the poor because the rich can import marine delicacies. You say that those who are not strong enough for fasts should secure papal dispensations. But that entails no end of bother and expense. Incidentally, just exactly what is fish? Are snails fish? [Erasmus refrains from raising the question in *The Letters of Obscure Men* whether embryo chickens are meat or fish like maggots in cheese.] If the purpose of the fast is to curb lust some vegetables might better be banned. Since Christ said, "Not that which goes in defiles," and Paul said that all meats are clean, why treat the eating of meat on Friday as if it were as bad as parricide? To be sure, Paul said we should have consideration for the weak but how about weak stomachs? All of my diseases would kill me if I could not eat meat.

As for holy days on which no work is to be done, we find none of them in the New Testament, where all days are equal. After a time Sunday was made a legal holiday. Then other days were added, often for the most trivial reasons. A mother has a daughter named Barbara, so she wants a day set aside for St. Barbara. The soldiers want one for St. Martin and the Parisians for St. Geneviève. On these days no work is to be done. Would not a working man do better to support his family than to honour a saint? Shall a farmer let his crop rot in harvest rather than take advantage of a good day because it is dedicated to some saint?

I do not say that the people should of their own accord disobey the regulations, but let the bishops remember that their sheep belong to Christ rather than to themselves. Let them remember that laws rest on the consent of the governed. Listen to the groans of those on whom intolerable burdens are laid.

As for celibacy, it was of late introduction. And it was more successful when priests were fewer. Bishops should not ordain such a horde as we now have. Only a few are chaste. The unchaste would do better to acknowledge their children and give them a liberal education. I do not say that those who are ordained *should* get married. It were better that they devote themselves exclusively to the Church, but, if they cannot contain themselves, better that they marry.[11]

During the years 1522 to 1524 Erasmus brought out some of his most piquant colloquies replete with allusions to churchly practices. Despite his disclaimers of any desire for total eradication, his satire was so disparaging that others might well be induced to give up pilgrimages, the cult of the saints, indulgences, monastic vows and habits, and even the very sacraments in favour of an interior piety. In the colloquy on *Rash Vows* several friends go on a pilgrimage. Two of them die en route and one is left deathly sick at Florence, but confident of heaven because of a bag bursting with indulgences. A doubt is cast on his assurance since heaven is a long way off and he may be robbed on the way. He replies that he is protected by bulls. "In what language?" "Latin." "Suppose you meet a spirit who does not know Latin. You'll have to trot back to Rome for another bull." With regard to monasticism Erasmus again slurs contemporary usage in the name of the founders of the monastic orders, for they did not institute official habits. Dominic took the simple garb of Spanish farmers, Benedict of Italian peasants, and Francis of Umbrian tillers of the soil. As for breaches of clerical celibacy, Erasmus makes a wicked thrust. A youth goes to a harlot to convert her by means of Erasmus' New Testament. "Erasmus!" says she. "He is half a heretic, I hear." "From whom did you hear that?" "From my clerical customers."

The most telling scoffing at the cult of the saints is in the colloquy *The Shipwreck*. A vessel with a heavy cargo is caught in a storm. Waves so high that the Alps in comparison are but warts heave the ship to within a finger of the moon and plunge it down to the gates of hell. The cargo is jettisoned. There are prayers to the Virgin, the Star of the Sea. "Why is she called Star of the Sea? She never went to sea." "No, but Venus protects sailors and the Virgin has taken over her role." One of the passengers bellows to St. Christopher the promise that if saved he will give him a candle as high as the loftiest spire in Paris. A friend suggests that he should not promise more than he can perform. The other whispers confidentially that if he touches land he won't give a tallow candle. The narrator, having been asked why he is not calling on the saints, explains that Peter, the doorkeeper, would be the first to hear, but while he was going to God the Father the boat might go to the bottom. Better to talk to God straight. An aged priest in his underwear stands in the middle of the ship delivering a sermon on Gerson's five reasons for confession. As the ship is breaking up he is slow to leave because he continually recalls something unconfessed and has to start over again. The narrator confesses silently to God. A Dominican strips and jumps in calling on St. Catherine. "How is she going to recognize him without his uniform?" A woman with a child is strapped to a spar from the mast and given a paddle. She and the child reach the shore. So also, of course, does the narrator. They are hospitably treated by those on land, who are Hollanders.[23]

After such sallies one can understand why Erasmus was credited with covert, if not overt, support for Luther, particularly when he wrote to Zwingli saying, "I seem to myself to have taught what Luther teaches, only not so savagely and without paradoxes and enigmas."[24] Not unnaturally even more perfervid appeals were addressed to Erasmus to declare himself and defend the Church. One

came from Cuthbert Tunstall, Bishop of London, Keeper
of the Rolls, royal ambassador, a humanist willing to be
an inquisitor. Erasmus had known him in England and
had renewed contacts when Tunstall was on diplomatic
missions in the Low Countries. Tunstall wrote:

> I am delighted to learn [from lost letters] that you dispel the
> suspicion of supporting Luther. The pope calls upon you to
> refute him. No more pernicious heresy was ever voiced than
> his. What greater glory can ever come to a scholar than to
> have refuted heresy? See how Jerome confounded Jovinian,
> how Origen refuted Celsus, how Augustine disposed of
> Pelagius! If we may repel barbarians invading our hearths
> shall we not repel heretics invading our altars? Who is better
> equipped to refute Luther than you and especially because in
> so doing you can clear your reputation? Following Wycliffe,
> new heresies have arisen with the poison of asps. The
> Lutherans say that all Christians, men and women, are priests,
> yes, and all even are kings. Where will this come out if not
> in sheer anarchy? Luther would abolish the Mass. What is left
> if not to abolish Christ? For the blood of Christ, shed for the
> redemption of the world, for the glory which you expect in
> heaven, I beg you, I beseech you Erasmus, the Church herself
> begs and beseeches you to grapple with this hydra and plunge
> the sword of the Spirit into the guts of this Cerberus.[25]

Plainly if Erasmus wished to stay in the Roman Catholic
Church he would have to write something or other
against Luther. Before launching any sort of a refutation
he laid the ground carefully. In a tract *On the Immense
Mercy of God* he enjoined the imitation of the divine mercy
in dealing with the weak, the erring, and the offending,
whether in deed or creed. Passages from the Old Testament and the New are cited on the loving-kindness of
God. Then Erasmus asks how God's mercy is to be
obtained. Shall it be by tears, fasting, sprinkling ashes,

CDe immensa dei misericordia.

CA sermon of the excedynge great mercy of god made by the most famous doctour maister Erasmus Roterodamus, Translated out of Latin into englisshe at the reqst of þ most honorable & vertuous lady the lady Margaret Coūtese of Salysbury.

Title page of an English translation of *De immensa dei misericordia*.

and by heartfelt contrition? To be sure, but even more by the exercise of mercy toward one's fellows. We are summoned to exceed in mercy the ordinary man who will give alms to a beggar. We are to be merciful as our Father in heaven is merciful, who causes His sun to shine upon the just and the unjust. So must we also be kind not only to friends but also to enemies and the unworthy. "I am greatly vexed, therefore, when I see so little mercy among Christians. If they were merciful they would extend their benefits to the Turks and heap coals of fire upon their heads. But now Christians harass one another with wars, rapines, and thefts. By what do we live if not by mutual shearing?"[26]

This injunction to mercy embraced all offenders. A more specific statement was required as to heresy. Erasmus supplied it in his preface to the edition of Hilary.

The ancients philosophized very little about divine things. . . . The curious subtlety of the Arians drove the orthodox to greater necessity. . . . Let the ancients be pardoned . . . but what excuse is there for us, who raise so many curious, not to say impious, questions about matters far removed from our nature? We define so many things which may be left in ignorance or in doubt without loss of salvation. Is it not possible to have fellowship with the Father, Son, and Holy Spirit without being able to explain philosophically the distinction between them and between the generation of the Son and the procession of the Holy Ghost? If I believe the tradition that there are three of one nature, what is the use of laboured disputation? If I do not believe, I shall not be persuaded by any human reasons. . . . You will not be damned if you do not know whether the Spirit proceeding from the Father and the Son has one or two beginnings, but you will not escape damnation, if you do not cultivate the fruits of the Spirit which are love, joy, peace, patience, kindness, goodness, long-suffering, mercy, faith, modesty, continence, and chastity. . . . The sum of our religion is peace and unanimity, but these can scarcely stand unless we define as little as possible, and in many things leave each one free to follow his own judgment, because there is great obscurity in many matters, and man suffers from this almost congenital disease that he will not give in when once a controversy is started, and after he is warmed up he regards as absolutely true that which he began to sponsor quite casually. . . . Many problems are now reserved for an ecumenical council. It would be better to defer questions of this sort to the time when no longer in a glass darkly we see God face to face. . . . Formerly, faith was in life rather than in the profession of creeds. Presently, necessity required that articles be drawn up, but only a few with apostolic sobriety. Then the depravity of the heretics exacted a more precise scrutiny of the divine books. . . . When faith came to be in writings rather than in hearts, then there were almost as many faiths as men. Articles increased and sincerity decreased. Contention grew hot and love grew cold. The doctrine of Christ, which at first knew no hairsplitting, came to depend on the aid of philosophy. This was the first stage in the fall of the Church. . . . The injection of the authority of the emperor into this affair did not greatly aid the sincerity of faith. . . . When faith is in the mouth rather than in the heart, when the solid knowledge of Sacred Scripture fails us, nevertheless by terrorization we drive men to believe what they do not believe, to love what they do not love, to know what they do not know. That which is forced cannot be sincere, and that which is not voluntary cannot please Christ.[27]

In this exordium one observes two lines of thought. The one calls for an attitude of calmness, objectivity, and persuasion. The other asks what is heresy and answers that heresy is the rejection only of those beliefs to which subscription is necessary on pain of damnation. The distinction is thus made between the *fundamenta*, the essential dogmas, and the *adiaphora*, the non-essentials. Erasmus was the first to use this distinction extensively in the interests of religious liberty. He magnified the non-essentials in order to enlarge the area of beliefs immune to persecution. This is not an adequate and ultimate theory of religious liberty because with regard to the essentials persecution still remains possible. Yet to reduce their number to the beliefs at that time almost universally held was a tremendous gain. The distinction is important also for church unity, since, if the points of doctrinal division are seen to be non-essential, the dogmatic barrier to union disappears. The effort to isolate and state the fundamentals is the search for the essence of Christianity, *das Wesen des Christentums,* as it was phrased by the liberal Protestants of the nineteenth century.[28]

Erasmus gave more attention to listing the non-essentials than the essentials. He enumerated as unimportant, if not indeed trivial and impious, all the assertions and debates about the theory of the Trinity, the degree of absoluteness in God's omnipotence, the extent of papal authority – whether the pope is merely a man or almost a god; whether he can do more than Christ in letting souls out of purgatory – the nature of the pain in purgatory, whether material or immaterial, and so on.[29] Less frequently Erasmus summed up the doctrines by which the Church stands or falls. He appears to have been the originator of this expression,[30] which the Lutherans later restricted to the one doctrine of justification by faith. Erasmus gave a formulation in a letter to the Bohemians, who had sought from him support for their position. He replied sympathetically and urged the curia to give them a considerate hearing.[31] To them he wrote: "The sum of the Christian philosophy consists in this, to recognize that all our hope lies in God who freely gives us all things through his Son Jesus, by whose death we are redeemed, into whose body we are implanted by baptism, that we should be dead to the lusts of the world and live according to his teaching and example, bearing adversity with patience and looking for the recompense of the reward, undoubtedly in store for all the godly at Christ's coming, and that we should ever progress from virtue to virtue, ascribing nothing to ourselves but whatever is good in us to God."[32]

Erasmus was not a systematic theologian and was not at all inclined to formulate the essentials in numbered articles. If one may do for him what he was disinclined to do for himself, one may infer from the tenor of his works that he would regard as essential the following beliefs: the incarnation, the pledge of Christ's authority; the passion, the seal of our redemption; the resurrection, the token of our immortality; justification by faith, the ground of our hope; and the imitation of Christ, our obligation.

If these, then, are the fundamentals, manifestly Luther was not a heretic. Erasmus was not content, however, to make the point by so minimal a test. He would rather show how much Luther held in conjunction with the Church. With this in mind the colloquy, *An Inquisition Concerning the Faith*,[33] interrogates a Lutheran with respect to the Apostles' Creed, to which he subscribes on every article. More than that he gives an exposition of the articles in terms of the creeds of Nicaea and Chalcedon. Since the Apostles' Creed does not exclude Arianism, the Nicene Creed became more explicit and employed even words not in the Scripture in order to safeguard the meaning of Scripture from Arian misinterpretation. The Lutheran is fully in accord and accepts all of the great ecumenical creeds held in common by the Roman and the Eastern churches. Consequently Luther is not a heretic. Erasmus would nevertheless raise with him a non-essential point in a spirit of fraternal discussion.

The subject on which Erasmus chose to break a lance with Luther was the theme suggested by Henry VIII, the freedom of the will. Luther had laid himself open to challenge by his assertion in the Heidelberg Disputation of 1518 that "free will, after the fall, even when doing the

best it can, commits a mortal sin,"[34] and in his tract on
The Freedom of the Christian Man in 1520 had declared that
good works, if done with an eye to gaining credit with
God are "damnable sins."[35] Erasmus disputed these
assertions in a tract entitled *De Libero Arbitrio* (*Concerning
the Freedom of the Will*). Luther, in the *De Servo Arbitrio*
(*On the Enslaved Will*), thanked Erasmus for going to the
core of their difference instead of debating such trifles as
the papacy, indulgences, and purgatory. The courtesy of
Erasmus made it difficult to be angry with him. Luther
speedily surmounted the difficulty. Erasmus made a
rejoinder in a work called *Hyperaspistes*.[36]

The freedom of man was really not so much the subject
as the omnipotence of God. The debate as to the will was
made needlessly sharp by misunderstanding on the part of
Erasmus and exaggeration on the part of Luther. Erasmus
supposed that his opponent made man into an automaton.
But Luther granted freedom to the natural man in all of
the normal affairs of life, and even the Jew and the Turk
may be good parents and good magistrates, and may
perhaps be even better than the Christians. The point at
which man is not free is in his inability to fulfil perfectly
the demands of God who requires more than upright
outward behaviour. God calls for purity of heart, self
effacement, complete obedience to the divine will. Of this
man is capable. His will is not constrained. He sins
willingly, but his nature is corrupt. He is not predestined
to commit any particular sin, but he will at some point fall
short of the glory of God. Whatever he does of good is
the work of God in him, for man is a donkey ridden now
by God and now by the devil. This misleading metaphor
was lifted by Luther out of a work attributed to Augustine.[37] It did give a handle to the charge of making man
into an automaton and Erasmus then asked what is the

point of all of the exhortations in Scripture calling man to
be perfect as God is perfect. Luther answered that the
object is to convict man of his unworthiness. Confronted
by a standard, he perceives how far he has fallen short,
recognizes his shortcoming, ceases to rely upon himself,
and throws himself wholly upon God's mercy. The part
of man is to believe, accept, and trust in God's mercy.
This is justification by faith and this faith is itself a gift
from God.

Erasmus agreed that man cannot be perfect. He agreed
that salvation is by faith alone.[38] At the same time he
wished to do justice to the passages in Scripture which
offer rewards for good deeds. What is the meaning of the
saying, "and great shall be your reward"?[39] Luther
answered that the reward is simply the recognition of the
working of God's grace.[40] Erasmus insisted that it must
have reference to some sort of merit and here he was
inclined to accept a distinction made by some of the
scholastics between a genuine merit (*meritum de condigno*)
and an approximate merit (*meritum de congruo*).[41] Erasmus
quite agreed with Luther that genuine merit does not
exist.[42] No one is good enough to have a claim on God's
mercy. But God in his mercy treats the lower merit as if
it were the higher.[43] This is not far from Luther's
assertion that man is always a sinner, but is at the same
time just because God treats him as if he were just, though
actually he is not. Erasmus illustrated his point by the
analogy of a toddler starting to walk across a room to
receive an apple at the other side. The tot is about to
tumble when a hand from behind applies a little boost.
The babe recovers his balance and reaches the apple.
That little boost is the grace of God.[44] Without it man
can go no farther. With it he can in a sense co-operate
with God in working out his salvation.[45]

This fable might easily have been interpreted in terms
of the scholastic view that by doing the best he can man
acquires the lower grade of merit which God rewards
with the gift of a special grace whereby man can achieve
the genuine merit. The scholastics were not clear or
unanimous as to whether the special grace was a reward
or merely a recognition.[46] Erasmus later told Thomas
More that he would incline to the view that man by his
natural powers achieves the lesser merit, had not the
Apostle Paul ruled otherwise. In any case Erasmus agreed
that man cannot accomplish genuine merit and can,
therefore, have no claim upon God.

Yet Erasmus was willing to speak of man's co-operation with God. That word co-operation was anathema to
Luther. In no way whatsoever can man co-operate with
God towards his salvation, which rests utterly in God's
hand. Erasmus might perhaps have been willing to drop
the word "co-operate" if Luther had not made the further
assertion that all men, having fallen short of God's
demands, are worthy of damnation. Some He damns, as
they deserve. Some He saves, who are no whit better.
This is the doctrine of predestination. Erasmus did not
perceive that it is logically involved in the doctrine of
justification by faith alone. Because, if faith is a gift of
God, as all then agreed, and if God gives it to some and
withholds it from others, and if salvation is contingent
upon the gift, predestination inevitably follows. Un-
trammelled by logic, Erasmus branded the doctrine as
simply monstrous. God is a tyrant if He condemns man
for what he cannot help. It is as if a master should kill a
servant for having a long nose.[47] (Erasmus had a long
nose.) To damn some and save others who are no better
is unfair.

"Of course this is a stumbling block," answered

Luther. "Common sense and natural reason are highly offended that God by His mere will deserts, hardens and damns, as if He delighted in sins and in such eternal torments, He who is said to be of such mercy and goodness. Such a concept of God appears wicked, cruel, and intolerable, and by it many have been revolted in all ages. I myself have more than once been offended to the very depth of the abyss of desperation, so that I wished I had never been created. There is no use trying to get away from this by ingenious distinctions. Natural reason, however much it is offended, must admit the consequences of the omniscience and omnipotence of God." God is not a tyrant, but this only faith can believe. "If it is difficult to believe in God's mercy and goodness when He damns those who do not deserve it, we must recall that if God's justice could be recognized as just by human comprehension, it would not be divine. Since God is true and one, He is utterly incomprehensible and inaccessible to human reason. Therefore His justice also must be incomprehensible."[48] There are three lights given to man, the light of nature, the light of grace, and the light of glory, and only in the light of glory will this mystery ever be fathomed.[49]

Erasmus recognized that some truths elude the light of nature. Only by the light of grace can man understand the foolishness of God who chooses the weak things of the world to confound the mighty. But if only the light of glory will show us that a god who damns and saves at his caprice is not a tyrant, then all notions of human justice have lost their religious sanction. The debate with Luther had come around to the same point as the debate with the late scholastics and the medieval exegetes. The scholastics said that God can do anything according to His absolute power which ordinarily He does not exercise to the full.[50]

Erasmus would rather give up God's absolute power than to make Him no longer amenable to the canons of human reason and the moral sense. The medieval exegetes justified the immoralities of the patriarchs, because sanctioned and even commanded by God whose will, whatever it is, cannot but be right.[51] Erasmus escaped this conclusion by allegory. Luther said, "Let God be God." Erasmus said, "Let God be good."

"At any rate," said Erasmus, "do not exaggerate the difficulties. There are difficulties. God allows some children to be born monsters,[52] but why project the inequities of life into eternity? Let us not go beyond the plain, clear, manifest affirmations of Scripture. With regard to everything beyond the word of Scripture and the decrees of the Church I am a sceptic."[53] "You are indeed," commented Luther, "a sceptic, a mocking Lucian. But the Holy Spirit is not a sceptic. Don't you see that there can be no religion without affirmations?[54] You say you will accept the decrees of the Church. What is the Church? Are popes, bishops, and councils concerned only for dignities and incense, are they the Church?"[55] This rejoinder was not fair because Erasmus did make a number of great affirmations, but he wanted a warrant in a clear word of Scripture.

"And we have it," answered Luther. "The doctrine of predestination is perfectly clear in Scripture. The Apostle Paul bases it on two texts in the Old Testament. The first is the statement that God hardened Pharaoh's heart." "But," countered Erasmus, "this passage is susceptible of another interpretation." Following Origen he took it to mean not that God hardened Pharaoh's heart but that He gave Pharaoh repeated opportunities of disclosing how hard it was, in order that his punishment might be seen to be manifestly just. The other text was the word of God,

Martin Luther: a perforated drawing for making copies. The dots indicate the shading as well as the outline.

spoken before ever the twins were born, "Jacob have I loved. Esau have I hated."[56] Erasmus, following the consensus of the Fathers other than Augustine, said that

God passed this judgment because He foresaw how the twins would turn out. This explanation has had a vogue for centuries, but it is specious. There can be sure fore-knowledge only of that which is definitely fixed. A man can, of course, foresee that which he has not fore-ordained, but if there is only one God, there is no other on whom to lay the responsibility for the predetermina-tion. A single omnipotent and omniscient God can foreknow only what He has foreordained. Luther insisted on this squarely. And he was convinced that he under-stood the mind of Paul.

To this Erasmus replied by asking how he could be so sure.[57] The consensus of the Fathers was against him. Luther answered that the majority is not necessarily right. "Is the minority?" asked Erasmus. "Councils may be mistaken," said Luther. "And may not a conventicle?" queried Erasmus. "You tell us, Luther, that certainty in interpretation is given by the Spirit. How do we know who has the Spirit? If learning is the test, both have it. If goodness is the mark, neither has it. We are all sinners. The gifts of the Spirit are love, joy, peace, and so on. Do we see these in you?" Thus the debate began to centre on the clarity of Scripture. Both assumed that Scripture must be consistent. Both tried to harmonize apparent inconsistencies. Luther had a difficult time to explain the passages on reward. Erasmus had quite as much trouble in trying to dispose of predestination.

"But in any case," contended Erasmus, "since the matter cannot be resolved till the day of judgment, why not suspend judgment?" And above all, the simple should not be perturbed by the shock technique.[58] Paradoxes as such are admissible, but the shocking paradoxes of Luther are disquieting and, to the common man, un-intelligible. Luther says that good works are "damnable sins." Luther added, of course, "if performed with an eye to reward." Erasmus countered that he should make his meaning plain and not give the appearance of jettisoning the Ten Commandments. Luther is as bad as the scholastics, said Erasmus, who blurt out that philosophically speaking the doctrine of the Trinity adds up to three gods, though not theologically. The common man will never grasp this distinction between philosophy and theology.[59] "Quite right," agreed Luther, "this is not a point to divulge in the marketplace, but man's eternal destiny must be declared, and the paradox is not mine, but God's."

The difference between the two men was theological. One is tempted to suggest that it was rooted in variant concepts of salvation. This for Luther consisted in the forgiveness of sins by a sheer act of God's grace, for Erasmus in fellowship with God calling for a human response. But the difference was more than theological. Erasmus felt that after condemnation by the Church and the empire Luther should have subsided and awaited vindication at the hands of God, instead of starting a faction and disrupting the peace of Christendom.[60] "You with your peace-loving theology,"[61] retorted Luther, "you don't care about the truth. The light is not to be put under a bushel, even if the whole world goes to smash; God can make another world."[62] "But," responded Erasmus, "what happens to truth when men are embroiled in a war of religion?" *Concordia! concordia! concordia!*[63] This comports with the mind of Christ. This is the precondition for the matching of minds, for the achievement of a consensus. If one's opinion is not confirmed by the consensus then bow and wait. Here we have the deepest difference between Catholicism and Protestantism to this very day. The Catholic scholar, if reproved by authority, will put his manuscripts back into his desk and wait for time and God. The modern Protestant usually justifies intransigence on the ground that truth being the object of a quest, each Christian who thinks he has a discovery or an insight to offer should make it known so that under criticism it may be refuted or confirmed. This is curiously an Erasmian position. It was not Luther's position, who believed that he was proclaiming not his insights, but God's truths.

But if Erasmus believed in free encounter, why did he wish Luther to be silent, and why was he willing to defer to authority? Why would he not leave the Roman communion? Such questions were pressed upon him with great urgency by the Lutherans who felt that he properly belonged on their side, and by many Catholics who for once agreed with the Lutherans. Since Erasmus continued to say that Luther was not a heretic and since the Church said he was, how could Erasmus stay with the Church? Thus harassed, Erasmus in several works of his later period set forth his reasons for declining to break with the Church of Rome. Naturally in so doing he drew from the arsenal of arguments stock-piled by centuries of Christian apologetic, repeating the phrases which would carry weight with his critics. He described the Church as the bride of Christ,[64] the heavenly dove,[65] the temple of God,[66] the still waters beside which the shepherd led his flock,[67] and the mystical body of Christ.[68] Outside the Church there is no salvation.[69] Better to live unworthily within the Church than to be a heretic and a schismatic, without the saving doctrine.[70] The Church is the custodian of the revelation and the locus of the consensus of the ages. So many statements in this tenor can be culled from the works of Erasmus that he can rightly be called a precursor of the Counter-Reformation. On the other hand he so spiritualized everything within the Church and so denuded the hierarchy of all sanction save utility that the lines run also from Erasmus to the Sacramentarians; Zwingli, Oecolampadius, and Pellikan, and even to the spiritualists and rationalists such as Caspar Schwenkfeld, Sebastian Franck, and Sebastian Castellio.

We are constrained, therefore, to scrutinize the traditional phrases cited by Erasmus to see in what sense they are employed. What does he mean by saying that there is no salvation outside of the Church? What is the Church? Does he mean the Roman communion only? He sometimes defined the Church as "the consensus of the Christian people throughout the whole world."[71] This would include the Greek and Eastern churches. Again he defined the Church as "the hidden society of those predestined to eternal life of whom the greater part is now with Christ. No individual can be identified as a member, but we are to believe that there is such a society on earth which Christ united by his spirit, whether among the Indians or Africans or in any other part of the world not yet explored."[72] One wonders what he means when he speaks of the predestined since he did not believe in predestination. Again he says that those who are out of the Church as to the body may be within the Church as to the spirit.[73] He came close to canonizing pagans before Christ – Cicero, and especially Socrates – so that he could scarcely refrain from ejaculating, "Saint Socrates, pray for me."[74] He may have relegated the pagan saints to a lesser felicity than that in store for the Christians; he can scarcely have regarded them as damned. And as for Christian dissidents, could he have been so sympathetic towards the Bohemians and so cordial to Melanchthon had he scented brimstone on the hem of their garments?

Did he not say that those burned at the stake as heretics may be martyrs in the eyes of God?[75]

What then of the statement that it were better to live unworthily within the Church than to be a heretic or a schismatic, without the saving doctrines? This was the standard justification for leniency towards moral offenders and severity towards doctrinal offenders. Erasmus was not using the saying in this sense, but rather to reprove the censorious who, unmindful of the beams in their own eyes withdrew from the Church because of the motes in the eyes of others. In any case the statement would not exclude the Greeks, Bohemians, Lutherans, and Sacramentarians because they did accept the saving doctrines as formulated by Erasmus. The entire spirit of Erasmus was inclusive, not because like Cusa he hoped for a parliament of religions in which Christian doctrines were to be recast to make them universally acceptable, not because like Pico he regarded the pagans as near Christians because of adumbrations of the doctrine of the Trinity in their writings, but rather since as a disciple of the *Devotio Moderna* he acknowledged a fellow spirit, even a fellow Christian wherever he encountered a warm faith and an upright life. The line runs from Erasmus to Sebastian Franck. Erasmus, moreover, was constantly proclaiming the mercy of God and many passages in his work breathe the spirit of his favourite, Origen, who believed that even the Devil would be saved.[76]

Another of the Erasmian arguments was that the Church is the locus of the *consensus omnium*, the agreement of all men. He would regard as authoritative the decrees of the ancient synods particularly those confirmed by the consensus of so many centuries.[77] "Is it necessary to believe in Christ's descent into hell?" he asked and answered, "As it is Christian prudence not lightly to believe anything not expressly stated in Scripture, so it is the part of Christian modesty not to reject petulantly what the religious contemplation of pious men has given for the solace and enlightenment of believers."[78] The consensus of many celebrated persons is a very weighty ground for credence, provided it is perpetual.

The contention that the consensus of the many had evidential value went back to classical antiquity. We noted that adages were esteemed by Aristotle as the quintessence of universal wisdom. He attached weight in ethics to universal custom and Cicero in theology to universal consent.[79] This classical view was grounded on the assumption that truth is discovered from below by inquiring minds in collaboration. The Jewish-Christian view posits a revelation coming down from above. It is not given, however, to all but only to a few, to Israel or a remnant within Israel. In the New Testament that "which is hidden from the wise and prudent" is given to babes.[80] Hence Luther could say that the minority is always right.[81] Yet Christianity was able to incorporate the concept of consensus by restricting it to the babes to whom had been given the wisdom hidden from the wise and prudent. In time the babes turned into the bishops. When Athanasius proved to be right as against all the bishops of his day, then the valid consensus had to be the perpetual consensus, that which is accepted by all, everywhere and always.

Erasmus was torn by the different concepts. He did take seriously the consensus and avowed that save for its authority he might easily have been a Pelagian, an Arian, or a follower of Oecolampadius, the Sacramentarian.[82] Yet, as a matter of fact, he adhered to the consensus only on theological matters which he considered insoluble or inconsequential. On ethical questions with regard to which he had a profound conviction he flouted the consensus. This was true in the case of his pacifism. He could find a consensus in the early Church only up to the time of Constantine. After Augustine had formulated the theory of the just war his view held the consensus for over a thousand years. Again Erasmus in his plea for the liberalizing of divorce certainly diverged from the tradition which took literally the gospel injunction that divorce should be allowed only for adultery.[83] He spiritualized adultery so that it could be equated even with a cantankerous temper. In such a case Erasmus would try to show that there never was a consensus,[84] and in this instance he was correct that the consensus was not absolute, for Augustine had described unbelief as fornication and indeed any unlawful lust may be so construed.[85] Or else Erasmus would admit the consensus and then say that to follow it would be inexpedient.[86] He could discover infallibility nowhere, whether in popes,[87] councils, or the Fathers, but distrusting also himself, if he were not sure, he would defer to the judgment of others.[88]

What then did hold him to the Church of Rome? Tentatively one may suggest here as elsewhere a confluence of classical and Christian strains. On the classical side there was the Neoplatonic doctrine that the progression from simplicity to multiplicity is degeneration and the salvation of the soul consists in returning to the ineffable One. On the Stoic side was the rationality of the universe expressed in cosmic harmony of which the closest earthly concretion in the classical age was the *Pax Romana*, and in the age of Erasmus the Church of Rome. Not that he considered the Church as the successor of the ancient empire in a political sense, but only as the bond of a universal society. In his own day Erasmus saw no political unity and did not expect it to be restored by the Holy Roman Empire. Possibly because he acquiesced in political pluralism he was desirous of ecclesiastical monism.

Again only in the Church did he feel genuinely at home. He had no deep attachment to any country. The sodality of scholars was being disintegrated by nationalism and confessionalism. In the Church he had a multitude of personal friends whom he would rather die than renounce.[89] Personal attachments may lead to rationally indefensible behaviour. Luther did not renounce Melanchthon although he confessed that he was as much of a sceptic as Erasmus,[90] and Erasmus did not renounce Thomas More though he was as virulent and vulgar as Luther. Loyalties often defy analysis.

The question whether Luther should be silent involved more, however, than the rightfulness of the claims of Rome. After 1526 the controversy had degenerated to the point where calm and fruitful discussion had wellnigh ceased to be possible. In that case, thought Erasmus, better silence than violence.[91] His position was much like that of Caspar Schwenckfeld, the Silesian reformer, who later on declared a moratorium on the celebration of the Lord's Supper until it could be observed in Christian love.

CHAPTER NINE

No Abiding Place

*

ERASMUS foresaw that nothing he was able to write against Luther would satisfy his detractors. How could he appease them while saying, "Would that Luther's charges were not true against the tyranny, avarice, and turpitude of the Roman curia"?[1] Duke George despite the *De Libero Arbitrio* charged that Erasmus himself was responsible for all the tumult because he had not written this tract three years earlier. He must now retrieve his failure by protesting without end.[2] "Luther has written a vicious tract against monastic vows," said the duke. Let Erasmus tackle that.[3] But if Duke George did no more than exhort Erasmus to keep on with refutations of the heretic, other critics pointed to heresies in the writings of Erasmus himself. Fresh attacks came from France, Italy, and Spain.

In France the prime mover was Noel Beda, the one-time successor of Standonck at the Collège de Montaigu, now a syndic of the theological faculty of the University of Paris. His ire was stirred by the intemperate zeal of a disciple of Erasmus, Louis Berquin, who had translated works both of Luther and of Erasmus. In May 1523 the Sorbonne, incited by the *Parlement de Paris*, the court with jurisdiction over heretical cases, seized Berquin's papers with all of the translations and cast him into prison.[4] He was compelled to abjure the errors of Luther. He did so saying that although he repudiated the opinions of Luther he would not call him a monster from hell.[5] A thoroughly

Erasmian comment! A further prosecution was for the moment deferred because Berquin enjoyed the favour of Francis I.

By translating coincidentally Luther and Erasmus, Berquin hoped to show that Luther was not a heretic since he said the same thing as Erasmus, who was not a heretic. The argument could be reversed to read that Erasmus was a heretic since he said the same thing as Luther who was a heretic. Erasmus perceived the open flank and warned Berquin.[6] Beda pursued the scent and discovered unorthodox statements in the translations. Erasmus disclaimed the translations, saying that they contained interpolations.[7] Those examined by the Sorbonne do not. But a translation in the style of Berquin adroitly wove together passages from Erasmus, Luther and Farel.[8] The point was inconsequential for Erasmus, since Beda went back to the original. So did the Sorbonne which in 1526 condemned the *Colloquies* and selected portions of other works.[9] Beda remonstrated with Erasmus privately, saying, "I speak out of zeal for your salvation. Much of what you say gives grave scandal to Christian folk."[10]

Erasmus replied: "Most excellent sir [not "Dearly beloved brother"], I am deeply touched by your solicitude for my salvation. But why are you not worried about the salvation of those who rail with abominable calumnies, manifest lies, and virulent abuse? You cover their diabolical raging with the tender word of zeal. You reproach me for reading the poets. In my youth I loved the poets and considered that they contribute to a liberal education. I do not regret it. What do you think of those who spend their lives delving not in the poets but in Aristotle, Averroes, and 'the superfluous quibbles and sophisticated labyrinths of the Sophists?' "[11]

In response to the Sorbonne Erasmus adopted the tone prevalent in his later apologies which modern biographers commonly call reactionary. He did no more than to insist, however, that his earlier parenthetical disclaimers of absolute condemnations were not mere sops to Cerberus but were seriously intended. He was not now retracting his earlier strictures against the abuses which all along he had desired to see corrected in an orderly manner and he was no more ambiguous than heretofore as to what should be done. On the one hand he would hold up the pattern of the primitive Church as an ideal to be restored and then would introduce a doubt whether it could be restored, since the ethic of the Sermon on the Mount cannot be imposed on the masses only nominally Christian. More should indeed be expected of the bishops but they are encumbered in civil affairs. Most should be expected of the monks. This may explain why Erasmus lavished on their failures his most caustic comments.

The main points in his reply to the Sorbonne may be summarized under rubrics:

With regard to force in religion: "Faith desires to persuade rather than to compel. Are the converted Jews in Spain sincere Christians? Augustine said that heretics should be removed. He meant simply removed from the communion of the Church. The spirit of our Lord was merciful. Did he not say, 'Neither do I condemn you'? But," added Erasmus, "I would agree that an extremely contumacious heretic might be burned." He does not explain what would make a heretic "extremely contumacious." And there was no example of burning for heresy in his day which he condoned.

With regard to war: "I have said over and over that I do not condemn war *absolutely*, but the Lord did not want the gospel to be defended. What then shall we say of popes with armed guards, bishops travelling with thirty knights and cardinals called 'legates of the camp'?"

As to oaths: "I have not said that princes should not take oaths. I have said only that if they were genuine Christians they would not need to."

Re indulgences: "I have not utterly condemned them. If they lead men to confess their sins and amend their lives, that is excellent. But where ever do papal bulls promise release from purgatory? The pope has authority to remit only excommunications and other ecclesiastical penalties. Shall an indulgence excuse a robber from making restitution?"

The Apostles' Creed: "I have said that it was not by the apostles. The phrase 'He descended into hell' is not in the Old Roman Symbol, nor in the Eastern creeds."

The liturgy: "I have said that it should be understood by the laity. You say that the sound of the Latin, even though not understood, kindles the heart to piety. Would not the sound of French do the same thing?"

Scholasticism: "This I do not condemn in its entirety. But I would remind you that Wycliffe, Hus, Luther, Oecolampadius, the Anabaptists, and Hübmaier all had their training in scholastic theology. Heresy does not arise among the laity who have the scriptures in the vernacular, but among the doctors." (Erasmus thus comes close to saying that scholasticism is the mother of heresy.)

Salvation by faith: "I have said that our salvation depends not on our desert, but on God's grace. I highly approve of Luther when he calls us away from frail confidence in ourselves to the most safe harbour of trust in evangelical grace, though I do not approve of his reasons. Our hope is in the mercy of God and the merits of Christ."

Ecclesiastical ceremonies: "These are permissible for the weak, but instead of worrying whether one has swallowed something before communion were it not better to ask whether the heart is clean? There is no sense in bowing the knee and not the heart. The true Sabbath is to have the mind free from carnal desires."

The monastic habit: "I am accused of saying that the cowl of the Franciscan is of no more avail in curing a disease than the jacket of a pimp. I think that recovery from a disease is a matter of natural strength and medical care. And for that matter, a pimp can don a cowl."

The decline of the Church: "I have said that during the last four hundred years the vigour of Christianity has grown cold. You point to the great luminaries of the late Middle Ages. Yes, but they do not compare with the ancients. I can give you two hundred examples of unprofitable questions discussed by the scholastics."[12]

Such was the reply to the onslaught from France. From Italy came a two-pronged attack from Alberto Pio, who taxed Erasmus with the usual charge of heresy, and from Castiglione who made the unusual charge of a barbarous style. Alberto Pio of Carpi in 1525 had spread among the cardinals at Rome the accusation that Erasmus was responsible for the Lutheran turmoil.[13] In 1529 the controversy was renewed in a number of tracts. "You think I am responsible," answered Erasmus. "The source lies in the immorality of the priests, the superciliousness of the theologians, the tyranny of the monks. Just look at all the scrambles over tithes, indulgences, emoluments, dispensations, annates, confirmations, privileges, exceptions, suits, offices, feuds, and the like. Are not these enough to provoke tumult? Do I damn the cardinalate when I say that St. Jerome had never heard of it? I wish the cardinals would discharge their functions. I wish the pope, whose dignity exceeds that of kings, would promote concord among his sons. I said that priests are equal to bishops, not in function but in dignity. No, *I* did not say it. St. Jerome said it. He said that bishops are shepherds, not lords. He said the Church increases in wealth, decreases in virtues. What would he say if he were living now?[14] . . . There is such a thing as the old age of a declining Church. Nothing is more wholesome for Christians than a perpetual rejuvenation and a striving after pristine sincerity."[15]

As for the slur of Castiglione that Erasmus wrote a barbarous Latin, the reply was that some of the Italians were guilty of pedantry and paganism. The pedantry applied to those who wished to restrict the Latin language to the style and vocabulary of Cicero. The point may appear to have been only of antiquarian interest, but it affected the entire future of the Latin language as the *lingua franca* of Europe. We have noted the concern of Erasmus for the standardization of pronunciation. The question now raised applied to grammar and vocabulary. The language must be accommodated to the needs of a growing society without becoming so diversified as to be no longer universal. The Ciceronians proposed to hold Latin to the norm of Cicero and were reputed somewhat in caricature to be willing to say *amo, amas, amat,* but not *amamus* unless this particular form could be discovered in a glossary of Cicero. Erasmus felt that the norm should be not a single classical author, but rather the entire literature through the silver age and the patristic period. This would constitute a truer imitation of Cicero than a slavish restriction to his precise vocabulary.

The Ciceronians replied that they were justified in curtailing the vocabulary because they proposed to restrict the use of the Latin language to the Church and perhaps the courts. Everyday needs should be met by the vernaculars. Bembo, the great Ciceronian of Erasmus' day, aspired to create a normative Italian by building up the Florentine dialect in imitation not of one author, in this case, but of the triad Dante, Petrarch, and Boccaccio. History was with Bembo and Erasmus has in consequence been called fatuous for thinking that he could revive a dead language. But Latin in his day was not dead. It was killed subsequently by the spirit of nationalism, which is able both to kill and to make alive, as it has done in the revival of Hebrew. Erasmus was resisting the *Zeitgeist*, but fatuous he was not. He was battling for the cultural unity of Europe. On the linguistic side he lost.

A further criticism which he levelled against the Ciceronians was that a faithful adherence to their programme would require the use of pagan terms for Christian truths. Letters could not be dated "in the year of our Lord," *anno Domini*. God the Father would have to be called Jupiter Optimus Maximus, God the Son would be Apollo or Aesculapius, the Virgin Queen would be Diana, the Church the holy assembly or the republic, heresy would be faction, schism sedition, Christian faith would become Christian persuasion, excommunication would be consigning to the shades. The pope would be a *flamen*, the apostles *legates*, the cardinals *Patres conscripti*, the bishops proconsuls, Christ would be the first president of the republic, the Eucharist would be the sacred crust, absolution would become manumission. Take for example, said Erasmus, the following affirmation of Christian faith and see what becomes of it in a Ciceronian vocabulary. Here is the affirmation from current Latin:

Jesus Christ, Word and Son of the eternal Father, came into the world according to the prophets and was made man. Of his own will he gave himself to death to redeem his Church

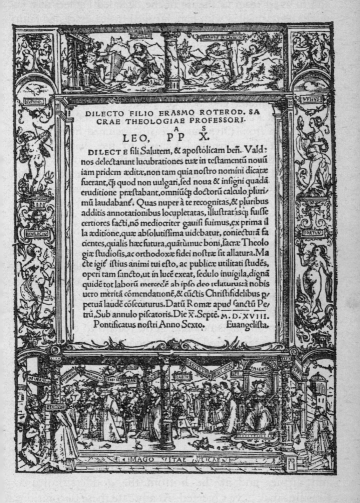

DILECTO FILIO ERASMO ROTEROD. SA
CRAE THEOLOGIAE PROFESSORI.
LEO, PP X.

DILECTE fili Salutem, & apostolicam beñ. Vald:
nos delectarunt lucubrationes tuæ in testamentũ nouũ
iam pridem æditæ, non tam quia nostro nomini dicatæ
fuerant, q̃ quod non uulgari, sed noua & insigni quadã
eruditione præstabant, omniũq̃ doctorũ calculo pluri-
mũ laudabant. Quas nuper à te recognitas, & pluribus
additis annotationibus locupletatas, illustratásq̃ fuisse
certiores facti, nõ mediocriter gauisi fuimus, ex prima il
la æditione, quæ absolutissima uidebatur, coniecturã fa
cientes, qualis hæc futura, quãrũmuc boni, sacræ Theolo
giæ studiosis, ac orthodoxæ fidei nostræ sit allatura. Ma
cte igit̃ istius animi tui esto, ac publicæ utilitati studes,
operi tam sancto, ut in lucẽ exeat, sedulo inuigila, dignã
quidẽ tot laborũ mercec̃ ab ipso deo relaturus: à nobis
uero meritã cõmendatione, & cũctis Christifidelibus p̃
petuã laude cõsecuturus. Datũ Romæ apud sanctũ Pe,
trũ, Sub annulo piscatoris. Die X. Septẽ. M.D.XVIII.
Pontificatus nostri Anno Sexto.   Euangelista.

IMAGO VITAE AVLICAE

Title page of Erasmus' New Testament in 1519 and 1522.

and to avert from us the ire of the offended Father, that we might be reconciled with him, justified by his grace and faith, liberated from the tyrant, grafted into the Church and that persevering in her communion we might after this life attain to the kingdom of heaven.

Now hear how this sounds in Ciceronian verbiage:

The Interpreter and Son of Jupiter Optimus Maximus, saviour and king according to the response of the augurs, came down from Olympus to earth, assumed human shape and voluntarily consigned himself to the shades for the welfare of the republic. He averted the thunderbolt of Jupiter Optimus Maximus pointed at our heads and returned us to his favour that restored to innocence by the munificence of persuasion and manumitted from the power of the sycophant we might be incorporated into the society of the republic and continuing therein might enjoy after this life the fellowship of the immortal gods.

This is, of course, caricature, but not altogether. Erasmus had heard a sermon in this vein at Rome as we noted earlier. And whereas Dante used some pagan mythology, in Sanazzaro and Camoēs it was luxuriant.[16]

At this point Erasmus had good reason to complain of two title pages inserted into the second and third editions of his New Testament by Froben. They were evidently pieces in stock because Froben used one of them also for the title page of Vives' edition of the *De Civitate Dei* of Augustine. They are startling decorations for an edition of a Church Father and even more for an edition of the New Testament. At the head of one Apollo is disporting himself with Daphne and on the sides are Cupid and Venus. Another page has the figures of the classical vices and virtues and at the bottom the goddess Fortuna. Erasmus may have objected. At any rate these decorations do not appear in later editions.

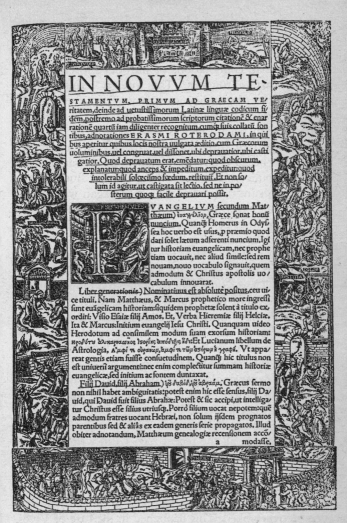

IN NOVVM TE-

STAMENTVM, PRIMVM AD GRAECAM VE-
ritatem, deinde ad uetustissimorum Latinæ linguæ codicum si-
dem, postremo ad probatissimorum scriptorum citatione & enar
ratione quartũ iam diligenter recognitum, cumᶜᵗ suis collatũ son
tibus, adnotationes ERASMI ROTERODAMI, in quĩ
bus aperitur quibus locis nostra uulgata æditio, cum Græcorum
uoluminibus, uel congruat, uel dissonet, ubi depravatior, ubi casti
gatior. Quod depravatum erat, emẽdatur: quod obscurum,
explanatur: quod anceps & impeditum, expeditur: quod
intolerabili soloecismo fœdum, restituitur. Et non solum id agitur, ut castigata sit lectio, sed ne in po-
sterum quoᶜᵗ facile deprauari possit.

EVANGELIVM secundum Mat-
thæum) εὐαγγέλιον, Græce sonat bonũ
nuncium. Quanᶜᵗ Homerus in Odys/
sea hoc uerbo est usus, ᵱ præmio quod
dari solet lætum adferenti nuncium. Igi
tur historiam euangelicam, nec prophe
tiam uocauit, nec aliud simile: sed rem
nouam, nouo uocabulo signauit, quem
admodum & Christus apostolis uo/
cabulum innouarat.

Liber generationis.) Nominatius est absolutè positus, ceu ui-
ce tituli. Nam Matthæus, & Marcus prophetico more ingressi
sunt euãgelicam historiam: siquidem prophetæ solent à titulo ex,
orditi: Visio Esaiæ filij Amos, Et, Verba Hieremiæ filij Helciæ,
Ita & Marcus: Initium euangelij Iesu Christi. Quanquam uideo
Herodotum ad consimilem modum suam exorsum historiam:
Ἡροδότε ἁλικαρνασσήος ἱστορίης ἀπόδεξις ἥδε: Et Lucianum libellum de
Astrologia, Ἀμφὶ τε οὐρανοῦ, ἐμφὶ τε τῶν ἀστέρων ἥ γραφή. Vt appa
reat gentis etiam fuisse consuetudinem, Quanᶜᵗ hic titulus non
est uniuersi argumenti: nec enim complectitur summam historiæ
euangelicæ, sed initium ac fontem duntaxat.

Filij Dauid, filij Abraham) υἱε Δαυίδ, υἱε ἀβραάμ, Græcus sermo
non nihil habet ambiguitatis: potest enim hic esse sensus, filij Da
uid, qui Dauid fuit filius Abrahæ: Potest & sic accipi, ut intelliga
tur Christus esse filius utriusᶜᵗ. Porrò filium uocat nepotem: quē
admodum fratres uocant Hebræi, non solum iisdem prognatos
parentibus sed & alijs ex eadem generis serie propagatos. Illud
obiter adnotandum, Matthæum genealogiæ recensionem acco/
a modasse,

Title page of Erasmus' New Testament in 1519 and 1522.

A serious and perennial problem was pointed up by the employment of all of this mythology. When Christianity takes over a new culture shall it invest indigenous words with Christian connotations or introduce foreign words into the native tongues? The foreign terms may be unintelligible, the indigenous may retain their former connotations. The danger was very real in the early Church when paganism was still alive. In the sixteenth century men felt that the use of pagan mythology was innocuous because no one would think of sacrificing a bull to Jupiter on the steps of St. Peter's. But Erasmus was not so sure that those who used pagan words were not thinking pagan thoughts. If one could speak of faith as no more than persuasion and grace as no more than munificence had one been touched by the finger of God?

There was also another point at least implicit in the controversy. The Ciceronians were addicted to the cult of *Romanitas*. They would like to revive the glory that was Rome. For them the Church was the successor of the empire. We have noted that for Erasmus also this was true in the sense that the Church as a visible institution gave a terrestrial embodiment to the harmony of the cosmos, as the empire had done in the days of the Roman peace, but never could he see the succession at the point of temporal power, which was the very mark of the Church's degeneration.

Erasmus concluded his tract against the Ciceronians with a survey of all the recent Neo-Latin writers for the whole of Europe with respect to their style. One is amazed at the range of his acquaintance with his contemporaries. But to assess contemporaries is a delicate venture. Ratings may displease and some writers may even be overlooked. This happened in the case of Vives, the distinguished Spanish scholar, the editor of Augustine's *De Civitate*. The oversight was pointed out to Erasmus who made amends in the next edition and excused himself to Vives on the ground that by reason of age he had had a lapse of memory. Vives replied, "To have been mentioned by you would have been pleasing. If by reason of age you overlooked me I forgive you, and equally if you meant to leave me out. I know that you are without malice, and no wonder that you should forget me when you have so much to do. I love you none the less, my dear teacher. How vain is fame which does not rest on merit, and let us not forget that speedily we shall all stand before that Judge whose judgment is just."[17]

Not all Spaniards were as charitable as Vives. The spirit of some was epitomized by a friar, who, commenting on the dictum that Erasmus laid the egg which Luther hatched, exclaimed, "May God smash the eggs and kill the chickens."[18] The Franciscan Carvajal said that the verse in the Psalm, "He shall tread upon the lion and the adder," had reference to Luther and Erasmus. By such exegesis, retorted Erasmus, the plagues of Egypt may be referred to the monks.[19] A coalition of Spanish monks, Dominicans, Franciscans, and Benedictines, attacked Erasmus. They by no means dominated the Spanish scene. The emperor and many at court were favourable to Erasmus, including the Grand Inquisitor, Alonso Manrique, the Archbishop of Seville, to whom Erasmus addressed himself.[20] Stung by the recriminations of the monks he sent them as usual an apologia.

They had complained of his statement that no affirmations should be made beyond the clear word of Scripture. They pointed out that this principle would leave the Arians unrefuted, for they accepted all of the Scripture. The monks had a point and Erasmus replied not very satisfactorily that men should not pry where angels adore.

The most spirited dispute was as to the meaning of the parable of the tares with the injunction, "Let both grow together till the harvest." Erasmus identified the tares with the heretics who should not be rooted out. "I am not objecting to the Inquisition," says he, "but only to the sycophant Inquisition. When I consider the compassion with which Christ planted his Church I do not see by what right we send a priest to the flames who prefers a wife to a concubine. Augustine did not approve of the death penalty for the Donatists although they disturbed the peace and shall we penalize those who would rather address their prayers to Christ than to the Virgin Mary, who doubt whether canonical hours were instituted by Christ and whether clerical celibacy is of divine institution? I would not take away the sword of princes, but they should exercise clemency. Let them not burn men over articles dubious, controverted, and newly contrived. Today he is sent to the fire who doubts whether the Roman pontiff has power over purgatory. The maximum penalty in the old days was exclusion from the Church."[21]

The Spanish affair was more ominous than all of the others because the pope for the first time began to withdraw support. Erasmus was continually asserting that he enjoyed the favour of Clement VII, but he was beginning to wonder[22] and with better reason than he knew, because when Clement was privately asked why he had not suppressed Erasmus, he answered that it was not because he agreed with him, but for fear of driving him into the Lutheran camp.[23] In other words tolerance was only strategic. The pope went so far as to give a directive for the appointment of four doctors in Spain to investigate the works of Erasmus.[24] They should see whether any portions needed to be expunged. Those containing no heresy were not to be banned, for Erasmus was a great

Was Kayserliche Maiestät erfordert
von dem Künig von Franckreych/Auch was
sich der Künig von Franckreych erbeüt/da
mit loß zü werden/Vnnd anders
meer rc. fürtzlich begriffenn.

The war between Charles V and Francis I: title page of a tract
published in Augsburg in 1526.

scholar and had done great service for the Church. Yet
that the pope should suggest expurgation was almost a
repudiation. Then Charles V told Erasmus not to worry,[25]
and one of the imperialists proposed that he edit Dante's
De Monarchia in which the empire was given a commission
directly from God and not through the mediation of the
Church, wherefore Peter should not interfere with

Caesar. The suggestion amounted to this: that the empire back Erasmus against the papacy. Just as Frederick the Wise had supported Luther against Leo X, so Charles should back Erasmus against Clement VII.[26]

Behind this willingness of the empire to use Erasmus against the pope lay several years of political manœuvrings. In August of 1521, just after the Diet of Worms, war had broken out between the most Christian king of France and the Holy Roman Emperor.[27] Erasmus wrung his hands.[28] The Defender of the Faith, England's king, supported the emperor. The coalition unseated Francis I, who was defeated on the field of Pavia in 1525 and taken as a captive to Madrid. "If I were the emperor," said Erasmus, "I would say to Francis, 'You fought well but Fortune was against you. Next time it may be my turn to lose. To continue the conflict injures us both. I will restore to you your kingdom. Let us cease to strive to extend our boundaries and rule well what we have. Mercy will bring me greater fame than were I to annex France and your gratitude will redound to your glory better than if you had driven me out of Italy'."[29] Charles did release Francis on oath to refrain from molestation of the empire and Francis, released, declared that he had sworn under duress and promptly formed a coalition of weaker powers to unseat Charles. This was invariably what happened whenever Charles was in the ascendant. In that case the pope would join the coalition as he now did. Then the imperial troops in northern Italy, mutinous for lack of pay, broke loose, swept down Italy, captured and sacked Rome with incredible barbarities. The pope barely escaped by fleeing to the *Castello di Sant Angelo* and then became the captive of the emperor. Erasmus was aghast. "What calamities have ensued through this fatal tempest! What part of the world has escaped this tornado!

We see Rome more cruelly captured than by the Gauls and the Goths. We see Clement, the head of the Church, inclemently treated. And we behold the two most powerful monarchs striving with each other in implacable hatred and, if rumour is true, fighting with each other for the mastery of the world."[30]

Would Erasmus now be willing to have the emperor support him against the pope? Should he become a shuttlecock between Caesar and Peter? What a ghastly proposal! He would have nothing to do with an edition of the *De Monarchia* of Dante.

The outlook was increasingly depressing. In 1523 two Austin friars were burned in the Netherlands for Lutheran opinions. Erasmus commented that they died "with incredible constancy for the paradoxes of Luther."[31] In the same year a hermit was burned in Paris for asserting that Joseph was the father of Jesus.[32] Also in 1523 Berquin was first arrested and then released on the king's intervention. Three years later he was again imprisoned and again released on the interposition of Marguerite, the king's sister. Grown overbold, Berquin then preferred charges of heresy against his accuser, Noel Beda, and in consequence was himself once more imprisoned. Erasmus wrote on his behalf to Francis[33] and to Marguerite[34] and warned Berquin not to tempt *Fortuna*.[35] In 1525 the emperor made peace with France on condition that the Lutheran faction be extinguished. Erasmus commented, "I would rather dissimulate on ten ambiguous articles than give a handle to such ills."

During all of this turmoil Erasmus again did not temper in the least his attacks upon what he deemed to be abuses in the Church. Further satirical colloquies were issued after the rupture with Luther in 1526 and the departure from Basel in 1529. *The Pilgrimage* derides the

Supstitio
sus cultus
imaginum

inanities attendant upon the cult of the saints. This colloquy contains the letter from the Virgin Mary to Ulrich Zwingli. The name Ulrich is taken to mean the rich owl (Ul-rich=Eul-reich) and is translated into Greek as *Glaukoplutus*. The Virgin thanks him for his attack upon her cult by reason of which she has been relieved of a plethora of petitions, as, for example, from a seafaring merchant to guard the chastity of his sweetheart during his absence, from a mercenary to give him booty, from a pregnant woman for an easy delivery, from a hag to be relieved of her cough, from a bishop for a benefice, and from a farmer for rain. On the other hand the Virgin complains that, while relieved, she is also impoverished,

since the offerings at her shrine are now scarcely sufficient
to pay a sacristan to light for her a tallow candle. Zwingli
is warned against expelling all of the saints, for if he
ejects St. Peter the gates of heaven may be closed against
him. We have also in this colloquy an account of a visit
to the shrine of St. Mary at Walsingham in England. The
quantity of the Virgin's milk on display exceeded what
the mother of one child could have produced even had
the infant not imbibed a drop. Besides, the milk on
exhibit looked like powdered chalk mixed with the white
of an egg, and as for the Holy Cross, the number of pieces
extant would make a full load for a freighter, whereas
Christ was able to carry his cross. One must, however,
remember that he was omnipotent. There is further an
account of the pilgrimage to the shrine of St. Thomas à
Becket at Canterbury in the company of Colet, who
sniffed derisively at a martyr's bone not clean of bloody
flesh, a handkerchief with recent snivel, and a slipper held
up for kissing. Erasmus reflected that the saint was able
to accomplish more dead than alive, for after his demise
one slipper could support a convent.

The colloquy called a "Fish Diet" begins with an
interchange of billingsgate between a fishmonger and a
butcher who resents the curb on meat eating during holy
days. The Jews, he complains, have greater freedom than
Christians because they are permitted throughout the
year to eat sheep, capons, partridges, and kids. Christianity
would the more readily be accepted in the non-Christian
world if irksome restrictions were rescinded by the pope.
The fishmonger replies that the decisions of popes are
binding and the butcher retorts that one pope can suspend
an enactment of another. The dialogue then passes into
an indictment of the ceremonial rather than the ethical in
religion. A priest who lets his hair grow over his tonsure

goes to prison. If he boozes in a brothel he is still a pillar of the Church. A Franciscan with an unknotted girdle, an Augustinian with one of wool rather than leather, a Carmelite with none, would "stir up the Tyrian seas." What an outrage to take communion with an unwashed mouth, though not with an unclean heart! How men pile up images and candles before the Virgin and think she will help them because at eventide they chant to her a hymn they do not understand, while to Christ they do not turn! The colloquy "Charon," after the manner of Lucian, portrays the ferryman of classical mythology conveying souls across the Styx to the lower regions. He complains of the overloading of his ferry. He is consoled that he will not have so many passengers because those who die in a just war do not go to hell. "I don't know," he answers, "but I do know that whenever there is a war such a crowd come down here that I wonder whether any are left on earth." He fears he will have to build a new boat and at that out of bronze because forests are being denuded to provide wood for burning heretics.

In the *Polyphemus* we are introduced to a guzzler carrying an embossed book. He is told that it ought to bear his coat of arms, the head of Bacchus peering through a wine jug. He calls this sheer blasphemy because the book is none other than the gospel. "And what has Polyphemus to do with the gospel?" "You don't think I live according to the gospel?" "You can decide for yourself. What would you do if some one called you a liar?" "Punch him." "And if he slugged you?" "I'd break his neck." "But the gospel says, 'Turn the other cheek.' " "O, I forgot . . . But I do believe in defending the gospel. When a Franciscan reviled the New Testament of Erasmus from the pulpit I collared him afterwards and gave him a wallop. And I banged him over the head with this book, once for the Father, once for the Son, and once for the Holy Ghost." There are two dialogues about funerals. One scoffs at the prevalent practice of being buried in the cowl of a Franciscan. The claim that devils are more frightened by the cowl than by the cross raises a query as to whether the exposed hands and feet are also protected and whether the garment will kill the lice. A negative answer prompts the ejaculation, "O blessed creatures to inhabit so holy a garment!" The other dialogue describes the passing of a godly man. He receives extreme unction without prior confession. He has no interest in indulgences. His confidence is solely in the Lord Jesus who takes away his sins, nailing them to the cross. "Far be it from me," says he, "that I should come armed with merits and briefs to summon my Lord to enter into judgment with his servant, certain as I am that in his sight no man living shall be justified! For my part, I appeal from his justice to his mercy, since it is boundless and inexpressible."[36] That statement would have satisfied Luther.

But if Erasmus continued thus to pour scorn on abuses in the Church why did he not take practical steps for their eradication? He was being called amphibious, two-faced, a Nicodemus who came to Jesus only by night,[37] a Balaam, who to please king Balak prophesied falsely until rebuked by the ass.[38] Luther said, "Erasmus is the king of Amphibians."[39] And Hutten had called him a renegade.

This charge came nearer to being just when a new reform movement arose among the very disciples of Erasmus who supposed that they were simply implementing his own ideas. They were the heirs of his stress upon the spiritual as over against all of the outward forms of religion. Relics, pilgrimages, indulgences, dietary regulations, monastic vows and habits, invocation of the saints,

ANNO AETATIS EIVS XLVIIL.

Ulrich Zwingli.

and a pompous liturgy, these are not the essentials of religion. Nor does the essence consist even in eating the bread and drinking the wine upon the altar. Erasmus himself had referred to the Mass as a mystical sign, a memorial of Christ's death, the bond of believers with each other and with their Lord, and a commitment to

William Farel.

follow in his steps. The mere corporeal presence of Christ, said he, is useless for salvation. The eating of his flesh and the drinking of his blood are worthless unless in the spirit. The sacrament is a celestial food in which Christ is present beneath the bread and the wine.[40]

For all the variations this was basically the position of Carlstadt, who said that the words "This is my body" were spoken by Christ as he pointed to his body; basically the position of Zwingli, who said that the word *is* in the above expression meant *signifies*; and likewise of Oecolampadius, the reformer of Basel, who saw a figure of speech in calling bread and wine body and blood.⁴¹ This group wished to sweep away all of the external practices, to remove the images, smash the organs, reduce the Mass to a very simple Lord's Supper. Like Luther they rejected the authority of the pope. Unlike Luther they regarded the Bible not only as the source of true teaching, but also as a law book. For all their spiritualizing they were in danger of a new externalism of reductionism.

This movement began to agitate Basel. The incursion of outsiders had something to do with the ferment. Carlstadt, expelled from Saxony, visited Basel. Thomas Müntzer, that fiery, tormented genius of religious and social unrest, came to Basel. But the outsider who most upset Erasmus came from France and his reproaches made plain that in France as well as in the Low Countries, Germany, and Spain a cross-fire existed between conservatives and radicals with Erasmus in the middle. The man was William Farel. He came from the circle of Bishop Briçonnet of Meaux, who had introduced many liberal reforms into his diocese, but submitted eventually to ecclesiastical authority. Another of the circle was Lefèvre. Farel was the most bellicose of them all. He it was who in later years by his thundering threats of hellfire intimidated John Calvin into becoming the reformer of Geneva. He it was who still later accompanied Servetus with harangues to the stake. When persecution broke in France Lefèvre, as we have noted, went to Strasbourg, Farel to Montbeliard and then to Basel, where he gave his support to the "sacramentarians," as they were called, and stigmatized Erasmus as a Balaam. "I turned down a benefice and an offer of money from the pope," said Erasmus. "I suppose that makes me a Balaam." Farel called on Erasmus. They discussed the invocation of the saints, which Farel would renounce completely, because not enjoined in Scripture. "But," objected Erasmus, "the Scripture does not enjoin the invocation of the Holy Spirit. Would you then refuse to invoke the Spirit?" "The invocation of the Spirit is enjoined," answered Farel, "because the Spirit is God and God is to be invoked." "Where does the Scripture say that the Spirit is God?" "In I John 5: 7, 'The Father, Son and Spirit are one.' " "It does not mean 'are one,' " retorted Erasmus. "It means 'of one mind.' Besides, the verse is not in the early manuscripts." "There is no use arguing with him," commented Erasmus. "If I had known what he was like I would not have been at home. In the olden days the gospel made the ferocious mild. It does not have that effect on these hot gospellers. I have never known any one so inflated, bombastic, and virulent. . . . He says I am no more of a theologian than Froben's wife. I'd be a great theologian if I called the pope Antichrist, human constitutions heretical, and ceremonies abominations." Unhappily Erasmus allowed himself to be carried away beyond his wont into Latinizing the name Farel not as Farellus but as Phallicus.[42]

But Farel, though galling, was only a fleeting irritation. Continued pressure on Erasmus was exerted by his old friend and helper in the edition of the New Testament, Oecolampadius, now the minister of St. Martin's church. He was abetted by Conrad Pellikan, professor of Hebrew at the university. Basel was falling into factions. On the conservative side were Ludwig Ber, rector of the university, and Boniface Amerbach, professor of law, who was not exactly charitable to Oecolampadius in his report that "A decrepit old man [he was forty-five] with trembling head and body, so emaciated and wasted that you might well call him a living corpse, has married an elegant and

blooming girl of twenty, more or less."[43] Erasmus was
even less kind when he wrote, "A few days ago Oecolampadius married a not inelegant girl with intent to castigate
his flesh during Lent."[44] Oecolampadius himself would
have preferred that she were older, but he had seen in her
no signs of unseemly levity and she had had several years
of experience in bearing the cross. She was a widow.[45]

The "living corpse" was lively enough in prosecuting
the reformation. He was impatient with the tolerant
attitude of Erasmus and of the Basel Town council which
was "trying to sit on two stools"[46] by repeatedly enacting
that every one should be free in faith and no one should
be compelled to go to Mass or to the reformed preaching
services and each should be free to follow his own conscience. This meant religious pluralism in a single city.[47]
Oecolampadius stigmatized as badly educated that conscience which after five years of preaching still held to the
Mass and the cult of images, which are a worse abomination than adultery. "Is adultery against God more to be
tolerated than adultery against man?" "Robbery, whoring,
adultery, treason, manslaughter, and murder are not so
bad as the blasphemous conduct of the servants of the
Mass. If one may and should punish thieves, murderers,
and the seditious, then in these dangerous matters the
magistrates should not look through their fingers."[48]
There should be but one religion in Basel. The Mass
must go.

The Evangelicals won five of the churches from which
the images were removed by the magistrates. But this did
not suffice. The Mass must go. The radical reformation
was reinforced by the influx of refugees, monks, and nuns
who had left their cloisters.[49] But also by a coalition of
the forces of social and political discontent, the manual
labourers who were in revolt against the patricians.[50]

The whole city was seething. Erasmus was trying to translate Chrysostom in Froben's garden[51] while a gunpowder explosion, pestilence, and rumours of war excited the people. There were riots, parleys with the council, negotiations and concessions. In January 1529 the Mass was restricted to three celebrations a day in Basel until May when a public disputation should decide for the future. This did not suffice. The Mass must go.

On the eighth of February, 1529, before dawn eight hundred men gathered in the *Barfüsserkirche*. They demanded from the council the abolition of the Mass and the retirement from the council of the twelve Catholic members, and also a reform of the political constitution. In the early morning the council began its deliberations. When by night no decision had been reached, the men took arms and possessed themselves of the *Marktplatz*. On the next day the council again sat while thousands gathered. By noon the shivering mob surged up the hill to the cathedral square and began hacking and smashing the images of the Münster and other churches. The council still sat. The twelve Catholic members resigned. The iconoclasts intimidated the rump which capitulated on the evening of the 9th of February, 1529.

In the morning Basel looked upon the broken idols, torsos, heads, arms and legs in wood and stone, shreds of painted canvas, fragments of stained glass and glittering decorations, all in heaps of rubble. The wood was offered to the poor and when they quarrelled over the pieces, the council ordered all to be burned. For two days and two nights fire consumed the residue of generations of piety. The images were gone. The Mass was gone.[52] Everyone had now to attend the reformed services and participate in the reformed Lord's Supper. Amerbach said, "Oecolampadius is so hospitable he *makes* us come to his table."[53]

The comment of Erasmus was that happily no blood had been shed and the chief syndic had escaped hanging. "When I consider what happened to those who mocked the wounds of St. Francis, I marvel at the patience of Christ and the Virgin this time."[54]

The riot was not to the taste of Erasmus even though he sympathized in a measure with its intent. His spirituality inclined him to agree with the more radical reformers. He confessed that Oecolampadius set forth his views with a persuasiveness that would deceive the very elect.[55] Nevertheless Erasmus refused to join the radicals because of his regard for *concordia* and consensus. He would not have these disrupted by constraint from either side. While the Catholics were still in the ascendant in Basel he disapproved of war on Zürich to stop the innovations,[56] and after the Evangelicals had won he declined to write against Carlstadt[57] and Oecolampadius[58] lest he increase the tumult.

Preserving the *concordia* was a matter of strategy, adhering to the consensus a matter of truth. When uncertain or not profoundly concerned, Erasmus, as we noted, adhered to the consensus. In this instance he declared: "The opinion of Oecolampadius would not displease me if it were not contrary to the consensus of the Church."[59] To Pellikan he was more explicit. "I agree with you that it would be simpler to say merely that Christ is present in the sacrament and leave the manner to God. The Christian, lest he fall into a labyrinth, should not depart from the authority of the councils and the consensus of all the churches throughout all the ages. That God should wish us to feed on His body and blood in an ineffable manner is congruous with His ineffable love by which He redeemed the world through the body and blood of His Son. I am willing to discuss the prob-

John Oecolampadius

lems with learned friends, but never have I said joking or serious that the Eucharist is nothing but bread and wine. I know you have little respect for the authority of the councils, but I do not despise the Roman church, especially when supported by the consent of all the churches [presumably the Greek and Eastern churches]. The Scripture speaks of a body, not of a figure of a body. To be sure we are commanded to be spiritual, but the presence of the flesh does not prevent us from being spiritual."[60] Pellikan answered: "I will love you just the same. I have read your *Paraphrases* with great profit and

I do not find you saying that Christ is present bodily, carnally, substantially and actually. You talk about an ineffable mode. Cannot one be saved by Christ's oblation made once and for all without believing that he is impanated corporeally by transubstantiation? As for the consensus of the primitive doctors of the Church one finds nothing in them about the Parisian definitions. Do you think the Catholic Apostolic Church is to be found in the works of Noel Beda, Sutor, Egmond, Latomus (and the rest of your opponents)?"[61] Erasmus responded in a tract that whereas he had spoken of the Eucharist as mystical food he had never talked of symbolic bread.[62] He had insisted very strongly that what the eye sees, what the ear hears, what the hand handles, what the mouth tastes is profitless apart from that which the heart feels.[63] He had said that the body and blood are symbols of the concord among Christians and a memorial of Christ's death, but he had never said that the Eucharist is merely symbolic.[64]

Another test which he applied to any theology was whether it bore fruit in Christian deportment. He became very critical of those who styled themselves Evangelicals and exhibited little of the quality of the evangel. When the church at Strasbourg was distraught by upheavals like those at Basel, he wrote, "I am called timid. I would not be timid if conscience constrained me, if I saw fruits of the gospel. A nice fruit of the gospel it is that a city should cast out all of its magistrates! Would that they might cast from their hearts the images which seem to me to be the most prodigious among those who call themselves evangelicals! At one time men gave up their wives for love of the gospel. Now they think the gospel flourishes if some take wives well endowed. The point is not that I condemn clerical marriage altogether, if there be necessity, honourable intent, the consent of the authorities, and no sedition. Now I am afraid there are some who marry simply because it is against the law." [65]

Erasmus had been thinking since the beginning of the commotion that he would have to leave Basel.[66] Life was growing unbearable.[67] Better to live among the Turks than amid such contention.[68] "I would rather be stoned like Stephen or perforated with arrows like Sebastian than have to endure for so many years the poison of the asp."[69] But where should he go? Where could he go? He had no lack of invitations from England, France, Spain, Vienna, Hungary, and Poland.[70] He had in fact a considerable following in Poland, seeing that Polish students, speaking Latin, of course, frequented the European universities and particularly Basel.[71] Among them John Laskey, subsequently the great Protestant reformer, was willing to pay his own expenses for the privilege of serving as secretary to Erasmus and paid the money in advance for the purchase of Erasmus' library to be transported after his death to Poland. But this land was difficult to reach. The most natural place was the Netherlands, because Erasmus was a councillor of the emperor; but only when the emperor was actually in residence at Brussels would there be any respite from the machinations of Hochstraten. France was promising and Erasmus said that he loved no people more than the French, though on occasion he would say the same of the English. But while in the service of the emperor he could scarcely go to France so long as the emperor was warring with that land.[72] England was appealing, but one could not predict what political entanglements Henry would undertake. Spain never did attract Erasmus,[73] perhaps because of the virulence of the Spanish monks, perhaps because friends like Busleiden and his brother died promptly when they went to Spain. As for Rome, Erasmus was nostalgic for a drink from the waters of the Tiber[74] (metaphorically presumably). If he were at Rome, however, mediation with the Lutherans would be precluded. Among all the possibilities the most promising seemed to be either the court of the emperor at Brussels or of the pope at Rome. He started for the Netherlands but the torment of the kidney stone turned him back at Schlettstadt. He started for Rome and was turned back at Constance.[75] Plainly his maladies restricted his movements to a small radius. The choice was Freiburg in Breisgau, not far distant from Basel, with much of the journey by water. And Freiburg was in the territory of the Archduke Ferdinand, who had invited him to Vienna.

When Erasmus announced his intention of leaving Basel there was universal dismay. The most implacable reformer, Oecolampadius, besought him to stay. Erasmus replied that he had already sent on his luggage. Then let him come back soon, urged Oecolampadius. The conversation was without contention. They shook hands in parting. Erasmus wanted to slip away unnoticed by boat down the Rhine. The council for some reason required him to embark at the bridge. A crowd in silence watched him board *magno cum dolore*.[76] Erasmus averred that he left for no other reason than religion.[77] He loved Basel. Not quite all of his goods had preceded him. He sent a little poem to a newlywed couple telling them that he had intended to leave with them his chickens, but had discovered too late that his housekeeper had found for them another disposal.[78]

CHAPTER TEN

The Cultivated Man

*

BEFORE going on to the Freiburg period we do well to
review the productions of the Basel sojourn insofar as
not already noted. Apart from continuing translations and
editions of Jerome, Augustine, Chrysostom, Hilary,
Seneca, Suetonius, Aristotle, Plutarch, and Galen there
were non-controversial tracts on a variety of subjects: on
marriage, confession, prayer, and so on. The range of
Erasmus' interests raises the question whether he should
be considered an example of the universal man of the
Renaissance, like Michelangelo proficient in painting,
sculpture, and poetry, Leonardo in art and mechanics,
Reuchlin in jurisprudence and Hebrew, Linacre in
medicine and Greek, Paracelsus in medicine, philosophy,
and sociology, Servetus in medicine, theology, and
geography, and their like. Erasmus does not quite fit the
picture. He was a literary man and that only. To be sure
his range in literary subjects was vastly greater than that
which any modern man would undertake. But he restricted himself to this. In his youth he dabbled in painting,
but not thereafter. And within the literary pursuits he
restricted himself rigidly. He gave up trying to master
Hebrew and knew only enough of the vernaculars to
enable him to get around.[1] The mastery of Latin and
Greek was quite enough for one lifetime. But if he was
not the universal man he was the cultivated man with a
wide range of interests. At the same time he was the

Christian man. The ideal of the cultivated man is to expand his interests, if not his skills, to the uttermost in order to develop to the full his own personality. The Christian man is ready to sacrifice the rounding out of his personality in order to meet the needs of his fellows. Erasmus might be called the cultivated Christian man, who would enlarge his interests insofar as compatible with his obligations.

Now let us investigate the range of his concerns as exhibited in the works of this period. We look first at the treatise on marriage dedicated to Catherine of Aragon, the saintly queen, as he called her, whom none could but love.[2] The object of this tract is to set forth the nature of Christian marriage and how it can truly be achieved. "Marriage is the most appropriate of all unions," he declared, "because based on nature, law, and religion. It should be for life, and any marriage which is capable of being dissolved never was marriage at all."[3] Here again the spiritualism of Erasmus comes to the fore. Marriage is not primarily of the flesh but of the spirit.

Because marriage is for life it should not be entered into lightly, but soberly, advisedly. Marriage should not be without the consent of parents, but they should not force the unwilling. Never let your daughter marry a leper or syphilitic. Better a healthy vendor of figs or olives; nor give her to a dissolute knight, better to a solid farmer. As between the bride and groom, the Church holds that marriage rests on consent. But does silence constitute consent? If a boy gives consent to one maid and then to another shall he be held to the first? Better not be too stringent in forcing him to carry through. If a girl will not receive a boy inflamed with wine unless he promises to marry her and he complies, do you call that consent?[4] I will give you an example of genuine consent and marriage. A lame man married a blind woman that they might help each other in their infirmities. Never an unkind word passed between them. They had twelve sons, all healthy. I knew one of them, a priest in Britain. That's what I call a real marriage.

If wedlock does not start off well, wait for the bitter wine to mellow. Nothing so helps conciliation as mutual consideration and talking things over. "A soft answer turns away wrath." Blow gently, for the flowers bend to the zephyr, then lift again their heads. Let the wife study her husband. Lions resent a corral, elephants are irritated by noise. Let the wife discover what sort of an animal she has married and avoid that which grates upon him. Let her be gay when he is at home and not talk about him in his absence. Let the husband yield to her in her proper domain. She is the mistress of the kitchen, finances, children, and the maids. (Let the husband not be familiar with the maids.) In this area the weaker sex is often mighty. Let the husband recall that God told Abraham to listen to Sarah.

The husband shall say to his wife: "My dearest, my sister in religion, my partner in marriage, God is pleased that we be bound in this most holy bond. I am ready to place you above my parents, who next to God are most dear to me and you are to put me above all else. We are united to our parents by blood but with each other we have become one flesh. We accept the yoke till death do us part. If we are of one mind we shall live sweetly and joyously, even though our lot be meagre, if there but be between us the same love as that between the soul and the body, between Christ and the Church. If our attachment is built on nothing more than age and comeliness, the desire of the flesh or wealth, there is no sound basis for concord. But if we are bound by devotion to God, neither poverty, nor sickness, nor age, nor any other fortune shall be able to separate us from joyous companionship. I will do my best to be to you a husband of whom you will not be sorry and I am sure you will try even to outdo me. I will approach you for progeny, not lust. We shall divide our functions. You will take care of the domestic, I of the professional, and we shall have nothing, save in common. If I do what I ought not, I will not take it amiss to be admonished by the companion of my fortunes. The authority which nature and the apostle give to the husband I hope you will not resent and mutual love will sweeten all things. You will sit on the eggs, and I shall fly around and bring in the worms. We are one and, as Scripture says, God rejoices when we dwell together in unity."[5]

Then follows a prayer for blessing upon their union:

O Thou founder of the human race, who first brought together our forebears in paradise, whose only begotten Son commended to us in many ways this sacrament, first by taking to himself our nature, as it were in marriage, again by making the Church his bride, then by his presence at the wedding when he turned water into wine, and finally by declaring that no man should put this bond asunder, we beseech Thee that, as we enter into this holy union, Thou wilt grant Thy perpetual favour that we may serve Thy will with equal acceptance and fervour. Cast from our hearts all impurity and discord. Give to us that peace which the world cannot give. Grant unto us life's necessities and children to be reared to the glory of Thy name, that persevering ever in Thy precepts, we may be made ready to enter into the celestial inheritance.[6]

Erasmus was well aware that many marriages did not fulfil this prayer. In that case it seemed to him monstrous that a couple should be compelled to stay together in the flesh when no longer and perhaps never united in the spirit. Thus the spiritualizing of marriage led to a readier dissolution of marriage. In a way this might be called the spiritualizing of annulment, for the Church recognized that a marriage was no marriage if there had been a violation, albeit in ignorance, of the prohibited degrees of consanguinity. Erasmus makes more of the spiritual impediments. He does not, however, use the word "annulment," nor did his generation. The dissolution of

he marriage of Henry VIII with Catherine of Aragon
vas called divorce, though in modern parlance the word
be annulment. Erasmus dealt with the entire subject in
everal writings; in his notes on the New Testament he
ntroduced a long excursus in the commentary on I
Corinthians 7 in 1519 and more fully in 1527,[7] again in an
nterpolation in the *Ratio Theologiae* in 1523,[8] and a
separate treatise was devoted to the subject in 1532.[9]

In his discussion Erasmus took his departure from two
biblical texts. The first was Matthew 5: 31, where divorce
was prohibited save for adultery. The other was Mark
10: 4, where Jesus said that Moses, "because of the
hardness of men's hearts," permitted divorce. Erasmus
understood this to mean that Jesus approved of the
concession to those whose hearts were hard.[10] In dealing
with the first of these texts Erasmus asked, What is
adultery? The Church herself had already spiritualized this
concept by calling heresy spiritual adultery.[11] "I have
myself," said Erasmus, "seen marriages in Britain
dissolved for heresy which were most unquestionably
marriages.[12] By this sort of exegesis any crime might be
called adultery and as a matter of fact there are many
crimes which are more disruptive of marriage than
physical adultery, which can be forgiven if not habitual,[13]
but what shall one say of homosexuality, infanticide, and
poison?"[14] Then take the second text. Moses allowed
divorce not for an outward act but for a spiritual state,
for the hardness of the heart. The Church herself recognizes spiritual impediments to marriage.[15] [Erasmus here
has reference to the ruling that a sponsor in baptism
incurred such a relationship that his own children could
not marry his god-children, and if such a relationship,
unwittingly incurred, were subsequently discovered, the
union was to be dissolved.]

"The Church herself, going beyond Scripture, sees the essence of marriage in consent; but [asks Erasmus] suppose the consent has been obtained on false pretences? I do not mean if the bridegroom claimed to have ten acres when he had only nine, or to be thirty years old when actually thirty-six, but if he concealed syphilis,[16] is a girl to be condemned to a life-long crucifixion?[17] Forcing a couple to stay together when they detest one another is dangerous. It may end in poison.[18] Those whose marriage is already on the rocks should be granted a divorce and permitted to remarry. Paul's dictum that it is better to marry than to be tormented by passion is not inapplicable to persons once unhappily married and now separated."[19]

Erasmus saw perfectly well in all of this argumentation that he was going counter to current practice. In his controversy with the Protestants he said commonly that he would be guided by the consensus of the Christian centuries. In this instance he undertook to demonstrate that there had been no consensus.[20] Popes had disagreed, canon lawyers had disagreed, Church Fathers had disagreed. But often the examples of disagreement which he cited dealt with questions other than marriage and divorce and were so broad in scope as to undercut the whole concept of consensus. The Church must not be bound by the past, he would say. He would ever be ready, he averred, to dissent from himself, if a better argument were adduced even by one without learning.[21] We have already remarked that Erasmus appealed to consensus only on theological points about which he was not deeply concerned. On a matter of ethics, like marriage, he was ready to contravene the consensus for the sake of humane legislation.

In the tract on marriage Erasmus assigned to the

mother the early education of the girls and then proceeded to discuss in general the education of women. Girls, he said, are harder to train than boys. Both are slippery, but girls are more crafty. Their disposition is weaker and they make a bigger fuss over a failure. Like boys they are to be treated with gentleness. A mother who beats her daughters deserves to be beaten. The first step in physical education is physical care. Girls are not to be victimized by parental pride into wearing heavy and cumbersome attire, pompous headpieces, superfluous underwear, dresses trailing to the ground and impeding movement.[22] How long should the education of women continue? It should never stop. The mind of the adolescent girl is to be filled with study. She should be shielded only from obscenity in art and music. After marriage, though encumbered with children, her interests should be cultivated. Her husband will rejoice in partnership on an intellectual level.[23] This point is made by a married woman in a discussion with an abbot who insists in one of the colloquies that women should confine themselves to the distaff, or if they have books, certainly let them not be in Latin. The lady reminds him that in pictures of the Annunciation the Virgin Mary is commonly shown reading a book. "Yes," rejoins the abbot, "she was reading the canonical hours of the Benedictine order." The lady informs him of the learned women in Spain, Italy, England, Germany.[24]

Erasmus was personally acquainted with a number of them and enjoyed their companionship. In several instances we can fill in the details. His commentary on the nativity hymn of Prudentius was dedicated to Margaret More,[25] who in turn translated into English his meditation on the Lord's Prayer. Erasmus rejoiced that the Princess Mary was able to write Latin letters and, as we noted, save for ill health, she would have done the translation of John for the English version of the *Paraphrases*. Mary of Hungary, the sister of Charles and Ferdinand, delighted in Latin codices, and to her Erasmus dedicated his work on the *Christian Widow*.[26] The tract *On Matrimony*, as already observed, was dedicated to Catherine of Aragon. The sisters of Pirckheimer, Caritas and Clara, both nuns, elicited the praise of Erasmus.[27] But the most interesting of his relations with learned ladies to be recorded was the case of Margareta Peutinger, the wife of Conrad, famous among other things for having discovered an ancient road map of the Roman empire. Margareta compared Erasmus' New Testament of 1519 with an old German translation and discovered that where in Matthew 20: 22 Jesus says, "Are you able to drink the cup that I am to drink?" Erasmus adds, "And to be baptized with the baptism with which I am baptized?" (which is in Mark 10: 39). Margareta and her husband wrote to Erasmus: "We looked up Jerome and found that he did not have this addition. I examined your translation and found you saying that these extra words belong in Matthew as well as in Mark. Then my wife wanted to examine Origen and Chrysostom in Greek and from these we learned that you had made the addition on the basis of the text used by these Greek Fathers." In her own hand Margareta copied out the old German translation interlarded with her comments in Latin.[28] That the Erasmian reading is not confirmed by modern scholarship is irrelevant here. The point is rather that Margareta was in a position to compare the German, the Latin, and the Greek and to carry on a discussion with Erasmus quite on his own level.

In the realm of music Erasmus was capable of appreciation rather than performance. He could not play an instrument like Zwingli, Luther, or More. He praised

The family of Thomas More as sketched by Holbein. In the centre is Thomas More, flanked by his father on his right and his son on his left. Daughter Margaret, who translated Erasmus' exposition of the Lord's Prayer, is seated on the right. Dame Alice is on the far right with a monkey near her foot.

More for teaching his wife to play the lute[29] and spoke with enthusiasm of the singing he had heard at Constance. He was not interested in musical theory like his friend Glareanus and at that point went scarcely beyond Plato's harmony of the spheres. Like the early Church Fathers he had no use for erotic and military music and deplored borrowing tunes from such sources for sacred use. His interest was in church music. Had he been inclined he would have had difficulty in banishing music altogether from the churches unless he were ready to dispose of all the biblical references by allegory, like Augustine who on occasion interpreted the lyre as the mouth, the drum as the skin, and the strings as the nerves.[30] This Erasmus would not do. Zwingli and the early Anabaptists spiritualized church music on the basis of Colossians 3: 16 which speaks of "psalms, hymns and spiritual songs" to be sung *"in your hearts."* This was taken to mean "not with your voices." So far Erasmus would not go. "What does the apostle mean," he asked, "by 'in your hearts'? He means that no one should think to please God by bellowing, or by modulated neighing, or by the organs which now blast in our churches. Not that I condemn all audible music, provided it be moderate, sober and appropriate."[31]

Sometimes, however, Erasmus did come close to allegorizing the music of the psalms. "The body of Christ," said he, "is itself the lyre which never ceased to sound forth the glory of God; when by his word he healed the sick, gave sight to the blind, cured the demented, and supremely when with his arms outstretched upon the cross he prayed, 'Father forgive them.' So mighty was his music when he yielded up his spirit to the Father that the veil of the temple was rent. What human music ever had such power? It is able to cure insomnia, put babies to sleep, and incite men to war. There is no age or sex which music does not stir, for according to Plato the soul of the world is attuned to musical intervals. Yet, though the harp of David expelled from Saul the evil spirit, it came upon him again. How different the lyre of Christ! For a moment it was silent in the tomb. Then the Father said, 'Awake O harp and lyre.' And each responded, 'I will awake with the dawn' [Psalm 57: 8]. This word was prophetic, for with the dawn the Lord Jesus arose to declare the glory of God over all the earth."[32]

This occasional allegorization obviously did not mean that Erasmus would give up church music, provided that like all else it should minister to piety, learning, and Christian deportment. As to the kind of music which would serve this end, he was as usual influenced by both the classical and the Christian heritage, by the humanists who called for monody, and by the Brethren of the Common Life who objected to organs. The humanists for the most part rejected polyphony, sometimes because unknown in antiquity, sometimes as obscuring the sense of the words on which they relied for moulding the minds of men.[33] This point entered into the dispute between Erasmus and the Sorbonne when he insisted that in France the liturgy should be in French.[34] The Sorbonne replied that the Latin had an emotive power even if not understood. Presumably they had in mind Latin chants. Erasmus asked whether those chants would be any the less emotive if in the vernacular and understood. Had the Sorbonne retorted that the French would not match the notes, Erasmus would surely have called for changing the notes to fit the words. He would subordinate the musical to the didactic. Music has the power to create moods of adoration, penitence, praise, and resolve, but it lacks conceptual precision. This may be why in modern times the symphony is preferred to the sermon. The writing of Erasmus was basically sermonic.

The humanist educational ideal, with reliance on the word, produces a distaste for polyphony which obscures the word. It certainly does in church music if in the treble the angels are warbling praises while in the bass the devils are shrieking imprecations. Erasmus said that he did not condemn polyphony absolutely.[35] He hesitated to condemn anything absolutely, but his comments point in that direction. To his mind there should be simple plain-chants only. The sense should be conserved by setting a single note to a single syllable. This principle, adopted by the Lutherans, did not impede a rich musical efflorescence in the service of religion. There were, however, those in the Church who feared that music, unless severely curtailed, would do a disservice to religion by way of distraction. For this reason the Brethren would have no organs. Erasmus agreed. "The rumbling of organs is distracting[36] and even more the sound of the trumpet, sackbut, flute and sambuke [a triangular stringed instrument with a shrill tone].[37] Heart and voice must be in accord.[38] Musical display justifies the scriptural reproach, 'This people honours me with its lips but its heart is far from me.' "[39]

Another principle enunciated by Erasmus calls for simplicity in music. He insisted that it should be congregational. When Christ walked with his disciples to the Mount of Olives they sang a hymn *together*. He did not sing a solo. Music is a bond of community, the expression of *concordia*.[40] "If we would be blessed let us with one mind praise the Lord, like the angels among whom there is no dissension. The universal creation in its own way praises the Lord: sun, moon, cattle, fish, mountains, streams, but evil men cannot join in this symphony."[41]

The thought of Erasmus is well epitomized in this passage: "Let us sing as Christ did with his disciples and as Paul and Silas did in prison. They did not chant words not understood, nor with indecorous bellowing or the chirping of birds. How the angels sang when Christ was born I do not know, but Luke indicates that they cut it short. Now in some of the churches and monasteries the chants wear out the congregation. New forms have broken in. The monks think the Virgin will be displeased if she does not have a mass to herself every day and if it is not said in advance of that of her Son. She will not be pleased, moreover, if it be not sung in various voices. The primitive church had none of this, nor of organs. Now in the very churches we have dissolute Dionysiac airs so that youth grows up good for nothing but crooning and guzzling."[42] In his own day Erasmus was a conservative, resisting the polyphonic music then flourishing in the Netherlands. In our day he might be a patron saint of the liturgical reform.

The attitude of Erasmus to the graphic arts has been variously assessed. Some have portrayed him as an enthusiast because he dabbled in painting in his youth, but the doodlings in his manuscripts are not distinguished. Others think him to have been devoid of interest because he never mentions the art treasures of Italy. One must remember, however, that they were not on display in museums. He was interested in sacred art and passed severe strictures on those who overdid the macabre, making the torments of Christ exceed anything save the pangs of the damned in hell and depicting the dead Christ with a ghastliness alien to the gospels. Erasmus may have been thinking of Holbein's *Dead Christ*, now in the museum at Basel. "Let us give up the cult of wailing," says Erasmus, "unless it be for our sins rather than for his wounds. Rather with joy we should proclaim his triumph."[43] Holbein's depiction of the fool must have pleased Erasmus. He is looking at himself in a mirror with a quizzical self-scrutiny.[44]

Erasmus did have contacts with artists, inevitably, because he was depicted by three of the greatest masters of his generation, Metsys, Holbein, and Dürer. Each caught a different aspect. Dürer portrayed the scholarly editor of Jerome, of Augustine, and of the New Testament. There is a delightful touch in the vase of flowers on the table. Holbein caught the author of the *Praise of Folly* and the *Colloquies*, with a slight ironic smile. Metsys saw

the Erasmus of the *Contempt of the World* and the *Preparation for Death*, refined, sensitive, and pensive. This portrait was done in 1517 in the form of a diptych of Erasmus and his friend Peter Gilles as a present for Thomas More, who was lyrical in his praise of the likeness of Erasmus.[45]

Holbein first did a little sketch among the illustrations for the *Praise of Folly* which he drew in the margins of Myconius' copy. When Erasmus saw the sketch, he ejaculated, "Good grief, if Erasmus still looked like that, he could readily get a wife."[46] The portraitists Holbein and Metsys, though not Dürer, made the error of having Erasmus pose seated. He worked habitually standing.[47]

Erasmus had the greatest admiration for Dürer, who sketched him twice in the Netherlands, once at Antwerp, once at Brussels.[48] When Dürer was later executing the well-known copperplate, Erasmus wrote to Pirckheimer,

Myconius, to whom this copy of the *Praise of Folly* belonged, wrote above the sketch the words: "Dum ad hoc proveniebat Erasmus se pictum sic videns exclamavit, Ohe, ohe, si Erasmus adhuc talis esset, duceret profecto uxorem."

"I will not decline to be painted by such an artist as Dürer, but I don't see very well how he can. [There was no chance for a sitting.] He sketched me once at Brussels, but was interrupted by callers. Although at that time I was a bad subject, since then I have grown worse."[49]

When Dürer died Erasmus wished to pay him a tribute. The only work going through the press at the time was the treatise on the correct pronunciation of Greek and Latin. This theme did not offer an obvious opening for the encomium of an artist. But in it Erasmus had said that boys should be trained in language by writing, and calligraphy would be helped by exercise in drawing, of which the great master was Albert Dürer. Then followed a eulogy full of phrases culled from ancient authors in praise of ancient artists, but not thrown together without discrimination or discernment. Erasmus observed that Dürer went beyond the ancients, for he obtained his effects solely by the use of perspective and he had the capacity to convey the emotions of his subjects. The passage reads:

If the ancient Greek painter Apelles were here he would yield the palm to Dürer. I confess that Apelles was the foremost of his craft and his fellow artists could criticize him only because he never knew when to leave a picture alone. A specious reproach! Apelles was aided by colour, even though applied only with parsimony, but what marvellous effects Dürer has achieved only in black and white! shades, light, brilliant illumination, heights, depressions! He shows an object not simply in a single dimension but observes precisely symmetry and harmony. He paints what cannot be painted, "clouds," as they say, "on a wall," the senses, the emotions and the soul in its entirety shining through the vesture of the body and almost the very voice itself. He does this with such singular felicity by lines only that if colour were added it would detract.[50]

Erasmus very seldom in his letters makes mention of the beauties of nature, but, after all, the letters deal usually with immediate concerns. In one instance, however, in describing the home of a host at Constance, he dilated on the elegance within and the majesty without.

Here we were received by that most excellent man John Botzheim, the canon. No one could be more gracious. You would say he had been born of the Muses and Graces. His home is a veritable abode of the Muses, exhibiting nothing if not lustre and elegance, and never mute, for the pictures seem to speak and attract the eyes to themselves. In the sun-court, placed at my disposal, stands St. Paul instructing the people. On the other wall Christ is seated, delivering to his disciples the Sermon on the Mount. Then we see the apostles travelling over the mountains and proclaiming the gospel. In the heated room are the Scribes and Pharisees and the elders conspiring to subvert the gospel. Elsewhere the nine sisters of Apollo are singing and in another place are nude Charities, the symbol of unvarnished benevolence and friendship. But how in a single letter shall I describe all the delights? Ten days would not suffice. Of all the graciousness nothing exceeded that of the host himself, whose manners surpassed his murals. He was very considerate. I begged him not to invite guests, for I was not up to conviviality. Vain precaution! There was Hugo, the Bishop of Constance. The host begged him to defer his visit and he did not take it amiss. After a little I was better, though never without torment from the stone. Then, Immortal God! what hospitality, what a host, what elegant servants, what choice dinnerware, what stories, readings, songs, what banquets of the gods! Had I only felt better I would not have envied them their nectar and ambrosia. And the scenery! The lake of Constance is spacious in width and length and ravishing, nestling amid wooded hills and distant mountains. The Rhine, as if released from Alpine crags, disports itself in pleasant relaxation and glides into the lake of incredible depth, from which we had a huge trout fit for a king. Then sportively leaving the lake the Rhine forms an island on which stands the city of Constance. Everything was superb except the wine which was fit only to be served to a heretic.[51]

With regard to medicine Erasmus naturally had no specialized knowledge. When Paracelsus diagnosed his maladies he marvelled that any one could so well understand his condition, "not that I understand all of your technical terminology which I have not studied."[52] Erasmus praised medicine in the most general terms. When he edited a treatise of Galen, the ancient Greek medical authority, he chose not a medical work properly speaking, but a plea that the physician be acquainted with letters.[53] In a tract of his own in praise of medicine

Erasmus lauded the doctors because thanks to them many persons survive who otherwise would die at birth. Doctors, said he, are the most powerful men in society because popes and emperors must obey their orders. Some doctors are poisoners, yes, and some priests are adulterers and some monks are pirates, but that is no reason for condemning their professions.[54] Better to trust to nature and the doctor for healing than to the saints. In any case prevention is better than cure. Let princes suppress the sale of acrid wine and putrid fish.[55] As for self-care Erasmus wrote to his friend Gilles, "Avoid drugs which sap the strength. Don't overdo. Avoid excitement. Don't laugh to bursting, nor walk to exhaustion. Don't study too hard and don't get angry."[56] Healing involves the soul as well as the body. Wherefore theologians also are doctors. If Caligula had had spiritual healing he would not have gone mad.[57]

Erasmus had wide personal acquaintance with medical men, though frequently not for medical reasons. They also were humanists. This was true of Lister, Linacre, and Cop, though of the last two he did seek professional counsel.[58] He needed it, for his diseases were many: in his youth, quartan fever; after the residence at Venice, excruciating kidney stone; in his later years, arthritis and gout. On the journey to Louvain he suffered from what he variously described as tumours, carbuncles, or ulcers.[59] Some medical men today think he may have had a mild attack of the Bubonic plague.[60] At Cambridge he was severely ill, perhaps of the sweating sickness, though there was no epidemic at that time.

The most surprising result of the exhumation of Erasmus' bones was the discovery of marks of syphilis:[61] asymptomic, so that he would not have known that he had it, not congenital, contractable by contact with any

open sore such as his ulcers, or even by a kiss. If he was afflicted nothing can be inferred as to the manner of infection. Though he did not pretend to have been free from all the vices of youth, he had not been addicted to Venus.[62] The medical report on the exhumation at Basel is very exact as to the state of the skeleton and inexact as to its identification. The bones had earlier been disturbed by the laying of pipes and the marking stone had been lost. The skeleton claimed to be that of Erasmus has an abnormally small skull. When the Holbein profile is superimposed the gap between the base of the skull and the nape of the neck is incredibly great. The assumption has been made that Erasmus, to conceal the smallness of his cranium, wore a large stuffed cap. Plausibility for this surmise is found in some doodlings in his manuscripts which are taken to be self-caricatures.[63] The back of the head is small. The nose is preternaturally large. A depiction with such deliberate exaggeration is hardly to be rated for accuracy above the Holbein portrait. One is left dubious as to the identity of the bones.

The caricatures are of quite independent interest. Two profiles appear back to back. The one has the quizzical Holbein smile, the other a lugubrious expression and the dripping nose from which Erasmus often suffered. A modern art historian claims that Erasmus is the first in the western world to leave caricatures of himself both literary and graphic.[64]

In general Erasmus was not interested in the science of his day. Like other humanists he drew his science from antiquity. When advising a young mother on the care of her child he drew his psychology from Aristotle.[65] In his edition of the *Geography* of Ptolemy Erasmus did no more than to print the Greek text. He did not, like his friend Pirckheimer, introduce maps, descriptions, or place names. In correspondence with Brunfels and Fuchs he never mentions their herbals. The new geographical discoveries interested him but little. In a letter of congratulation to the king of Portugal on the exploits of his explorers, Erasmus took occasion to express the hope that the king would not establish a monopoly on spices.[66] In general Erasmus feared that geographical expansion would make world government more difficult.[67] He was interested in missions, but the place mentioned is Ethiopia,[68] of which he would have heard from his friend Damião de Gois, the Portuguese.[69] There is no mention of Franciscan missions in the New World. Erasmus was a European.

Although he was the cultivated man, his main interests and primary vocation were religious. During the Basel period he wrote a tract on confession, and another on prayer:[70]

צִיר אֱמוּנִים לְמַרְפֵּא׃

ፈቀርዮሃናፍተ አቆኖምየሃ

Orandum ut fit mens sana in corpore sano.

ልሳን፡ዘየአምን፡በ፡ሉ፡ወአኔ፡፡

APVD INCLYTAM COLONIAM
IO. SOTER EXCVDEBAT
ANNO MDXXII.
MENSE OCTOB.

Ethiopian script on a work of Erasmus. Ethiopian (Amharic) script appears as a part of the printer's mark on the edition of Erasmus' *Colloquies* by Johann Soter (in German, Heil) at Cologne in October, 1522. His name is given in Greek in the genitive at the bottom of the printer's mark. His interest in Ethiopia is further evidenced by the publication of an Amharic alphabet with a key. Around the device are legends in four languages, all having reference to health. The Latin says, "Pray for a sound mind in a sound body." The Hebrew is from Proberbs 13:17, "A faithful envoy brings healing." The Greek means, "Nothing in life is better than health." The Amharic has, "The knowledge of the spoken word is like medicine to man."

(*I am indebted to Michael Lund for the translation of the Amharic.*)

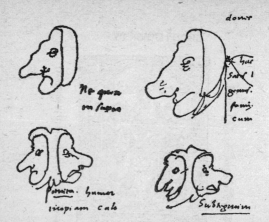

Confession, though not instituted by Christ, is useful. Its form has changed since the days of the early Church when it consisted in an act of public humiliation before the congregation. Today it is private. Confession requires genuine contrition. Do not, therefore, run immediately after an offence to confession, but search your heart as to whether your contrition is genuine and make your first confession to God. Do not repeatedly confess the same offence. Once is enough. Be not perpetually dissolved in tears. The confessor can be of great help as a spiritual guide. He should cast down the proud, encourage the despairing, and relieve scrupulants – young priests, for example, who worry over nocturnal pollutions and whether they have pronounced every syllable correctly in saying the Mass. The confessor must guard himself. He will hear things he would not believe people capable of doing and this may put ideas into his head. His health may be endangered when he confesses lepers and syphilitics. Nothing is more dangerous than to inhale their breaths. He should not allow the penitent to go into too great detail. *Pas d'histoires!* That leads to desperation, especially in the case of boys, women, and the aged, of whom I have known not a few.[71]

This last remark implies that Erasmus had heard a good many confessions. There is also another confirmatory passage where he says that there are many persons fifty years of age who have no idea of what was vowed for them in baptism. "This we know from familiar conversation and from the secrets of the confessional."[72] These statements are of interest for their bearing on the question whether Erasmus performed his priestly function. In all of his bulky correspondence he never once mentions having said Mass. True, but the letters do not detail the whole of his experience. They deal with immediate preoccupations, the publication of books, religious controversies, finances, diseases, and the like. They do, however, disclose that Erasmus carried his prayer book.[73]

His treatise on prayer from this period breathes very much the spirit of the *Enchiridion*. He reviews the varieties of prayer in the Bible, prayer as praise, thanksgiving, and petition, and then poses some questions.

To whom shall we pray? To God. But how shall a miserable little creature like man come before Him in whose presence angels tremble? What could be more sublime than God, what more abject than man? Shall he then lift himself up and talk with Him who inhabits eternity? Yet the publican cried unto Him and was heard. Shall we pray to Christ? We may, but not on the assumption that he will do for us what the Father would not. May we invoke the saints? They are not invoked in Scripture, but there is no reason why we should not, provided superstition is avoided. The saints have become the successors of the gods. The cult of Proserpine became the cult of the Virgin. Apollo and Aesculapius became St. Roche and St. Anthony. Juno was invoked for a safe delivery, now St. Jodocus. The sailors used to call on Venus and the Gemini, now they cry *Salve Regina*. What could be more revolting than the cult of relics? Prayers to the saints should be appropriate.

I knew a dear old priest at Louvain who would go around saying "Our Father who art in heaven" to St. Barbara or the Virgin and *Ave Maria* to St. Christopher.

How shall we pray? Not interminably. If you are going through a round of prayers you might as well be rolling rocks like Sisyphus. Don't bellow like a soldier or croon like a singer. Don't recite "Have mercy upon me, O lord, according to Thy tender mercies," while ogling the ladies. Your whole life should be a prayer and it may be said in bed, in the bath or in the work shop, for to pray is to desire the highest good. Prayer need not be vocal. God said to Moses, "Why are you crying to me?" though Moses had not opened his mouth.

For what may we pray? If it be for material things, then add "Thy will be done." And think not that your prayer is unanswered if you ask for prosperity and receive calamity. Then say, "Thy grace is sufficient for me." Above all, rise above the carnal to the spiritual and cry, "O that I had the wings of a dove."

Public prayers should not be tedious. Pray that rulers may be given wisdom rather than victory in war. Pray not for one king but for all rulers and for the Turks that they may be given mercy rather than destruction.

Erasmus in his later years brought together a collection of prayers which were long to be used in devotional manuals in Germany and England and probably elsewhere.[74] Many of them have reference to a particular occasion. The two following are from those devoted to the seasons. The first, on spring, is addressed to God the Son, the second, on winter, to God the Father:

Omnipotent Lord Jesus, initiator of all things, who for our sakes hast established this world most fair and hast adorned the heavens with such great delights for use by day and solace by night, the earth Thou hast tempered by the cycle of the seasons that she should be to us and to all creatures a gracious mother. Now in Thy rising all things revive and confirm for us the hope of the resurrection which Thou hast promised. The barren fields are reclad with verdure and bedecked with jewel-like flowers, the grain matures, the seeds burst their tombs, stark trees put forth fronds, then burst into a shower of bloom, the harbingers of fruit. The sun himself augments his gracious light and the universal face of nature, wherever the eye is cast, bespeaks, as if reborn, Thy loving-kindness to the race of men, whose merited expulsion from paradise Thou dost assuage with such delights. Grant unto us, once reborn in baptism, that we may put off the old man and having become new creatures, may never again wither but be invigorated by the bracing air of Thy spirit to walk in unfailing innocence, that more and more adorned with the flowers of virtue, we may bear fruit worthy of the gospel, O Thou, who with the Father and the Holy Spirit livest and reignest world without end.

For winter:

O God most wise, founder and governor of the world, at whose behest the seasons revolve in stated changes, like unto sere death is winter, whose desolateness and hardship are the better borne because soon to be succeeded by the amenity of spring. Like the year our outward man is in childhood vernal, in youth torrid, in maturity ripe, and in age declining. But the horror of death is softened by the hope of renewal of which we are most certainly assured by the promise of Thy Son, who is eternal truth, who can no more deceive or be deceived than he can not be Thy Son, through whom our inward man knows not age and through his constant aid is vernal in innocence, fervent in the zeal of piety, bears fruit, and passes on to others that which also it has received. The more the vigour of the body declines, by so much more the spirit flourishes. We beseech Thee that what through Thy Son Thou hast conferred upon us, Thou wilt deign to guard and increase through the same who reigns with Thee, world without end, Amen."[75]

CHAPTER ELEVEN

A Voice Crying in the Wilderness

*

At Freiburg Erasmus received a very cordial reception. The Archduke Ferdinand placed at his disposal the house which he had intended for his own old age. A few years later Erasmus built another for himself. Several beloved friends accompanied him in the transfer from Basel: Louis Ber, one-time rector of the university, and Glareanus, who had assisted in the publication of the New Testament and for whom Erasmus had secured a post occupied for a time in Paris. Boniface Amerbach went with them for a portion of the journey, but then returned to his family in Basel. He shared the views of Erasmus as to the innovations, but was resolved neither to leave nor to comply.[1] Erasmus did not reproach Amerbach for remaining in Basel. After all, "Peter held the faith among the pagans at Rome, whereas Judas was a traitor among the apostles."[2]

Among those at Freiburg to extend a welcome was the distinguished jurist Ulrich Zasius, in age but slightly older than Erasmus. His delvings into legal theory and history, both civil and ecclesiastical, had caused him to be well versed also in theology. At the outset he had been enthusiastic for Luther but recoiled from the attack on the authority of the pope and the disparagement of good works. In 1521 he wrote to Amerbach saying, "If only Erasmus had the boldness and acuteness of Luther and Luther but had the fecundity, eloquence, modesty, and discretion of Erasmus, how could the gods have created a more excellent creature? I favour both, but I prefer Erasmus. He unravels Scripture. Luther twists it in knots."[3] Zasius was outraged by the more extreme position of Zwingli and Oecolampadius and wished that Erasmus would renounce them unequivocally. Comparing now himself with Erasmus he said, "If only he had my courage and I his astounding esprit."

Freiburg was a quiet little country town, but not shut off from news of the world, and from without the news was disquieting. Berquin had been burned at Paris. Charges of heresy had been renewed against him. A committee of twelve examined him and passed sentence that he must abjure. His books should be burned, his tongue bored, and he should be imprisoned for life. He appealed at once to the king and the pope. Had Marguerite, the king's sister, not been at Blois, she might at once have intervened. The judges forestalled a recognition of the appeal by sending Berquin the very next morning to the stake. "I am sure he was of a good conscience," said Erasmus. "He died with constancy and tranquillity. How often I warned him to be less provocative."[4]

In 1531 Zwingli, with sword and helmet defending the gospel, was struck down on the field of Kappel, quartered, and burned. Erasmus wrote to Amerbach. "Zwingli has received his judgment among men. May he find God more merciful."[5] Oecolampadius was badly shaken by the news and died shortly thereafter.[6]

For some time now the chain of events was being forged which culminated in the English schism and the execution of some of Erasmus' dearest friends. On first hearing that Henry was minded to put away Catherine, Erasmus was outraged, but later on began to see something to be said for Henry,[7] as indeed there was. For

Henry found himself regarded as a national stallion to provide an heir for the throne on pain of civil war, should he fail. At the age of eighteen in the year of the coronation (1509) he had been married against his inclination to the Spanish princess Catherine, the widow of his brother Arthur. The queen had had many miscarriages and babies lost in infancy. Only one child survived to maturity and at that a girl, the Princess Mary. Catherine was older than her husband and by 1525 there was scant reason to believe that she could have further offspring. The English a century later would not have been appalled by the prospect of a woman ruler, but early in the sixteenth century England had experienced but one instance of female rule and that one disastrous, under Mathilda. Good Queen Bess's golden age was yet to come. All felt that England must have an heir. The simplest solution would have been for the pope to annul the marriage with Catherine and permit Henry to take another wife. The normal procedure in such a case was to discover some flaw in the marriage, which made it no marriage at all, so that it might be annulled. In this instance there was no difficulty in discovering the flaw because the book of Leviticus in the Old Testament forbade marriage with a deceased brother's wife. On that account both Catherine and Henry had been reluctant to marry till a dispensation from Pope Julius II had removed the impediment. But did not the failure of this union to supply an heir indicate the displeasure of God because of the violation of the Levitical injunction? Had the pope any authority to dispense with the law of God? Henry may perfectly well have believed himself to be under divine judgment and the king's conscience was not at first twinged by the sight of Anne Boleyn who, when the divorce was first bruited, was not yet in the picture.[8]

A further canonical question was whether a pope could declare invalid a dispensation granted by a previous pope. Catherine stood firmly in the way of any annulment because she affirmed that the marriage with Arthur had never been consummated. She was a virgin when she married Henry and no impediment to their marriage existed. The dispensation granted by Julius had not been necessary and there was nothing to set aside. Had Catherine been willing quietly to withdraw into a nunnery she might have saved England for Rome, but she was of the same stuff as Luther and More. Truth is truth.[9]

The pope and the canon lawyers under normal circumstances would have been able to come up with a solution agreeable to Henry, but the circumstances were not normal. Catherine was a Spanish princess, the aunt of Charles, King of Spain and Holy Roman Emperor, and he was of no mind to see despite done to his house and land. The case was referred to the pope. Clement shrank from alienating the emperor, whose prisoner he had lately been. Why risk another *sacco di Roma*? He shrank equally from pushing Henry into schism. The wise course was to stall and this the pope did. Judgment in the case was committed to Cardinal Wolsey, the papal legate in England, but since he would undoubtedly rule in favour of his king, a coadjutor was named in the person of Cardinal Campeggio, with instructions to reach no conclusion.

While all of this was going on Henry undertook to marshal the opinions of the universities and learned men. There is no evidence that a direct inquiry was addressed to Erasmus, but friends solicited his opinion. He was gravely embarrassed because he continued to regard Catherine as "the most saintly queen" and his mind had never been disabused of the image of the glorious prince

Henry. To the king he had dedicated his *Paraphrase of the Gospel of Matthew*, and to the queen, the *Treatise on Matrimony*. When she requested it he had no inkling of what was in the wind, but being secretly apprised, so wrote as to discountenance divorce. Then came a request from Thomas Boleyn, the father of Anne, for a commentary on the twenty-third Psalm. Erasmus had heard enough by now to suspect that his sanction was being solicited by both sides in an impending crisis. "If the twenty-third Psalm had mentioned marriage," said he, "I would never have touched it." Thomas Boleyn was a rare nobleman versed in philosophy and theology. Why affront him by rebuffing so innocent a request? By responding to both parties Erasmus hoped to avoid a rupture with either and thought to have succeeded. But the issue of divorce came into the open. What now did Erasmus think? "I do not wish to be involved in this affair," said he. "What is above us is beyond us," meaning that the case involved intricacies of the canon law in which he was not versed. He saw well enough that the basic immorality in the whole situation lay in the system of dynastic marriages which he abhorred. But since the system was in vogue, and since the peace of the realm depended on having a legitimate heir, the marriage might have to be sacrificed. Erasmus turned for counsel to his legal friend Boniface Amerbach, who proposed adoption.[10] Erasmus for all his disclaimer of competence did render a judgment. "I would rather," said he, "that Jupiter take two Junos than that he put away one."[11] In other words, Erasmus recommended bigamy. So did Martin Luther. And the pope himself proposed an arrangement involving an overlapping of wives.[12]

Henry, unlike Philip of Hesse later on, never entertained this expedient, but he did move in the direction of adopting his natural son by Elizabeth Blount, the cousin of Lord Mountjoy. The lad was now made the Duke of Richmond and was evidently being groomed for the succession. But by this time Anne Boleyn had come upon the stage. She was resolved not to be Henry's mistress, like her sister before her, but England's queen. That ambition disposed also of the suggestion that the Princess Mary be married to some nobleman in the hope of progeny, of which, however, the doctors thought her incapable.[13]

When all of the arguments were in, Campeggio declined to render a decision and prorogued the case from June to the next September. At this point Wolsey might have rendered a judgment as the pope's legate and having done so might have received papal endorsement, but this time Wolsey served, if not his God, at any rate God's vicar rather than his king.[14] Knowing that he would forfeit his position and perhaps his life, he held out for a verdict to be rendered by the pope. Then Henry took over himself and started that train of legislation which culminated in the schism. Thomas More resigned from the chancellorship rather than appear to favour the divorce. Bishop Fisher wrote against it. Archbishop Warham died and was succeeded by Cranmer. The Anglican Church was declared in 1534 to be independent of Rome with the king as the Supreme Head. Refusal to recognize that title would soon bring Erasmus' best beloved friends in England to the block.

Erasmus' spirit was breaking. He was experiencing in any case the loneliness of one who outlives his generation. Where were the friends of yesteryears? Fausto Andrelini had died in 1518. Ammonio, that Italian of whom he was so fond and who had managed for him the dispensations from illegitimacy, had been carried off in forty-eight hours by the sweating sickness when only thirty-three. Batt, who had been so helpful in the years of penury in the Netherlands, had long since been gone, Busleiden too. Colet had been taken and Peter Gilles, with whom Erasmus had been painted by Metsys. Now Warham was gathered to the others and Mountjoy as well.[15]

Erasmus had long been weighed down by diseases.[16] The kidney stone was so excruciating that he envied the martyrs who had to endure only one stroke of the axe or one flare of the faggots.[17] Illness and the rasping of so many attacks made him irritable. This had been true for some time. While he was still in the Netherlands an amanuensis said, "Erasmus is continually blowing up. I simply would not stand for it if I did not know him."[18] His infirmities and nervous depletion made him suspicious. Beneath every diatribe he thought to see the hand of Aleander. There was some ground for his surmise during the Diet of Worms when Aleander was writing to Rome that Erasmus was responsible for the Lutheran affair, but since then there had been a reconciliation. Nevertheless suspicion continued. Aleander tried to allay it and wrote saying, "No one loves you more than I." But on the appearance of the next anonymous attack Erasmus again suspected his old friend.[19] Against known opponents he was forever writing devastating refutations. He did not, like Luther, wield a broadsword, but his rapier was no less deadly. A friend remonstrated: "If any one scratches your cutex you howl as if you had received a lethal wound: can't you understand that men are hurt by your thrusts?"[20] Erasmus claimed that he sought always to conduct a controversy so as never to lose a friend. He came remarkably close to succeeding, but there were periods of intense strain.

At one point the outward circumstances of Erasmus

Freiburg im Breisgau in the age of Erasmus.

were improved. There came a new pope, concerned for reform and favourable to Erasmus. Paul III appointed a committee of high-minded cardinals to advise him as to what was needful by way of reform, and they produced a very frank document. Little came of it, but hopes at first were high.[21] This same pope conferred on Erasmus a prebend at Deventer.[22] Rumour had it that this appointment was designed to supply Erasmus with the funds which would enable him to accept a red hat. Friends were lobbying for him at Rome, but he would have none of it. To empurple his ailing frame would be like decking out a cat in saffron, not to mention all the other objections valid in any case.[23]

Did Erasmus pay a price for this evidence of papal favour? Such insinuations were made in his own day and Huizinga in our day has felt that in the last period he had become simply a reactionary. Indisputably his tone changed. Already in the Basel period he was insisting that he had not been throwing sops to Cerberus in his earlier writings, when he inserted parenthetically that he did not *absolutely* condemn this or that teaching or practice of the Church. The qualifications were sincerely meant and now the refrain was coming to be, "I did not *utterly* condemn monasticism. I did not *utterly* condemn the invocation of the saints or the reverence for images." There is one letter of the Freiburg period which sets forth his position in this regard with great clarity, even though only the saints and the images are involved. To Cardinal Sadoleto he wrote:[24] "I have never condemned either the one or the other, but only superstition, as that a soldier going out to butcher should pray for a safe return, that St. Barbara should be addressed with magical incantations, that the saints should be invoked as if Christ were dead, that particular saints should be given specialities so that Catherine would grant what Barbara would not, that images should be treated as if they were alive, and that folk should bow the head before them, fall on the ground, crawl on the knees, kiss and fondle the carvings." The poem of gratitude to St. Geneviève for a cure, published in the old age of Erasmus, had been composed in his youth.[25] When he prepared a liturgy for the shrine of Loretto, Zasius wrote in surprise to Amerbach, "I like Erasmus' poem, but I don't know what stars impelled him to assign the Virgin to Loretto. I'd leave Loretto to the Italians and revere her in heaven. Don't show this to Erasmus." There was no retrenchment here. Long since Erasmus had derided the superstitions attached to the shrine of the Virgin at Walsingham and at the same time had composed a prayer befitting her cult.[26]

There are other points on which he is alleged seriously to have receded. One is with respect to the Lord's Supper. We have already seen that his position was matured in the controversy with Oecolampadius. His spiritualism inclined him to reject a physical presence. But the words of institution, "This is my body," and the consensus of the Church inclined him to accept it. As to the manner of the presence the Church had given no ruling to be received as dogma. Such statements and no more he was repeating in the Freiburg period.[27] The question became poignant when his friend Amerbach sought his counsel. He agreed with Erasmus on the Lord's Supper. He did not join Erasmus in Freiburg. He did not leave Basel. And in defiance of the order of the town council he did not come to the Lord's Table as interpreted by Oecolampadius. Three times he was brought up before the *Bannherrn*, who had authority to banish.[28] Should he submit? Should he migrate? Erasmus answered:

There is no ambiguity about the presence of Christ's body. As to the manner there is room for doubt. Here the Church disputes rather than pronounces. If your conscience is to be clear you must bear in mind that by submission you may confirm many in their error and you may let yourself in for yielding all down the line. You may tell the *Bannherrn* that it is absurd for them to exercise the constraint of which they complain in the pope. If I were you I would say, "My conscience is not in the clear and he sins who goes contrary to conscience. Let me have more time to think it over. Rather than forfeit integrity I will accept the penalty." If you say that, they may relax rather than lose such a citizen. Don't irritate them by sharp words. I realize it is no easy matter for you to leave. You have your fatherland, relatives by blood and by marriage, wife, home, family, and property. Emigration is burdensome and costly, especially when you are married.[29]

All that we can say in these instances is that loyalty to the Church and her tradition curbed the spiritualist tendencies of Erasmus, but by no means suppressed them, as we shall shortly see.

Did he retrogress as to religious liberty? He did concede
that a seditious and blasphemous heretic might be
executed,[30] but did not define in what extreme contumacy
consisted and never condoned an execution occurring
during his day. But there are two cases in which one may
feel that he did not act in accord with his declared
principles. In 1533 he sent a letter to James VI in Scotland,[31] commending a work of Cochlaeus directed
against Tyndale's translation of the New Testament, the
point being that James should impede its publication in
his domain. Such advice conflicts with the expressed
desire of Erasmus to see the Scriptures disseminated in
the vernaculars. But he did not wish to spread a translation which insinuated heresy, and on this score he would
probably accept the judgment of Thomas More who had
written against Tyndale. Erasmus himself could not read
English. But the point may also have been to avoid the
disturbance which might arise were approval given to an
opponent of the Church. There may be a parallel in the
coincident attempts to stop the burning of Luther's books
and to dissuade Froben from publishing any more. There
is a direct parallel in Luther's suppression of a low
German translation of the New Testament issued by the
Brethren of the Common Life at Rostock on the ground
that it was based on the translation of Luther's rival
Catholic translator, Emser.[32]

A second example is the case of Sebastian Franck, who
is commonly believed to have been banished from Strasbourg at the instance of Erasmus. Franck had published
a world history including an alphabetical list of heretics
in the eyes of the Roman Church. Under the letter E were
the names Eunomius, Eutyches, and Erasmus. Moreover
Franck had applied specifically to the device of the Holy
Roman Emperor the Erasmian stricture on the use of the

eagle, a bird of prey, on the arms of rulers. Erasmus ought not to have taken umbrage at this for what else could he have meant? But now that he was a councillor of the emperor he did not relish so pointed a thrust at his chief. Erasmus remonstrated with the magistrates at Strasbourg for allowing the publication. He suspected at first that Butzer was responsible for the work. Apprised of the mistake Erasmus apologized. Butzer, perhaps the better to clear himself, pushed the case against Franck before the magistrates who expelled him from the city. Whether Erasmus recommended or approved the penalty, we do not know.[33]

Another area in which Erasmus is claimed to have retrogressed is with respect to war. The Turks had invaded Hungary, and at Mohacs King Louis had fallen. They threatened Vienna. Might they be resisted? The answer of Erasmus may be abridged as follows:[34]

The Scripture does not forbid a just war. Paul said that the magistrate bears not the sword in vain to protect the good and punish the bad. And what is war if not the punishment of the many by the many? But we shall have no success against the Turks unless we first mend our lives, free our hearts of all lust of power, of all vindictiveness, unless we stop cheating the people. Flanders was recently inundated. Indulgences were proclaimed and huge sums collected which were then diverted to other ends than relief. Wars cost money. Let monarchs raise it, while at the same time reducing that taxation which causes peasants to die of hunger. Let the clergy withdraw from wars and devote themselves wholly to the things of the spirit. Let us not in fighting the Turks degenerate into Turks. "Well now," you will say, "what is the purpose of this harangue? Do you or do you not approve of fighting?" I answer, "If the Lord were to speak to me I might answer decisively. I do not dissuade from war, but am concerned that it be fought favourably. The best way to subdue the Turks would be to conquer them as the apostles did the Roman empire. If by arms the Turks are conquered they should enjoy all the benefit of our laws and we should seek gradually to bring them to our faith."

The tract is mainly an excoriation of Christian princes for all the ills they have inflicted on each other. Just what does it add up to?

The polemic of Erasmus in his last period against the Protestants became sharper, but it was directed not so much against Luther as against those who were his torment, the Sacramentarians. After the deaths of Zwingli and Oecolampadius the target shifted to Strasbourg where the church was headed by Erasmus' old disciple Martin Butzer, seconded by Capito, who had assisted Erasmus with the printing of the New Testament at Basel, not to mention an entire circle imbued with Erasmian concepts but more radical than he in their application. And the application was the point of the debate. Doctrinal differences became subsidiary, except that Erasmus was at pains to point out that the Evangelicals could not all be right on doctrine since they disagreed with each other. "You wrangle among yourselves," he wrote to Pellikan, "Zwingli and Oecolampadius against Luther and Bugenhagen, Hübmaier against them, and Farel against you[35] . . . not to mention the prophets and the Anabaptists and all the squabbles between Luther, Oecolampadius, and Osiander."[36]

The chief complaint of Erasmus was that the Evangelicals had not brought to pass an improvement in life, in piety, in tolerance, and humility. *Against the Pseudo-evangelicals of Strasbourg*[37] was the title of a tract in which he said:

Where is your dovelike spirit? Did the apostles spread the

Rew zeytung.
Die Schlacht des Turckischen
Reysers mit Ludovico etwan König zu Vngern geschehen am tag Johannis
entheuptung .1 5 z 6.

Item des Türcken feyndtsbrieff / König Ludo-
uico zugesandt vor der schlacht.

Item eyn kleglicher Sendbrieff so die Vngern
dem König jn Polen zugeschickt /
nach der schlacht.

Item etlich naw gezeyten aus Polen.

Rew zeytung vom Habst zu Rome
am.xxvij.tag Septembris geschehen .1 5 z 6.

The King of Hungary routed and killed by the Turks in 1526: the title page of a contemporary account.

gospel after your fashion? You cry out against the luxury of the priests, the ambition of the bishops, the tyranny of the Roman pontiff, the loquacity of the sophists, against prayers, fasts, and masses. But your object is not so much to reform as to destroy. You would root out the wheat with the tares. Look at these Evangelicals. Are they any less addicted to luxury, licence and lucre? The gospel is supposed to make the drunkard sober, the cruel kind. But I can point to some whom it has made worse than they were before. Images are thrown out of the churches, but what good is that if the idols of vice remain? The solemn prayers of the liturgy are ended and some now do not pray at all. The Mass is abolished. I would not abolish the Mass even if it has degenerated into a sordid sacrifice. What better has taken its place?[38] I have not been in these evangelical churches to see for myself, but I have seen people coming out with a fierce mien. Who ever saw any one in their churches beating his breast and weeping? Instead they lacerate the priests in a way conducive to sedition rather than to piety. The cowl is gone. Would that vice had gone with it. And as for freedom, there are those who would rather go into exile than live under your liberty.

How far do you think you have progressed in reforming the Church of Rome? What you have done is to harden it. Formerly one could discuss papal power and purgatory. Now one dares scarcely to whisper. Now we are forced to believe that a man of himself can perform works of genuine merit and that the Virgin can prevail on the Son to influence the Father. Formerly no one was molested for a breach of dietary regulations in private. Now death is the penalty for eating an egg in Lent.

Your principle is unsound that in every respect we can return to the pristine condition of the Church. The primitive state was not altogether ideal. There was drunkenness at the Lord's Supper, debauchery at midnight vigils, and riots attending the election of bishops. In other respects I agree that there has been degeneration, notably in the elaboration of church music and in the punishment of heretics, but on the whole I think, if the Apostle Paul were to return, he would lament not so much the state of the Church as the vices of men.

Among the sects separated from Rome Erasmus had the highest respect for the Anabaptists. Just before leaving Basel he wrote to his friend Ber: "An Anabaptist has just experienced the fate of John the Baptist, except that the one was decapitated, the other burned. Although this sect is of all the most hated by the princes because of anarchy and community of goods, these people have no temple, they establish no kingdom, they defend themselves by no violence and they are said to have many among them much more sincere in morals than others, though what can be sincere if the integrity of the faith is corrupted?"[39] Erasmus apparently regarded as invidious the appropriation by Oecolampadius of all the churches in Basel, giving none whatever to the Anabaptists, though they were numerous.[40] To Cardinal Campeggio he wrote from Freiburg, "I am grieved for the Anabaptists. We might come to an understanding with them if it were only a matter of baptism, but they bring everything into confusion. Yet I hear there are many fine people among them."[41] To Cardinal Fonseca he wrote: "In innocence of life they excel all others. Nevertheless they are oppressed by the sects as much as by the orthodox."[42]

The statement that an understanding might be reached on the subject of baptism is very interesting in view of a passage in Erasmus' preface to his paraphrase of the gospel of Matthew. There he proposed that at the age of puberty the rite of baptism should be re-enacted. The young candidates should first be instructed as to the meaning of the baptismal vow. Then with great solemnity they should publicly make this vow their own. "We actually put on plays in our churches," noted Erasmus, "showing the resurrection, the ascension, the descent of the Spirit, and these performances I do not wholly condemn, but how much more glorious a spectacle it would be to hear the voices of so many youths dedicating themselves to Christ, so many initiates pronouncing their vows, renouncing the world, abjuring Satan; to see new Christians bearing the mark of the Lord on their foreheads, to behold the great crowd of candidates coming up from the sacred laver, to hear the voices of the multitude acclaiming the beginners in Christ. . . . If this were done, we should not have so many at the age of fifty who do not know what was vowed for them in baptism and have not the faintest notion of the meaning of the creeds, the Lord's Prayer, and the sacraments. I know this from conversations and from hearing confessions. And what is worse, there are priests among us who have never given any serious thought to what Christianity is all about. . . . You say that this is the repetition of baptism. No indeed, not any more than daily sprinkling with holy water."[43] That was an unfortunate comparison, for what would one call daily sprinkling if not repetition? Erasmus' opponents with no little plausibility taxed him with subterfuge[44] and indeed it is not too far-fetched to say that he was the only Anabaptist in the sixteenth century, because the Anabaptists insisted that they were simply Baptists, not Anabaptists (that is, repeaters of baptism), since the first baptism in their eyes was no baptism at all. For Erasmus it was, and the difference between his "re-enactment" and "repetition" was purely verbal. No wonder that his strictures on the Anabaptists were comparatively lenient and directed at their social radicalism, notably after the beginnings of the Münster affair.

Yet for all his criticism of the Evangelicals Erasmus did not desist from his efforts at mediation. The Diet of Augsburg in 1530 revived the hope that counsels of moderation might prevail. The leaders on both sides at the Diet felt themselves being sucked into a morass and

frantically turned to the apostle of mediation in the hope
that he might fling some barrier across the path of their
descent. The situation had greatly changed since the Diet
of Worms nine years earlier. In the meantime Lutheranism
had come to be entrenched not only in Saxony but in
other regions of Germany, including Hesse. And other
varieties of Protestantism had arisen. The Diet was not
willing, however, to take cognizance of the Zwinglians
and Anabaptists. The latter had been placed under the
penalty of death by the Diet of Speyer, the year previous,
in 1529. At Augsburg, as at Worms, there was an align-
ment of parties. The emperor hoped for a tentative
compromise, pending a definitive solution by a general
council. If the Lutherans then refused to accept its ruling
they should be constrained by war. The pope did not
want a council lest it clip his wings. The alternatives for
him were a compromise with minimal concessions, or war.
On the Protestant side the Lutherans were ready to "let
goods and kindred go, this mortal life also," rather than
renounce the Augsburg Confession. If confronted by war
the majority would go no further by way of resistance
than to seek the deposition of the emperor through the
electors. There was, however, also a revolutionary party.
Erasmus had little hope that a council would be called,
or, if assembled, would accomplish anything. He favoured
concessions to the Lutherans, which if they would not
accept, they should be accorded the same toleration as the
Jews and the Bohemians. His proposal was the only one
which could have averted the wars of religion, and none
of those in power would listen.[45]

He did not attend the Diet. To a friend he wrote from
Freiburg on July 19, 1530: "Many have urged me to
attend the Diet, but the emperor has not invited me and
if he does I have a better excuse than I relish. I suffer from

vomiting and insomnia."[46] The correspondence was
brisk. Fourteen letters of Erasmus to members of the Diet
are extant, and eight replies. The correspondents on the
Catholic side were members of the entourages of the
emperor and Duke George, and the papal emissary,
Campeggio. On the Protestant side the only one was
Melanchthon. Erasmus had sharp comments for them all.
He cannot be accused of trimming in this instance.

On August 1st Melanchthon wrote from Augsburg:[47]
"The ferocity of Eck is incredible. The princes are
inclined to clemency but he stirs them up. I hear that you
have sought to moderate the emperor. I hope your letters
will have great weight with him. Nothing is worthier of
your wisdom and authority. Nothing will so redound to
your glory as to compose this tumult. We wish to make
it plain that we do not disdain counsels of peace on
equitable conditions. Great changes are under way. May
rulers so act that the Church shall not be prostrated. I beg
you in the name of Christ to exhort the emperor not to
take up arms against those who will accept just conditions."

Erasmus replied the very next day:[48] "No, I have not
written to the emperor. I have written to the Bishop of
Augsburg and to others. You ask me not to desist from
these efforts. Why don't you exhort the other side to
refrain from provocation? I assure you that I will always
seek to curb the rage of the theologians and the cruelty
of the princes." On August 18 Erasmus addressed
Campeggio:[49]

If the emperor awes his enemies by the threat of war I
cannot but laud his prudence. If he seriously intends war I do
not want to be a wet blanket but I am appalled by the thought
of what will happen if once arms are used. Already this evil
is widespread. I confess that the emperor has the greatest

power, but not all nations acknowledge his name. The Germans do, but subject to conditions so that they rule rather than obey. Consider how the resources of the emperor have already been wasted in wars. Consider how such regions as Frisia, Denmark, and Switzerland are disaffected. If the emperor in his piety follows the behest of the pope, he will have still less on which he can rely. Add the Turkish danger which can scarcely be repelled even if we all act together. How useless it is to fight with unwilling soldiers has been made evident in the *sacco di Roma* and the siege of Vienna.

I do not doubt that the emperor is inclined to peace, clemency, and tranquillity. But I do not know by what fate he is constantly dragged despite his intent from war to war. How France has been ravaged! How Italy has been despoiled! The greater part of the world seems to be inundated with blood. The worst of all the vice of war is that the Church herself may be subverted when the people is persuaded that back of all this are the pope and even more the bishops and the abbots. There is reason to fear that the emperor himself may be in peril. May the gods avert this omen!

I execrate the impudence of those who abet the sects, but we must consider not so much what they deserve as that which ministers to the tranquillity of the whole world. Up until now we have not had reason to despair of the Church. Consider how much worse was her plight in the days of Arcadius and Theodosius. Every city had its Arians, pagans, and orthodox Christians. In Africa there were Donatists and Circumcellions. In many places the virus still lurked of the Manichees and of Marcion, not to mention the barbarian invasions. Nevertheless in the midst of such disorders the emperor held the reins without the shedding of blood and gradually the monstrous heresies died out.

Time itself cures irremediable ills. If under certain conditions the sects are tolerated (as in the case of the Bohemians) it will be bad, I admit, but by no means so bad as a war and what a war!

This letter was intercepted and quickly published in a

German translation. Whether Campeggio ever saw it is not known.

To a friend Erasmus wrote on the first of September: [50] "The Augsburg Confession has been submitted. If only the emperor will follow the pope and the pope will consider the Church. The number of cardinals has been increased. I doubt whether this is a good omen. At one time the cardinalate was an honour, now it is a kingdom. When the emperor seems inclined to peace the Evangelicals clamour for war and portray the emperor as a seven-headed monster."

We today know, of course, what happened. The emperor gave the Lutherans a year in which to submit. If they refused, then war and war it would have been had not the emperor been so involved in other wars with Christian kings and prelates.

Erasmus grieved the more because all of the disturbances were emptying the universities and rendering futile the work of his lifetime. The enrolment in the university of Basel in 1521 was sixty, in 1528 only one, and in 1529 none at all. Erfurt likewise declined. So also did Vienna and Wittenberg. There were sometimes more professors than students. Of course later on there was to be a great resurgence. [51] But that which cannot be foreseen is not too great a comfort.

The best way to answer the question whether Erasmus was a reactionary in his last years is to look at his own productions. He wrote commentaries on a number of the psalms, a catechism, a treatise on preaching, and a meditation on preparation for death. All breathe the spirit of the *Enchiridion*.

From the commentaries on the Psalms a few excerpts will suffice:

PSALM 34: *I will bless the Lord at all times.* This you can well do while eating, drinking, sleeping, yes, and I dare say even in playing and in telling yarns for diversion. He who fasts to save money or gain a reputation does not praise the Lord. He who does not fast, if he exercises himself in labours of the body, cares for wife and children, teaches the people or engages in some other work of love, he praises the Lord. He always gives praise whose mind is disposed to prayer, when there is time for praying.[52]

PSALM 84: I do not object to a reverent picture, and to kiss it is like the act of a lover who kisses his beloved's ring in her absence. I do not object to relics, but it is much better to imitate the lives of the saints than to kiss their bones.

Some object to the adoration of the Eucharist, but, if Christ is present, why not? But he should be received in purity of heart, not paraded around in a cart. . . . No one knows whether the priest actually consecrates, but Christ is always present in any case. The Catholic Church teaches that the body and blood are really there. If the divine nature was not separated even from the dead body of Christ why should we not believe that he is in the elements? But there is no need to go beyond this affirmation.[53]

The commentary on the eighty-sixth Psalm reiterates the familiar themes of universalism, the divine mercy, inwardness in religion, emancipation from the thraldom of the senses, the great miracle of a noble character, despondency over the times, the hope of a blessed immortality, and the obligation during this earthly pilgrimage so to live as to glorify the Father. Here are some excerpts:[54]

VERSE 9: *All the nations Thou hast made shall come and bow down before Thee, O Lord.* "All the nations." Not all men have received the gospel, but there is no nation which does not receive the doctrine of Christ. [Does he mean the moral teaching?] What wonder that He who created the nations should restore the nations! What he created through His Son He has recreated through the death of His Son. All the nations, without distinction, will come, for in the amplitude of the people lies the glory of the King. He invites all to the wedding and desires His house to be filled. They come from the shades of ignorance to the light of the gospel, to the worship of the true God, to a life of holiness, to the home of Him who invites them, that is to the Church. Here they are reborn in the sacred laver. Here they put off the old man and put on the new. Here the hands of the priests are laid upon their heads and they receive the Holy Spirit and begin to speak with new tongues. Not in their own righteousness do they come, for they have none. They shall come and bow down before Thee, O God. And what is the meaning of "before Thee"? What place is this? No place at all, for God is a spirit. In thy heart is He. There adore Him. The Church spreads out her tent to receive all nations that in every place they may offer a pure sacrifice in the spirit, dispelling from the mind all human fantasies arising from the senses. Should you rise beyond the angels you would be infinitely removed from Him who inhabits light inaccessible.

VERSE 10: *Thou art great and doest wondrous things.* What wonders He performs! In fountains and streams, in woods and herbs, in precious stones, in sun and stars, and above all in man! What miracles He has wrought in prophets and apostles, in martyrs and saints! The magicians of Egypt turned a rod into a serpent. It is no great miracle to turn a rod into a serpent or a louse into a camel compared with the miracle of turning an idolater into a devout worshipper of God. It is no miracle to wipe out this city or that with bombardment. It is a very great miracle to bring the whole world to the one religion of the gospel by the whole power of the Word.

VERSE 14: *Insolent men have risen up against me.* There is no age which does not have its Herod slaughtering the innocents, which does not have its Annas and Caiaphas, its Scribes and Pharisees, even in the most tranquil times of the Church, let alone in this most turbulent century, in which the nets are rent by dissensions of opinions and spirits. Is then the Church called upon to tolerate within her bosom those who under the name of Christians live like pagans and by their evil words and examples kill more than ever did Herod or Nero? These tyrants destroyed only the body. But evil Christians send many souls to hell. The Church weeps for the massacre of her children and like Rachel refuses to be comforted.

VERSE 17: *Show me a sign of Thy favour.* The time is short. Let us then watch, knowing that God is merciful and gracious. Help is at hand and the assurance of eternal solace, when God shall wipe all tears from our eyes. While, then, upon this our pilgrimage, let us not spurn the aid and solace of God, but sustained by hope, let us co-operate with His grace that men may see our good works and glorify our Father who is in heaven.

In the year 1533 Erasmus again responded to a request from Thomas Boleyn, this time for a catechism. Erasmus may have complied in the hope of conserving the essence of Catholicism within the framework of the Anglican Church. His catechism took the usual form of an exposition of the Apostles' Creed and the Ten Commandments.[55] A persistent note is the distinction often made by Erasmus between the fundamental beliefs requisite for salvation and the points of indifference. Here, as in many other of his writings, we have a partial enumeration of the inconsequentials. The *filioque* clause which divides the Greek and Roman churches is one, and whether those who are alive at Christ's coming will be directly invested with immortality without prior death. As for the disputes about the Eucharist, Erasmus simply passes them over this time and restricts himself to this statement: "In the sacrament of the altar we are enriched with copious grace through the commemoration of the death and in a mystical manner, insofar as may be, we renew in ourselves that one sacrifice to which we owe our salvation."[56]

The Apostles' Creed, he says, though not the work of the apostles, is to be received because of the consensus of the Church, for she had to become more precise in defining the faith after it had been challenged. We have already discussed Erasmus' deference to and defiance of the consensus. We may add here his assertion that every one of the Church Fathers slipped at one point or another. "We are not obliged to believe everything in their writings and if we are in error we are not necessarily heretics. Not every error is heresy. One who is excommunicated is not necessarily cut off from communion with the true Church. A heretic burned at the stake may be regarded by God as a martyr and the one who burns him may be worthier of being burned. But, as a matter of fact, there is more latitude in the Church of Rome than among the heretics."[57]

Once again the whole emphasis of the *Catechism* is on the inwardness of religion. Faith is not mere belief, but rather total commitment. "Faith it is which joins us to God the Father, binds us to Christ our head, and through his spirit adopts us into the number of the sons of God, introduces us to the eternal fellowship of angels and all the saints, dispels the darkness of this life, makes us invincible against all the darts of Satan, consoles us in sorrow with the hope of celestial delight, having always on our lips the words, 'If God is for us who can be against us?'[58] Without faith the sacraments are of no avail. Images are the books of the unlearned but so readily lend themselves to externalism that it might be well if bishops in an orderly fashion should remove them all except the cross."[59] Erasmus at this point conceded more than he had done when writing against the iconoclasts. "War," he continues, "is not absolutely forbidden, but it were better to be killed than to kill."[60]

Erasmus is most consistently himself when, with the medieval mystics, he stands before the cross. "He who with full face fixes his eyes upon Christ crucified and fears to crucify him afresh, when he considers how much he suffered for us who was without blemish, will surely bear with greater patience the afflictions of this life. Who would be so inhuman and ungrateful as not to love in turn him who first loved him and by such benefits prompted him to a life of love?"[61]

The *Catechism* of Erasmus has been said to be closer to fideism than to rationalism, and that is true,[62] but when one considers the many qualifications it is certainly not a lapse into obscurantism.

The treatise *On Preaching* is the proof that despite all disillusionment Erasmus had not lost his faith in the power of the word proclaimed. He would instruct the preacher, after the manner of Augustine, to employ it effectively, using the arts of the rhetorician in sincerity and without rhetorical embellishments. "If elephants can be trained to dance, lions to play, and leopards to hunt, surely preachers," said he, "can be taught to preach."

The preacher should exhibit purity of heart, chastity of body, sanctity of deportment, erudition, wisdom, and above all eloquence worthy of the divine mysteries. Let him remember that the cross will never be lacking to those who sincerely preach the gospel. There are always Herods, Ananiases, Caiaphases, Scribes and Pharisees. There are men of Ephesus who incite the mob and there are those like the Jews before Pilate who cried, "Crucify him! Crucify him!"

The role of the priest is not to kill, but to make souls alive. It is far easier to compel by force than to persuade by speech, much simpler to destroy the body than to convert the mind.

A miracle is considered to be that which goes counter to normal experience as when the Master multiplied the loaves, but is it not a greater miracle that daily a single grain brings forth sixty-fold? It is deemed a miracle that Peter at Pentecost spoke in the languages of all his hearers, but was it not a greater miracle that a fisherman converted three thousand men?

The most important function of the priest is teaching by which he may instruct, admonish, chide, and console. A layman can baptize. All the people can pray. The priest does not always baptize, he does not always absolve, but he should always teach. What good is it to be baptized if one has not been catechized, what good to go to the Lord's Table if one does not know what it means? How shameful that popes should leave this most important function to subordinates and devote themselves to the care of horses, building triumphal arches, favouring satellites, and fawning upon monarchs! Are such men priests of the Church?

In the delivery of sermons do not strive for effect. If you pronounce the word "grunt," don't sound like it. Don't ejaculate everlastingly "O!O!O!" Don't imitate a priest who drilled his congregation when he was reading the account of the passion to shout in unison, "Crucify him! Crucify him!" Don't make a feat of jerking tears. The Italians tell the story of a certain Robert who boasted that he could wring tears from any one. His vicar scoffed. "You sit in my congregation tomorrow and I will make you weep," boasted the preacher. The vicar accepted the wager. Robert gave a moving peroration on the amazing mercy of God and upbraided his audience for ingratitude. "You hard of heart, do you begrudge God even a tear?" The vicar wept. The preacher said, "I win," and sat down. That evening at supper he crowed over his victory. The vicar replied, "I did not weep because of what you said, but to think that a man should so prostitute his gift."[63]

In the *Treatise on Preparation for Death*, more than in all else, Erasmus brings us back to the mood of the *Enchiridion*. "Meditation on death is meditation on true life," he tells us. "Consider all of the promises":

We are assured of victory over death, victory over the flesh, victory over the world and Satan. Christ promises us remission of sins, fruits in this life a hundred-fold, and thereafter life eternal. And for what reason? For the sake of our merit? No indeed, but through the grace of faith which is in Christ Jesus. We are the more secure because he is first our doctor. He first overcame the lapse of Adam, nailed our sins to the cross, sealed our redemption with his blood, which has been confirmed by the testimonies of the prophets, apostles, martyrs, and virgins and by the universal Church of the saints. He added the seal of the Spirit lest we should waver in our confidence. . . . What could we little worms do of ourselves? Christ is our justification. Christ is our victory, Christ is our hope and security. "Unto us a child is born." Unto *us*, born for us, given for us. He it is who teaches us, cures our diseases, casts out demons, for us suffers hunger and thirst, is afflicted, endures the agonies of death, sweats blood, for us is conquered, wounded, dead and resurrected, and sits at the right hand of God the Father.

As we approach death the sacraments are not to be despised, but of greater importance are faith and charity without which all else is vain. I believe there are many not absolved by the priest, not having taken the Eucharist, not having been anointed, not having received Christian burial who rest in peace, while many who have had all the rites of the Church and have been buried next to the altar have gone to hell. There is no point in putting on a cowl. Better to resolve to live a better life if you get well. I knew a noble woman who gave a large sum to a priest to have masses said for her soul at Rome. Her money might better have been spent to obligate the priest never to go to Rome. Some leave everything to a particular monastery for its prayers. Better to turn to all the saints from the foundation of the world than to those of a single order. Christ said, "Come unto me all ye that labour." Take refuge then in his cave in the rocks. Flee to his wounds and you will be safe. The way to enter paradise is the way of the penitent thief. Say simply, "Thy will be done. The world to me is crucified and I to the world."[64]

These, then, are the writings of the Freiburg period. A shift of emphasis they do indeed disclose, but they so far repeat the teaching of a lifetime that one finds them at times somewhat repetitious.

Erasmus was not altogether happy at Freiburg. The city, he said, was costly and dirty and might be captured by the Protestants. Of course he was not altogether happy anywhere, partly because he was in pain so frequently and grew the more petulant. He complained even of his faithful Margaret, the housekeeper who had been with him for twelve years and had followed him from Basel. He grumbled over her vigour in rubbing the laundry until after three washings it was worn through.[65] But if not Freiburg where then? Besançon was attractive because of the Burgundian wine. Were he to go back to the Low Countries would Mary, the regent, welcome him now that he had so long been deaf to her entreaties to return? As far as religion was concerned the location did not greatly matter because every place had become intolerant. He advised a Catholic at Augsburg not to leave if the city became Protestant.[66]

The decision was to return to Basel. The city was tranquil now,[67] and if there, he could see to the printing of his treatise *On Preaching*, though this could have been done also at Freiburg as in earlier cases. An important reason may well have been that his friend Amerbach had found a solution for his crisis of conscience. In 1534 the city of Basel submitted to the inhabitants a new confession which Amerbach found he could sign after the council declared itself willing to accept his interpretation that the body of Christ is substantially present upon the altar but our eating of his body is sacramental. "Whether the bread remains I do not know. The main point is that by faith the soul should be exalted to contemplate on this holy table the Lamb of God that takes away the sins of the world." Basel was satisfied and Amerbach went to the Lord's Table.[68]

He was thereupon made the rector of the nearly extinct university. The date was the first of May 1535. Two weeks later he went to Freiburg to bring Erasmus back to Basel. The suggestion is very plausible that he sought the help of the aged scholar for the revival of the university.[69] Erasmus came back. So enthusiastic was the welcome that the vigorous handshake of the young Oporinus made him cry out for pain.[70]

Basel was tranquil, but the world was not. In Paris *The Placards* were posted containing vicious denunciations of the Mass. In consequence there were some twenty-four burnings and hangings.[71] From England came the news that Fisher and More had been beheaded.[72] Erasmus wrote of More, "By his death I feel myself to be dead."[73] In the dedication of his work *On Preaching* to the Bishop of Augsburg he made mention of Fisher and More "whose like England has never before seen nor ever will again."[74] The young Portuguese guest of Erasmus, Damião de Gois, made him aware that many thought this was saying altogether too little.[75] The Bishop in acknowledging the dedication said that the work contained a comparison between Herod and present-day rulers. Erasmus should have been more specific and should have said that the new Herod had decapitated More and Fisher for the sake of a concubine.[76] Erasmus did not defend himself this time. He would probably have said that a simple statement of the fact would be more shaming than a denunciation.

Basel had its minor irritations. Visitors could not be fended off, and would not leave theology alone. One kept him sitting next to an open fire and argued for three hours. "He would have been at it all night. I had to break in and dismiss him."[77]

In June 1536 his protracted illness neared the end. When, a few days before the climax, Amerbach, Jerome Froben, and Episcopius came to call he twitted them as Job's comforters and asked why they were not tearing their garments and sprinkling ashes on their heads. That was said in Latin. A modern has remarked that no one can be profound in religion who does not express his faith in his native tongue. In that case Erasmus was profound once in his life. As the end approached he was heard to murmur first in Latin "*O Jesu misericordia*, O Jesus have mercy; *Domine libera me*. Lord deliver me. *Domine fac finem*. Lord, bring the end. *Domine miserere mei*, Lord have mercy upon me." And then in Dutch, "*Lieuer Got*, Dear God."[78]

His friend Amerbach reported that he died on July 11th.[79] The monument on his tomb has as the date the 12th. The reason for the difference is that the Europe of the sixteenth century had no Greenwich time with global zones. Each locality set its own clocks. A discrepancy of an hour obtained between the city of Basel and its suburbs. On the one time Erasmus died a little before midnight on the 11th, on the other a little after midnight on the 12th. The ambiguity which beset him in life pursued him in death.

Epilogue

*

ERASMUS at the end of his life felt that his lamps had been blown out by the Lutheran gust. Not that Luther was altogether to blame. The incredible ineptitude of the papacy bore a heavier responsibility. Nor was Luther to be held responsible for the excesses of his followers. On that score Erasmus himself was open to even greater reproach, for the Sacramentarians and iconoclasts claimed to be implementing his ideas. But blame apart, there was no gainsaying the debacle of the Erasmian programme. His followers on both sides of the confessional struggle were being sent by the Catholics to the stake and by the Protestants to the block. His spirit was being extinguished and his hopes belied. The universities were being emptied and the studies by which he hoped to refashion the mind of Europe were falling into desuetude. He could do no more than hope that God in His providence would cause the wrath of men to praise Him and that Christ, as the Master of the play, would give to the tragedy a happy ending.[1] His mood was that of Elijah: "It is enough. Now, O Lord, take away my life. . . . The people of Israel have forsaken Thy covenant, thrown down Thy altars, slain Thy prophets with the sword."[2] The Lord might have answered Erasmus, as He did Elijah, that there were yet in Israel seven thousand who had not bowed the knee to Baal.

The situation varied country by country and century

by century. In some lands by the time of his death he was already in eclipse, in others at the very peak of his influence. In Spain by 1533 his vogue was spent.[3] As the century advanced all traces of Catholic liberalism were extinguished. In Italy the great turning point was the year 1542 which saw the establishment of the Roman Inquisition. In 1559 Caraffa, the one-time friend of Erasmus, became pope as Paul IV and then placed everything Erasmus had ever written on the Index, even that which had nothing to do with religion. The Council of Trent was less drastic and allowed expurgated editions.[4] Among the Italians the vogue of Erasmus was perpetuated only by exiles, such as the Socinians, and such champions of religious liberty as Curio, Mino Celso, and Acontio. Poland, well into the sixties, was the land of refuge for those cast out by Catholics and Protestants. Here a number of the Italians found a refuge. Polish students at the European universities, notably Basel and Tübingen, brought home with them a very lively admiration for Erasmus. Hungary, too, for a time was hospitable.[5] France was divided. The Sorbonne had long since been hostile. An individual Frenchman, Sebastian Castellio, became a great proponent of Erasmian ideas on tolerance. In the age of the Enlightenment Voltaire loved the satire of Erasmus. In Germany Melanchthon, in accord with the spirit of Erasmus, established the pattern of humanist education which prevailed in the revived universities and continued to be dominant until, in the late nineteenth century, the natural sciences encroached upon the humanities and the vernaculars displaced Latin. In the period of the Enlightenment Herder and Goethe found the spirit of Erasmus congenial and Lessing was in his steps when he published the *Wolfenbüttel Fragments* that the devastating attack of Reimarus upon Christianity

Erasmus defaced.

might be refuted or confirmed by honest inquiry. The
Pietists also found much to their liking in the devotional
writings of Erasmus.[6]

England was the land where the influence of Erasmus
was paramount at his death. The entire English Reformation has been characterized as Erasmian, and with
justice, if it be remembered that the vogue of his ideas is
not necessarily to be attributed solely to his personal
impact, since other men of influence in England, like

Colet and More, were of like mind. None can deny the
immense popularity of Erasmian works during the latter
years of Henry VIII and well into the period of Elizabeth.
Thomas Cromwell initiated an extensive programme of
translation in order to bolster the Henrician reform.
Those works of Erasmus were chosen which by criticism
of the papacy could serve to justify the breach and by the
liberalizing of divorce could excuse the setting aside of
the queen. Erasmus, of course, approved of neither. At
the same time the orthodox party brought out one of his
works dealing with the Eucharist to demonstrate his
doctrinal rectitude. An irenic temper is evident on the
part of Catherine Parr, the last wife and widow of Henry
VIII, who sponsored the translation of the *Paraphrases* of
the Gospels under the supervision of the dramatist,
Nicolas Udall. The strongly Catholic Princess Mary would
have done the Gospel of John save for ill health, while
her half brother Edward VI, the most Protestant Tudor
sovereign of the century, decreed that the translation of
the *Paraphrases* should be set up in every parish church in
England. The Elizabethan settlement breathed the spirit
of the Erasmian attempt to achieve comprehension
through minimal doctrinal demands. During this period
the devotional meditations of Erasmus were not
neglected.[7] A survey of the English translations of his
works during the succeeding centuries discloses that the
seventeenth preferred the educational works – the *Colloquies* were used as a school book – the eighteenth the
satirical, notably the *Praise of Folly* and the *Colloquies*, the
nineteenth the pacifist treatises.[8]

The Low Countries were presumably the area where
Erasmus had the most unbroken influence, despite the
readiness of Louvain to follow the lead of the Sorbonne
and Trent. The liberals were Erasmian – Coornhert,

Arminius, Grotius. The Socinian Leclerc in the early eighteenth century brought out a complete, though not a critical, edition of the *Opera Omnia* at Leiden. Significantly Holland was the first country to grant toleration to the Mennonites. The reason for the continuous hold of Erasmus on this area may be that the temper of the land had long since been formed by that tradition in which Erasmus himself stood, the piety of the *Devotio Moderna*.

The twentieth century, particularly in its third decade, has seen a resurgence of interest in Erasmus. Two causes may be assigned. The first is the ecumenical movement. After four hundred and fifty years Catholics and Protestants have resumed the dialogue which was possible in the early years of Luther's revolt and which Erasmus desired to keep open until reunion was achieved. At long last we are ready to reopen the discussion.

The second reason is that our age, like the age of the Reformation – and to an even greater degree – is an age of revolution. Once again the liberals, who desire to bring about social change without violence, are caught between the upper and the nether millstone, and are ground not to flour but to dust. Is drastic reform possible without violence? At this point the discussion with respect to the sixteenth century generally assumes the form of a comparison between the methods of Luther and Erasmus. There are those who lament the roughness of Luther and say that if only he had been gentlemanly like Erasmus reforms would have been gradually achieved, wars of religion would have been avoided, and the Church would not have been rent. To say what would have happened if something had not happened which did happen is always precarious.

To begin with one must recognize that, whether because of or despite the violence, something of value was accomplished. Luther saved the papacy. Such was the judgment of Jacob Burckhardt in his famous study of the Renaissance. He pointed out with great sagacity that the See of Peter in the age of the Renaissance was on the way towards becoming a secularized Italian city-state. If that process had not been arrested the result for the papacy would have been far more drastic than anything which did happen. A secularized Italian city-state would not have continued to command the obedience of the nations, nor even of the other Italian city-states. Luther revived the religious consciousness of Europe. Luther was responsible for the calling of the Council of Trent. The popes persistently opposed the calling of a council lest their wings be clipped. The Lutheran peril at last compelled them to acquiesce in the demands of the emperor that a general council be summoned. These statements are, of course, not meant to imply that the positive contributions of Luther extended no further than the reform of Catholicism, but only to point out that in addition to the beneficial results in the Protestant world there were also beneficial results in the Catholic world.

Such assertions make the question worth asking whether a gentler approach could have accomplished the same results. One is not to forget that a reform of the Church in head and members was no light undertaking. Reforms initiated by individuals had been crushed in the past. Reforms undertaken by popes were circumvented by the curia, and when a pope with reformatory intent, like Paul III, appointed a body of estimable cardinals, who drafted a frank and searching programme of improvement, very little came of it.

To return to Erasmus and Luther, we must recognize that the differences between them as to the method of reform were not as great as is commonly assumed. Luther

was not as violent, nor Erasmus as gentle as generally
supposed. Luther could use intemperate language. He
could use vulgar language. But he was not vindictive
and, if the opponent showed the least sign of yielding,
would call off the fight. Luther's intemperance was con-
fined to words. He did not approve of the use of force on
behalf of religion and condemned Zwingli for taking part
in the battle of Kappel with helmet and sword. Luther
called for violence against the peasants because he disapproved of violence. The common man, he said, must
not take the sword to vindicate his claims, but should
seek redress through constitutional channels and, if these
fail, then through prayer alone. When the peasants
refused to heed his word and broke out in indiscriminate
looting and pillaging of cloisters and of the countryside,
Luther called upon the princes to use violence to suppress
violence. When that was accomplished he pleaded for
mercy towards the vanquished and sympathetic consideration of their legitimate claims. Luther would not
engage in rebellion against the emperor, not even in the
name of religious liberty. If the emperor sought by force
to exterminate Lutheranism, redress must lie through the
constitutional means of deposition by the electors. The
wars of religion did not stem directly from Luther, but
rather from his followers whom he was powerless to
control. He sought to restrain them and indeed returned
from the Wartburg to Wittenberg at peril to his life in
order to curb those who were smashing images and
dragging priests from the altars by their hair. Luther
pleaded for calmness and moderation. "Of course there
are abuses," he said, "but are they eliminated by destroying the objects abused? Men can go wrong with wine and
women. Shall we then prohibit wine and abolish women?
Such haste and violence betray a lack of confidence in

God. . . . Had I wished I might have started a conflagration at Worms. But while I sat still and drank beer with Philip and Amsdorf God dealt the papacy a mighty blow."[9] Luther's counsels of moderation went increasingly unheeded. The question then comes to be whether one is justified in starting a revolution which may well defy control.

On the other hand Erasmus was not so very gentle. He did indeed insist that debate should be conducted with civility. He was not blunt, smashing, and abusive, but he was cutting. If one is to be demolished, does it so much matter whether one is bludgeoned with a club or punctured by a rapier? In some respects Luther's technique was less galling. If he said to an opponent *Du Schwein* (you hog), the other could reply *Du Esel* (you ass), and they could have a merry bout with the same weapons. But when Erasmus lodged an oblique shaft of irony the victim might prefer to writhe in silence than by a retort to reveal how deeply he was touched and hurt.

Which strategy is kinder is hard to say. Erasmus insisted that he did not intend to leave an irremediable wound. He was loath to rupture friendships, but he did wound. And the judgment may be right that actually he did more to discredit monasticism than Luther. The Erasmian spiritualizing of religion, though utterly gentle, led to the drastic measures of Zwingli, Oecolampadius, and Pellikan, and though Erasmus disowned his children, they were not altogether wrong in regarding him as their sire. Ought he then never to have spoken? He declared that had he known what would happen he would have left some things unsaid.[10] Ought he to have left them unsaid for fear chaos would ensue? Luther reproached him saying, "You with your peace-loving theology. You don't care about the truth. Suppose the world does go to smash. God can make another world."[11] This was a characteristic exaggeration. When the peasants were raging Luther did not say, "Let them rage. If they destroy the world God can make another." He was concerned for social order. As for Erasmus, he would not yield on everything for the sake of tranquillity. He said, indeed, that for the sake of peace he would be willing to dissimulate on ten *ambiguous* articles,[12] but not with respect to those which he considered clear.[13] Nor was he at all sure that drastic reform could be accomplished without tumult.[14]

One wonders whether either man could have behaved other than as he did. Luther said, "Ich kann nicht anders" (I cannot do otherwise). And Erasmus said, "I cannot be other than what I am."[15] Are we then driven to assume a determinism of temperament? If that be so, may it not be that each temperament has its place in the strategy of reform which calls for a certain vocationalism? The variant methods complement each other. The one slugs, the other reasons. But if one had not first slugged would the one assailed have recognized that there was anything to reason about? One may bludgeon, the other pierce; one may denounce, the other ridicule. Both desire to keep the attack within bounds and by avoiding violence to keep open the channels of reconciliation. If instead violence is unleashed, what can they do but strive to bring it to heel? and if they fail, have they any recourse other than to repeat that truth is truth and right is right and vindication must be left to time and God?

E.

Notes

*

CHAPTER ONE

1. P. S. Allen begins in much this way in his *Erasmus Lectures and Wayfaring Sketches* (Oxford, 1934). Documentation for the statements can easily be found through the Index to the letters of Erasmus, Volume XII of the *Erasmi Epistolae* (hereafter referred to as *EE*) edited by P. S. and H. M. Allen (Oxford, 1906–1958). The invitation from Francis I is reproduced on p. 15.

2. The chronology of the early life of Erasmus is reviewed by P. S. Allen (*EE* I, app. 2). (Reader, see p. 389 for key to abbreviations in footnotes.) The case for 1469 as the date of birth is set forth by R. R. Post, "Quelques Précisions sur l'année de la naissance d'Érasme (1469) et sur son éducation," *BHR* XXVI (1964), 489–509. He combines the statement of the *Compendium Vitae* (*EE* I, p. 48, l.33) that Erasmus was nine when he went to Deventer and the statement of Erasmus in the *Exomologesis* (*LB* V, 153F) that he witnessed the Jubilee which Post shows to have occurred at Deventer in 1478 and not as at Rome in 1475. The case for 1466 is argued by E. W. Kohls, "Das Geburtsjahr des Erasmus," *Theologische Zeitschrift* XXII (1966), 96–121. He feels that no reliance can be placed upon the *Compendium Vitae* because its authenticity as a work of Erasmus has been impugned by Roland Crahay, "Recherches sur le *Compendium vitae* attribué à Érasme," *BHR* VI (1939), 7–19, 135–153. Kohls points out that nowhere is it said that Erasmus was nine at the time of the jubilee. The more exact statements of Erasmus point to 1466. Post replies that, since Erasmus is not consistent, even his more exact statements do not merit reliance, and one must take the date which best explains the sequence of his early studies. R. R. Post, "Nochmals Erasmus' Geburtsjahr," *TZ* XXII (1966), 319–33. Kohls replies (*ibid.*, 347–59) that the academic sequence is uncertain and we must rely on Erasmus' precise statements as to 1466.

3. *Adagia* 4635; *Auris Bataviae*, LB II, 1084. The name of Erasmus' father, Gerhard, meant "the beloved." Translated into Greek it became "Erasmus," though "Erasmius" was the more correct spelling, which Erasmus in after years regretted not to have adopted. In his first publications he spelled it "Herasmus." The Latin equivalent was "Desiderius," which he later added.

4. *EE* II, 517, l.8.

5. R. R. Post says that Obrecht never was the choir director at Deventer. "Erasmus en het laat-middeleeuwsche Onderwijs," *Bijdragen voor Vaderlandsche Geschiedenis en Oudheidkunde* VII (The Hague, 1936). Compare Jean-Claude Margolin, *Érasme et la Musique*, (Paris, 1965), Index.

6. Albert Hyma, "Erasmus and the Reformation in Germany," *Medievalia et Humanistica* VIII (1954), 99–104.

7. R. R. Post, *De Moderne Devotie* (Amsterdam, 1940). Also, Albert Hyma, *The Christian Renaissance* (New York, 1924).

8. *Imitatio Christi* I, 3, 6; IV, 8, 10; I, 3, 62.

9. Post, *De Moderne Devotie*, p. 134; and Werner Kaegi, "Erasmiana," *Schweizerische Zeitschrift für Geschichte* VII (1957), who cites an article by Kurt Ruh, *Bibliotheca Germanica* VII (1956) on the influence of Bonaventura on the *Devotio*.

10. *Opera Omnia* of Thomas à Kempis, ed. Pohl (1904) III, 55f. Paul Mestwerdt, "Die Anfänge des Erasmus," *Studien zur Kultur und Geschichte der Reformation* II (1917), p. 96. Cf. *Imitatio* I, 1, 7f.

11. *Imitatio Christi* II, 1, 5f.

12. *Ibid.*, I, 1, 43f.

13. The impact of the *Devotio Moderna* on Erasmus is treated by Paul Mestwerdt, "Die Anfänge des Erasmus," *op. cit.*, and by Otto Schottenloher, "Erasmus im Ringen um die humanistische Bildungsform," *Reformationsgeschichtliche Studien und Texte* LXI (1933).

14. Hyma, *Christian Renaissance*, p. 433.

15. Schottenloher, *op. cit.*, 13, note 48. *Lucubrationes* 144, 6.

16. H. E. J. M. Van der Velden, *Rudolphus Agricola* (Leiden, [1911]); Georg Ihm, *Der Humanist Rudolf Agricola* (Paderborn, 1893); Lewis Spitz, *The Religious Renaissance of the German Humanists* (Cambridge, Mass., 1963); and an article in *ARG* LIV, 1 (1963), 1–15.

17. *EE* I, p. 2, line 30f.

18. *EE* II, 447, line 88.

19. *EE* II, 447; possible to get along at the university, lines

166–68; regret not to have joined the Brethren without vows, line 127; age sixteen, line 242.

20. The Grunnius letter, *EE* II, 447.

21. Albert Hyma, *The Youth of Erasmus* (Ann Arbor, Michigan, 1930). The decline of the age is in the Gouda manuscript, p. 252. The specific strictures on the monastic orders are in the published edition, p. 276. The text is in *LB* X, 1691–1743. For a critique of Hyma's contentions, see Rudolf Pfeiffer, "Die Wandlungen der 'Antibarbari' " in *Gedenkschrift zum 400. Todestage des Erasmus von Rotterdam* (Basel, 1936), pp. 50–68.

22. *LB* V, 1239–62.

23. To *Clichthovius*, *LB* IX, 811–14.

24. *LB* V, 1259 A.

25. *Ep.* XIV.

26. *Controversia* I, 5–8.

27. *Omnium Operum Divi Eusebii Hieronymi* . . . Tomus Primus (Froben: Basel, 1516), copy in the Yale Divinity School Library, f. 3.

28. *EE* III, 867, pp. 267–68 (1518).

29. Erasmus did not coin the term. There is a section devoted to the theme in Jean Gerson, *Quarta et nuper conquisita pars Operum Joannis de Gerson* (Strasbourg, 1514), Tertia Pars, *De remediis contra Pusillanimitatem*, f. LXIX. The definition is *nimium timor, desperatio, timor pavidus*. Copy at the Yale Beinecke Library.

30. *EE* I, 8, and other letters to Servatius. This letter is more explicable if Erasmus was eighteen rather than twenty-one. The letter, having no date, can be dated by adding 18 to 1466 or 1469 accordingly.

31. "*Expedit etiam vitare singulares continuas familiaritates vel personarum acceptationes, quae interdum suspicione carnalis affectionis non carent.*" From the Institutes of the Brothers at Zwolle bearing the title *Jacobus Traiecti alias de Voecht Narratio de inchoatione Domus Clericorum in Zwollis*, ed. M. Schoengen, 1908, p. 265, cited by Mestwerdt, *op. cit.*, p. 201, n. 2.

32. *LB* VIII, 551–60.

33. Schottenloher, *op. cit.*, pp. 42–43. Note in particular *EE* IV, 1110 where he says that he wrote the *Antibarbari* to avenge himself with his pen for having been driven away from his beloved studies.

34. Vittorio de Caprareis, "Per la datazione dei due Lettere di Erasmo," *Rivista Storica Italiana* LXIV (1952), 222–31. He shows conclusively, I think, that the dates in the *Erasmi Epistolae* of Allen

for two letters of Erasmus referring to the *Antibarbari* should be
inverted. Both were written to Cornelius. The one indicates that
the work was in its inception and help is solicited. This one Allen
dates in 1494 (*EE* I, 37). The other indicates that a version drafted
some time earlier has been revised. For this one Allen gives the
date 1489 (*EE* I, 30). The dates should be reversed. But this procedure does not date the composition of the *Antibarbari*, which is
itself determinative for the dates of the two letters. Erasmus said
on one occasion that he wrote the first draft when a mere youth
("admodum adolescens," *EE* I, 1, 15–16) and in the preface to the
printed version he said more precisely that he was not yet twenty
("Nondum annum vigesimum," *EE* IV, 1110). Presumably this
means that he was nineteen and the year would be 1488, but
Erasmus was so inexact in his datings that one cannot be sure.

35. *LB* X, 1691.

36. The manuscript and the published versions are printed by
Albert Hyma, *The Youth of Erasmus* (Ann Arbor, 1930), app. B. On
the circumstances, *EE* I, App. V, p. 121.

37. Hyma, *op. cit.*, in particular pp. 327, 290, 251.

38. *Oratio de Pace et Discordia LB* VIII, 546–52. Cf. *EE* I, p. 121,
n. 16.

39. Full documentation in Roland H. Bainton, "The Complaint
of Peace of Erasmus, Classical and Christian Sources," *ARG*
XLII (1951), reprinted in *Collected Essays* (Boston, 1962), 217–36,
and my *Christian Attitudes to War and Peace* (New York, 1960). The
reference to Juvenal is *Satire* XV; to Ovid, *Metamorphoses*, 1, 98;
to Dion of Prusa, *Oratio* XL, 35, ed., Arnim II, p. 55.

40. R. R. Post, *Geschiedenis van Nederland*, Deel II, *Middeleeuwen*
(Amsterdam, 1935). Compare the poem by Erasmus' friend William
Hermann, *Hollandia: bello: penuria: morbo: factionibus iam diu vexata*,
in the collection *Guielermi Hermani . . . . Sylua Odarum*, which
Erasmus published for him in Paris in 1497. There is a copy in the
Morgan Library.

41. *LB* I, 1068.

42. *EE* I, 296, ll. 165–70.

43. *EE* I, p. 311, n. 103, and p. 318, n. 12. Cf. Francis M. Nichols,
The Epistles of Erasmus (see Bibliography under Translations), I, 92.

44. *EE* I, pp. 57–58. The poem is in the collection listed in note
40.

CHAPTER TWO

1. *EE* I, 49, p. 160.
2. *EE* I, 77.
3. *EE* I, 159, l. 24.
4. *EE* I, p. 590, App V.
5. Albert Hyma, *Youth of Erasmus*, pp. 265–267.
6. *Enchiridion*, ed. Holborn, p. 135.
7. *EE* I, 146, l. 25.
8. *LB* V, 68–70.
9. *EE* I, 22, ll. 18–19.
10. *EE* I, p. 58, l. 63.
11. *EE* I, p. 50, l. 103.
12. Augustin Renaudet, "Jean Standonck, un Réformateur Catholique avant la Réforme," *BSPF* LVII (1908), 1–81.
13. Pierre Imbart de la Tour, *Les Origines de la Réforme,* II *L'Église Catholique* (Melun, 1946²).
14. Augustin Renaudet, *Préréforme et Humanisme à Paris 1494–1517* (1953), p. 243.
15. Pierre Debongnie, *Jean Mombaer de Bruxelles* (Louvain, 1928).
16. *EE* I, 73. Mombaer is here spelled Mauburn. On this period compare Margaret Mann Phillips, "Autour du Paris d'Érasme," *Mélanges offerts à M. Abel Lefranc* (Paris, 1936), 113–29.
17. *EE* I, 130, ll. 59–65.
18. Marcel Godet, "La Congrégation de Montaigu 1490–1580," *Bibl. de l'École des Hautes Études,* No. 198 (Paris, 1912).
19. Colloquy, "Fisheaters," Thompson, *Colloquies,* pp. 351–52.
20. *EE* I, 50.
21. *EE* I, 154, ll. 45–47, and p. 50, ll. 107–08.
22. *EE* I, 55, p. 170.
23. *EE* I, 124, p. 287, l. 49. Cf. p. 279.
24. Colloquy, "Inns," Thompson, *Colloquies,* p. 148.
25. *EE* I, 64, pp. 190–92.
26. Ricardo G. Villoslada, "L'Universidad de Paris 1507–1522," *Analecta Gregoriana* XIV, Series Fac. Hist. Eccl. Sect. B (N. 2), cap II, p. 78f.
27. Henry D. Vocht, *Monumenta Humanistica Lovaniensia* (Louvain, 1934), pp. 87 and 265.
28. L. Vives, *Opera,* 2 vols. (Basel, 1555), I, pp. 390–92.

29. Louis Dulieu, "Les 'Théologastres' de l'Univeristé de Paris au Temps d'Érasme et de Rabelais 1496–1536," *BHR* XXVII (1965), pp. 248–71.

30. Bengt Hägglund, "Theologie und Philosophie bei Luther und in der Occamistischen Tradition," *Lunds Universitets Årsskrift* N.F. Avd. 1, Bd. 51, Nr. 4 (1955). See also my article "Michael Servetus and the Trinitarian Speculation of the Middle Ages," first published in *Autour de Michel Servet . . .* (Haarlem, 1953) and reprinted in my *Collected Papers in Church History, Early and Medieval Christianity* (Boston, 1962). Heiko Oberman, *The Harvest of Medieval Theology* (Cambridge, Mass., 1963) represents me (p. 85, note 94) as saying that Occam's position is "obviously indistinguishable from tritheism." I did not have in mind his theological position. He escapes tritheism by a double epistemology.

31. The opening section of the *De Libero Arbitrio.*

32. *LB* VI, 926 E. ff., where in notes on I Tim. 1: 12–13 he gives a long list of the questions which he deemed unprofitable. The Leiden edition does not distinguish the additions of 1519 and 1527, but they are not important as to the point of view.

33. *LB* IV, 469 C.

34. Preface to Hilary, *EE* V, 1334.

35. *LB* VII, 306 E.

36. *LB* VI, 927 C.

37. *LB* VI, 927 C, and *EE* 1, 108, pp. 246–48.

38. *LB* VI, 927 B.

39. Peter Lombard, *Sententiae.* II, I and IV, 5; Aquinas, *Summa Theologica* I, 45, 8.

40. Christian Dolfen, *Die Stellung des Erasmus von Rotterdam zur scholastischen Methode* (Osnabrück, 1936).

41. Paul O. Kristeller, "An Unknown Sermon on St. Stephen by Guillaume Fichet," *Mélanges Eugène Tisserant* VI, *Bibl. Vaticana* (1964), 459–99.

42. A brief sketch of Gaguin in *EE* I, p. 146. Fuller treatments: Louis Thuasne, *Roberti Gaguini Epistolae et Orationes* I (Paris, 1903) and Franco Simone, "Robert Gaguin ed il suo cenacolo umanistico 1478–85," *Aevum, Rassegna di Scienze storiche linguistiche e filologiche* XIII (1939), pp. 410–75.

43. *EE* I, 43.

44. *EE* I, 49. A copy of Hermann's poems is in the Morgan Library.

45. *EE* I, 45, abridged. Gaguin's history is in the Yale Library.

46. *EE* I, 44.

47. Ludwig Geiger, "Studien zur Geschichte des französischen Humanismus," *Vierteljahrschrift für Kultur und Litt. der Ren.* (Berlin, 1886), pp. 1–48. The Yale Library has six of Fausto's publications. The *Epistolae Puerbiales* (1508) has a preface by Beatus Rhenanus who says that in other works Fausto is *genuino poetarum more lasciviusculus*, but in this work he is *integer et modestus*. Cf. Rudolfo Reinier, "Fausto Andrelini," *Giornale Storico della Litteratura Italiana* XIX (1892), 185–93.

48. *EE* I, nos. 96–100.

49. *EE* I, 48, p. 159.

50. *EE* I, 70.

51. For a list of editions, see Margaret Mann Phillips, *The Adages of Erasmus* (Cambridge, England, 1964).

52. Here is a chronological list of the major educational treatises of Erasmus apart from the Colloquies: *Adagia* (1500), followed by ten editions during his lifetime; *De Ratione Studii* (1511); *De Copia Verborum* (1512); *Colloquia* (1519 ff); *De Conscribendis Epistolis* (1522); *De Pronuntiatione* (1528); *De Pueris Instituendis* (1529), of which there is a superb edition with text, translation, notes, and introduction by Jean-Claude Margolin, "Erasme Declamatio de Pueris Instituendis," *Travaux d'Humanisme et Renaissance* LXXVII (Geneva, 1966); *De Civilitate* (1530); *Compendium* of Valla's *Elegantiae* (1531); edition of Gaza's *Greek Grammar* (1516); and two letters in the Allen edition, Nos. 56 and 66.

53. Walter Ruegg, article "Humanität" in the *RGG;* Rudolf Pfeiffer, "Humanitas Erasmiana," *Studien der Bibliothek Warburg* XXII (1931); Helfried Dahlmann, "Clementia Caesaris," *Neue Jahrbücher für Wiss. und Jugendbildung* X (1934).

54. Hannah Holborn Gray, "Renaissance Humanism: the Pursuit of Eloquence," *Journal of the History of Ideas*, XXIV (1963), pp. 497–514.

55. Quintilian, *Institutio Oratoria*, especially the first two books. Jean Gerson, *Opera Omnia*, ed. Dupin (Antwerp, 1706) IV, *Doctrina de Pueris*. Erasmus, *Declamatio de Pueris*, ed. Margolin, see note 52 above. *De Ratione Studii* LB I, 516–30. *EE* I, 56.

56. Cornelius Reedijk, *The Poems of Desiderius Erasmus* (Leiden, 1956), p. 395.

57. *LB* I, 511 E.

58. *De Civilitate Morum Puerilium* LB I, 1034 C–35 B. French translation by J.-C. Margolin, *Érasme par lui-même* (Paris, 1965).

59. Jean Gerson, "De Parvulis trahendis ad Christum," *Opera* (1706) III, 296.

60. *LB* II, 6.

61. Margaret Mann Phillips, *The Adages*, Introduction and translations.

62. R. R. Bolgar, *The Classical Heritage* (Harper Torchbook: New York, 1964), p. 300.

63. Copies (Paris 1500), at Harvard; (Venice, 1508), at Yale.

64. *LB* I, 11.

65. *Colloquies*, ed. Thompson, pp. 585 and 563.

66. Rudolf Hirzel, *Der Dialog*, 2 v., (Leipzig, 1895).

67. *LB* I, 414–23. The biblical references are to Genesis 2:18 and 8:17.

68. *EE*, Index, under *Mountjoy*.

CHAPTER THREE

1. *EE* I, 118, p. 273.

2. *EE* I, 103.

3. On hunting, *EE* III, 894, l. 20. On kissing, *EE* IV, xx, and *LB* V, 678 A. Cf. Craig Thompson, *Colloquies* (Chicago, 1965), pp. 402 and 410. On the English custom, *George Cavendish, Life and Death of Cardinal Wolsey*, ed. Richard Sylvester (Early English Text Soc. 1959), p. 56, ll. 23f. and note on pp. 216–17.

4. *EE* I, 106.

5. *EE* IV, 1211.

6. *EE* I, 116, pp. 269–70.

7. Mark 14:36.

8. John 12:27.

9. *EE* I, 109, 110, and 111. *De Taedio, LB* V, 1263–94.

10. Thumbnail sketches in *EE*. Consult the Index and in *DNB* which gives the remark of Linacre and the sources.

11. *LB* IX, 917 B. In the *Adagia* of 1500, under *Sanctum dare canibus*, Erasmus refers to Dionysius as Paul's disciple.

12. *EE* IV, 999.

13. *EE* I, p. 6.

14. Reedijk, *Poems* No. 45.

15. *EE* I, App. VI, p. 592.

16. *EE* I, 124, p. 288.

17. Sears Jayne, *John Colet and Marsilio Ficino* (Oxford, 1963).

Colet never met Ficino. Also, Leland Miles, *John Colet and the Platonic Tradition* (La-Salle, Indiana, 1961).

18. *EE* I, 126 l. 133.

19. *EE* I, 118 l. 21.

20. M. Van Rhijn, *Studiën over Wessel Gansfort en zijn Tijd* (Utrecht, 1933), pp. 74–90.

21. Gal. 5:16; Rom. 8:13.

22. II Cor. 4:16.

23. II Cor. 4:18.

24. II Cor. 3:6.

25. John 6:53, 63.

26. Mark 7:18–23.

27. The claim that Colet decisively changed the course of Erasmus is suggested by Seebohm, positively stated by Huizinga, rejected by Phillips and Dibbelt. The opinions in question are set forth in: Frederic Seebohm, *Oxford Reformers* (London, 1896), p. 128; J. Huizinga, *Erasmus* (London, 1952), p. 33; Albert Hyma, "Erasmus and the Oxford Reformers" *NAKG* XV (1932), p. 1253 H. Dibbelt, "Erasmus griechische Studien," *Das Gymnasium* LVII (1950), p. 61.

28. *EE* I, 108, pp. 246–49. Cf. *EE* I, 181, pp. 405–06.

29. *EE* I, 48, p. 160.

30. *EE* I, 51, pp. 165–66.

31. *EE* I, 138, p. 320.

32. On the experience at Dover, see *EE* XII, Index, under *Dover*.

33. *EE* I, 181, p. 405.

34. His movements are traced by Allen, *EE* I, p. 357, footnote.

35. *EE* I, pp. 288 and 381. Greek only recently begun, I, 336.

36. *EE* I, 132, ll. 75–76.

37. *EE* I, 138, p. 321, note 41.

38. *EE* I, 152, p. 355.

39. *EE* IV, 1211, p. 508.

40. *EE* IV, 1211, p. 509, note 62.

41. *EE* IV, 1211, p. 527.

42. *EE* I, 182, p. 406.

43. *EE* I, 182, note 181.

44. *EE* VI, 1556, p. 42. Otto Schottenloher, "Erasmus, Johann Poppenreuter und die Entstehung des Enchiridion Militis Christiani," *ARG* XLV, 1 (1954), pp. 109–16.

45. Rom. 8:3.

46. John 16:33.

47. I Cor. 7:28–30.

48. Ex. 16:14.

49. II Cor. 5:16.

50. Luke 18:11–12.

51. Rom. 8:1–8.

52. Psalm 51:19.

53. *EE* I, 185.

54. *EE* I, p. 5. Cf. I, 188. Eulogy of Warham in *LB* VI, 903–05.

55. *EE* IV, 999, p. 18.

56. *EE* I, 7 and 8.

57. *EE* I, 191, p. 422, ll. 1–6.

58. David S. Wiesen, *St. Jerome as a Satirist* (Cornell, New York, 1964).

59. *EE* I, 193, pp. 425–26.

60. Craig Thompson, *Colloquies*, "Charon," and pp. 286, 289, 291.

61. *EE* I, 189, April 1506.

CHAPTER FOUR

1. *EE* I, 59, p. 427. On Erasmus in Italy: Pierre de Nolhac, *Érasme en Italie* (Paris, 1898); Augustin Renaudet, *Érasme et L'Italie* (Paris, 1954).

2. Deno J. Geanakoplos, *Greek Scholars in Venice* (Cambridge, Mass., 1962).

3. *EE* III, 809, p. 267.

4. Text in Cornelius Reedijk, *The Poems of Desiderius Erasmus* (Leiden, 1956). K. A. Meissinger makes much of the poem in his *Erasmus von Rotterdam* (Berlin, 1948). Many in this period considered themselves old at forty. Cf. Creighton Gilbert, "When Did a Man in the Renaissance Grow Old?" *Studies in the Renaissance*, XIV (1967), 7–32.

5. *EE* I, p. 432, note 8. For a conjecture as to the reason, see John J. Mangan, *Life . . . of Erasmus*, 2 vols. (New York, 1927), I, 222–23.

6. *LB* I, 685 A.

7. Ludwig Pastor, *History of the Popes* (English trans.) VI, 281–82.

8. *LB* VI, 455 and IX, 361; *EE* VI, 1756.

9. *LB* II, 338 A.

10. Geanakoplos, *op. cit.* p. 258–59, and "Erasmus and the Aldine Academy of Venice," *Greek, Roman and Byzantine Studies* III (1960), 107–34.

11. *EE* I, 207 and Introduction.

12. *EE* I, pp. 60–61.

13. J. Pasquier, *Jérome Aléandre* (Paris, 1900), p. 21.

14. *EE* I, 256, pp. 503–05.

15. *LB* IX, 1136 B–D, and Colloquy, *Fisheaters.* Erasmus elsewhere specifies kidney stone (*EE* V, 1283, l. 10). He reports passing a huge stone (*EE* VI, 1558, ll. 93–94), of necessity from the bladder. These descriptions do not fit gall stones.

16. *De Pronunciatione,* *LB* I, 914–67.

17. Engelbert Drerup, *Die Schulaussprache des Griechischen,* 2 vols. (Paderborn, 1930), I, 46–75.

18. Margaret Mann Phillips, *The "Adages" of Erasmus* (Cambridge, England, 1964), p. 68.

19. Edgar Wind, *Pagan Mysteries in the Renaissance* (New Haven, 1958). *Festina Lente,* *LB* II, 397 B; M.M. Phillips, *op. cit.*, pp. 171–90.

20. *LB* II, 951 A ff.: M.M. Phillips, *op. cit.*, pp. 308–53.

21. *LB* II, 869 A ff., M.M. Phillips, *op. cit.*, 229–63.

22. *LB* II, 770 C ff., M.M. Phillips, *op. cit.*, 269–96.

23. *EE* I, 207, p. 439.

24. *EE* III, 604, p. 16, note 2.

25. *EE* I, 216, Introduction. Cf. *EE* III, 756. On the forgery, *LB* X, 1688 C, and *EE* X, 2874; on tutoring, *LB* I, 363 B.

26. *LB* X, 1758 E, and *EE* III, 604, note 2. In view of Erasmus' continual preoccupation with death his disclaimer is convincing despite Edgar Wind, "*Aenigma Termini:* the Emblem of Erasmus," *Journal of the Warburg Institute,* I (1937–38), pp. 66–69.

27. *LB* X, 1676 F–1677 and 1758 F.

28. Adage *Spartam nactus es* of 1515, *LB* II, 42: Phillips, *op. cit.*, pp. 305–07.

29. *EE* I, 296.

30. *EE* II, 334, ll.80–83.

31. *LB* I, 993.

32. *LB* X, 1754 C–D. The bull ring may have been formed by a barricade (*LB* V, 458 F). Erasmus compares such fights to gladiatorial combats (*LB* V, 840 D).

33. *LB* IX, 1105 E–1106 A.

34. *EE* I, p. 37.

35. *LB* V, 898–99.

36. *EE* I, 215.

37. *EE* I, 214.

38. *EE* IX, 2465, pp. 206–07.

39. *EE* III, 611, pp. 26–27.

40. *Stultitiae Laus*, *LB* IV, 397–504. Critical edition, J. B. Kan (Hague, 1898). English translation, Hoyt Hudson (Princeton, 1941). Facsimile with Holbein illustrations, H. A. Schmid, 2 vols. (Basel, 1931). Interpretations: Walter Kaiser, *Praisers of Folly* (Cambridge, Mass., 1963); Walter Nigg, *Der christliche Narr* (Zürich, 1956); Clarence H. Miller, "Current English Translations of the Praise of Folly," *Philol. Quarterly*, XLV, 4 (1966).

41. Paul Joachimsen, "Der Humanismus und die Entwicklung des deutschen Geistes," *Deutsche Vierteljahrschrift für Literatur und Wissenschaft* VIII (1930), p. 456.

42. Werner Kaegi. "Hutten und Erasmus," *Historische Vierteljahrschrift* XXII (1924–25), p. 247.

43. *LB* V, 276 B.

44. There is an illuminating discussion of the theme of the fool in the Renaissance by Robert Klein, "Le thème du fou et l'ironie Humaniste," *Umanesimo e Ermeneutica*, *Archivio di Filosofia* (Anno 1963, N. 3), pp. 11–25. For Erasmus' cartoon of himself, see page 293. A literary caricature appears in the *Adagia*, *Herculei Labores*, English translation, Phillips, *Adages*, p. 194. Compare the article by Heckscher listed in the bibliography.

45. J. Huizinga, *Erasmus of Rotterdam* (London, 1952, first published 1924) p. 78.

CHAPTER FIVE

1. Clemente Pizzi, *L'Umanista Andrea Ammonio* (Florence, 1956).

2. *EE*, Index under *Alice More*.

3. H. C. Porter and D. F. S. Thomson, *Erasmus and Cambridge* (Toronto, 1963). On Erasmus' movements: *EE* I, 218, 221, 232, 252. Study of Greek, *EE* App. VI. At Cambridge *EE* I, 245, 281.

4. *Concio de Puero Jesu LB* V, 601 A.

5. J. K. Sowards, "The Lost Two Years of Erasmus," *Studies in the Renaissance* IX (1962), 161–86.

6. *EE* I, 255, p. 501.

7. *EE* III, pp. xxix–xxx.

8. Cornelis Reedijk, *Poems*, App. II, pp. 391–92, and "Een Schimpfdicht van Erasmus op Julius II," *Opstellen . . . . aan Dr. F. K. H. Kossmann* (Nijhoff, Hague, 1958), 186–207.

9. *EE* IV, 1211, pp. 524–26.

10. *EE* II, 333, p. 70.

11. *EE* I, 239, p. 481.

12. *EE* I, 245, p. 492.

13. *EE* I, 262, p. 513.

14. *EE* I, 273, p. 530.

15. *EE* I, 288, p. 553.

16. On May 1, 1519 Erasmus said he had leafed through it some five years earlier: *EE* III, 961 l.38. The text is critically edited by Wallace Ferguson, *Erasmi Opuscula* (Hague, 1933). Cf. R. H. Bainton, "Erasmus and Luther and the Dialogue *Julius Exclusus*," *Festschrift Lau* (Leipzig, 1967).

17. *EE* III, 749, p. 184.

18. The case for Fausto as the author is made by Carl Stange, *Erasmus und Julius II, eine Legende* (Berlin, 1937).

19. *EE* II, 416, pp. 247–48.

20. *EE* III, 809, pp. 266 f.

21. *EE* II, 470.

22. *EE* II, 436.

23. *EE* II, 474.

24. *EE* II, 476, p. 357.

25. Henry de Vocht, *Jerome de Busleyden* (Turnhout, 1950).

26. *LB* IV, 528 F and 540 D.

27. The political thought of Erasmus is treated more fully by: Adriana Wilhelmina de Jongh, *Erasmus Denkbeelden over Staat en Regeering* (Amsterdam, 1927); Ferdinand Geldner, "Die Staatsauffassung und Fürstenlehre des Erasmus von Rotterdam," *Historische Studien* CXCI (1930). Briefer treatments by: Lester K. Born, "The Education of a Christian Prince," *Records of Civilization* XXVII (New York, 1936), translation of the *Institutio* with a long introduction. Fritz Caspari, *Humanism and the Social Order in Tudor England* (Chicago, 1954), 28–49. Pierre Mesnard, *L'Essor de la Philosophie Politique au XVIe Siècle* (Paris, 1936). Wilhelm Maurer, "Das Verhältnis des Staates zur Kirche nach humanistischer Anschauung vornehmlich bei Erasmus," *Aus der Welt der Religion* XIV (1930). He holds that Erasmus went beyond the Middle Ages in treating the state as an entity apart from the rulers. But in medieval political thought, was not the empire an entity apart from

the emperors, at any rate for the philosophical realists? Leo
Spitzer, *Classical and Christian Ideas of World Harmony* (Baltimore,
1963). Erasmus on war: Robert P. Adams, *The Better Part of Valor*
(Seattle, 1962). R. H. Bainton, "The Complaint of Peace of
Erasmus . . ." *ARG* XLII (1951), reprinted in *Collected Essays* I
(Boston, 1962); also, *Christian Attitudes toward War and Peace* (New
York, 1960). The four adages are found in *LB II*, commencing on
pages 106, 551, 869, 951.

28. Eiliv Skard, "Zwei religiös-politische Begriffe Euergetes-
Concordia," *De Norske Videnskapsakademie*, Avh. II Hist.-Filos.-
Kl. No. 2 (1931). John Ferguson, *Moral Values in the Ancient
World* (London, 1958), Chapter VII, *Homonoia*.

29. *Oratio* XL, 35, ed. Arnim II, p. 55. Cf. Harald Fuchs,
"Augustin und der Antike Friedensgedanke," *Neue Philologische
Untersuchungen* III (1926), 101-03.

30. Article "Humanität" in *RGG* and Rudolf Pfeiffer, "Humanitas Erasmiana," *Studien zur Bibl. Warburg* XXII (1931).

31. R. H. Bainton, "The Unity of Mankind in the Classical-
Christian Tradition," *Albert Schweitzer Jubilee Book*, ed. A. A.
Roback (Cambridge, Mass., 1945), reprinted *Collected Essays* III
(Boston, 1964).

32. Rom. 12:16.

33. I Cor. 1:10.

34. I Cor. 12:14f.

35. Matt. 20:25.

36. Rom. 13.

37. Johann Huizinga, "Erasmus über Vaterland und Nationen,"
Gedenkschrift (Basel, 1936), 34–49.

38. *EE* II, 333, p. 70.

39. *EE* V, 1314 and 1342, ll. 536–40.

40. *EE* VIII, 2201, p. 247, and *LB* IX, 489 B.

41. *EE* VII, 1840.

42. *LB* IX, 285 F.

43. *EE* VII, 1885, ll. 47–49.

44. *Ibid.*, and *EE* VII, 2046, ll. 33–34.

45. *LB* VI, 695 C.

46. *LB* IX, 842 A–B.

47. Edward Surtz, *Utopia* (New Haven, 1965), p. 483. *LB* V,
648, 700. *Christian Prince*, ed. Born, p. 228.

48. *LB* V, 648 D.

49. *LB* V, 153 F.

50. *LB* IX, 839–40. Cf. 131–32, 462, 575. Cf. Guido Kisch, *Erasmus und die Jurisprudenz* (Basel, 1960).

51. *LB* IV, 601.

52. *LB* IV, 507–54 and 559–615.

53. Born, *Christian Prince*, p. 160, note 59.

54. *LB* IV, 568 A–B, 571 D. The Christian elements in the *Institutio* are clearly brought out in a discussion of this work in comparison with the writings of Isokrates in antiquity and the interpretations of Isokrates in the Renaissance by Otto Herding, "Isokrates, Erasmus und die *Institutio Principis Christiani*," *Dauer und Wandel der Geschichte,* Festgabe für Kurt von Raumer (Münster, 1966), 144–63.

55. *LB* VII, 265 E.

56. *LB* IX, 623, and VII, 494.

57. *LB* IV, 565 F–566 A, and *EE* VI, 1555.

58. *LB* IV, 562 E.

59. *LB* IV, 585 C.

60. *Ibid.*, 566 B.

61. *EE* IV, 1009.

62. *EE* II, 586, pp. 584–85.

63. *LB* IV, 591 A.

64. *LB* IV, 637 B.

65. *LB* IV, 604 E.

66. *Ibid.*, 603–04.

67. *Dulce Bellum,* Adage 4101, *LB* II, 956 C; *The Adages,* tr. Phillips, p. 320.

68. *EE* II, 586, p. 585.

69. In addition to the *Institutio Principis* cf. *EE* V, 1352, p. 261.

70. See the abundant notes in Edward Surtz, *Utopia.*

71. *EE* III, 603.

72. Gerhard Ritter, *Machtstaat und Utopie* (1940), rev. and tr. as *The Corrupting Influence of Power* (1952).

73. *Dulce Bellum, LB* II, 964 E–965 C.; *The Adages,* tr. Phillips, pp. 340–41.

74. *LB* IV, 609 E.

75. For a bibliography on medieval arbitration, see my *Christian Attitudes,* pp. 116–17.

76. *EE* IX, 2599.

77. Charles W. Ferguson, *Naked to Mine Enemies* (Boston, 1958), pp. 101 and 112.

78. Pierre Mesnard, *L'Essor de la Philosophie Politique au XVIe Siècle* (Paris, 1936), pp. 102 ff.

79. *The Complaint of Peace*, ed. William J. Hirten (*Scholars' Facsimiles and Reprints*, New York, 1946), p. xii.

CHAPTER SIX

1. *EE* II, 302 and 305.

2. Gerhard Ritter, "Erasmus und der deutschen Humanistenkreis am Oberrhein," *Freiburger Universitätsreden* XXIII (1937).

3. *EE* II, 440, p. 279.

4. *EE* II, 305, cf. 302.

5. Fritz Husner, "Die Handschrift der Scholien des Erasmus von Rotterdam zu den Hieronymusbriefen," *Festschrift Gustav Binz* (Basel, 1935), 132–46.

6. Wallace Ferguson, *Erasmi Opuscula* (Hague, 1933), p. 129.

7. Peter G. Bietenholz, "History and Biography in the Work of Erasmus of Rotterdam," *Travaux d'Humanisme et Renaissance*, LXXXVII (1966).

8. Ferguson, *op. cit.*, pp. 177–79, especially lines 1995–98.

9. *Omnium Operum Divi Eusebii Hieronymi* (Froben, Basel, 1516), I, fol. 6 verso and 80 verso.

10. *EE* III, 694, p. 117.

11. Froben asked for the New Testament, *EE* II, 330: The *Complutensian* was in circulation after March 22, 1520, *EE* IV, 1213, note 82; Erasmus did not receive the *Complutensian* until 1522, *EE* II, 373, Introduction. Cf. Aug. Bludau, "Die Beiden ersten Erasmus–Ausgaben des Neuen Testaments und ihre Gegner," *Biblische Studien*, VII, 5 (1902).

12. Franz Delitzsch, "Die Entstehung des Erasmischen Textes des Neuen Testaments, insonderheit des Apokalypse," *Handschriftliche Funde* (Leipzig, 1861).

13. Edited with Introduction by Hajo and Annemarie Holborn, *Desiderius Erasmus R. . . . Ausgewählte Werke* (München, 1933), abbreviation H. Erasmus' prefatory essays were called the *Methodus*, *Apologia*, and *Paraclesis*. In the second edition the *Methodus* was enlarged and entitled *Ratio Theologica*.

14. *EE* II, 337.

15. *Ibid.*, cf. II, 456 and *LB* IX, 752 f.

16. *LB* IX, 790 E–791 D.

17. *H* 152, 167, 169, 183.

18. *Novum Testamentum* 1516, p. 116. LB VI, 215.

19. *LB* IX, 297–80.

20. The statement is in the edition of 1527, p. 697.

21. *LB* IX, 275 B.

22. See note 20.

23. Bruce Metzger, *The Text of the New Testament* (Oxford, 1964), p. 102.

24. *EE* XII under *Lee* in the Index.

25. *LB* IX, 132–33. The statement is in the edition of 1516.

26. *EE* III, 652 and 707.

27. *LB* IX, 17–80.

28. *EE* III, 810.

29. *EE* III, 814, April 1518.

30. *EE* III, 855, 856, 906.

31. *EE* III, 953, April 1519.

32. *EE* VI, 1650, p. 234.

33. *H* 183.

34. *H* 168.

35. *EE* III, 844, p. 332.

36. The *Apologia* for *Sermo*, *LB* IX, 111–22, 446, and annotations on John 1:1.

37. *LB* VI, 335 C from the edition of 1522, vol. II, p. 183.

38. *LB* V, 772 B–C. Cf. the Preface to the Paraphrase of Matthew *LB*, VII**3v.

39. *H* 146–49.

40. *H* 142.

41. Preface to the Paraphrase of Matthew *LB* VII**2 v.

42. *LB* IX, 786 C.

43. *EE* II, 301.

44. *LB* IX, 783 D.

45. Roland H. Bainton, "Interpretations of the Immoralities of the Patriarchs," *Collected Papers* I (Boston, 1962), HTR XXIII, I (1930).

46. *EE* III, 701, line 35.

47. The wars of the Old Testament against the vices, *H* 199. Further examples: *LB* V, 301 C, 467 F, 480, 1028, 1031. The standard passage calling for allegory in the New Testament is Matt. 21:7 where Jesus is portrayed as riding on both the ass and the foal of the ass. Erasmus equates the animals with the Jews and the Gentiles. *LB* VII, 111 D and 242 F.

48. W. Schwarz, *Principles and Problems of Biblical Translation*

(Cambridge, England, 1955). Henri de Lubac, *Exegèse Mediévale* (Aubier, 1964). Sec. Partie II, pp. 427–87 on Erasmus and Christian humanism. Hermann Schlingensiepen, "Erasmus als Exeget," *ZKG* XLVIII NF XI, I (1929).

49. *LB* VII, 199 D–E.

50. *LB* VII, 207 D and 217 A–E.

51. *LB* VII, 220 B.

52. *LB* VII, 209 A–C on Mark 6:56.

53. *LB* VII, 339 F–340 A on Luke 5:19–20. Cf. VII, 170 B on Mark 2:4.

54. *LB* VII, 378 F–379 E on Luke 10:39–42, abridged.

55. *LB* VII, 407–08.

56. *EE* II, 335, p. 83.

57. *EE* II, 446, p. 289.

58. The debate of late as to whether Luther nailed his theses to the door of the church or mailed them to the archbishop is reviewed by Richard Stauffer, "L'Affichage des 95 Thèses Réalité ou Légende?" CXIII, *BSPF* (1967), 332–46.

CHAPTER SEVEN

1. *EE* II, 333, p. 72.

2. *EE* III, 798, 856, 967, p. 589; IV, 1006, pp. 46–47.

3. *EE* III, 697, 700, 701.

4. *Epistulae Obscurorum Virorum*, ed. and tr. G. Stokes (London, 1909).

5. *EE* II, 363; *LB* X, 1640 F–41 A.

6. *Op. cit.* in note 4 above, *Ep.* 59.

7. *Ibid.*, *Ep.* 68.

8. *EE* III, 622.

9. *EE* II, 365; III, 611, p. 28.

10. *EE* IV, 1135 and 1006; *LB* X, 1637 F–1638; *Ep. U. Hutteni*, ed. Böcking (1859), II, 192, 198.

11. Giulio Vallese, *Apotheosis Capnionis* (Naples, 1949), text and Italian translation. English translation, Thompson, *Colloquies*, pp. 79–86.

12. *EE* III, 967, p. 589.

13. *EE* II, 501, pp. 417–18, Dec. 11, 1516.

14. *EE* II, 933, March, 28, 1519.

15. *EE* III, 785, p. 239, l. 37.

16. Luther's Works, Erlangen ed., *ova* I, pp. 341–46.

17. *EE* III, 872, Oct. 17, 1518.

18. *LB* IX, 850.

19. *EE* V, 1299, l. 58; *EE* III, 786, l. 24; 858, ll. 405–08; IV, 1211, p. 512; VIII, 2285, ll. 86–87; *LB* VII, 851–52; IX, 850 C.

20. *LB* IX, 887; VII, 173 F.

21. *LB* X, 1658 B.

22. *LB* VII, 93 D.

23. *EE* IV, 1033, p. 103.

24. *EE* III, 858, p. 375 abridged.

25. *LB* VI, 64 D–E, ed. 1519, copy in the Yale Library.

26. *H* p. 198.

27. *Ibid.*, pp. 205–06 abridged.

28. *Ibid.*, p. 207.

29. *EE* III, 939.

30. *EE* IV, 1033.

31. *EE* V, 1528, l. 11.

32. *EE* IV, 1218; *LB* IX, 690 D.

33. *EE* III, 948, ll. 91–93.

34. *EE* III, 980, p. 606, ll. 53–54.

35. *EE* III, 983, p. 609.

36. *EE* IV, 1113.

37. *EE* IV, 1167, p. 403, ll. 121–22.

38. *EE* IV, 1044, ll. 69–74.

39. Luther's Works *WA* VI, pp. 178–80.

40. *EE* IV, 1030, note 16.

41. *EE* IV, 1040.

42. Luther's Works *WA* VI, 176–80.

43. *EE* IV, 1113, ll. 16–17.

44. *Ibid.*, ll. 33–34.

45. Ferguson, *Opuscula Inedita*, pp. 312–28.

46. Compare the phrases in *EE* IV, 1162 and 1173.

47. *EE* IV, 1153, p. 365; 1167, p. 409; 1183, p. 441.

48. Pacquier, *Aléandre*, pp. 151 ff; *EE* IV, 1195, p. 460.

49. Kalkoff, *Anfänge*, pt. I, p. 22. Other burnings, *EE* IV, 1186, p. 445.

50. *EE* III, 904, note 19; 967, l. 98; IV, 1167, p. 406, l. 273.

51. *EE* IV, 1102, p. 261; 1113, ll. 16–20.

52. *EE* IV, 1153, p. 362, ll. 15–18.

53. *EE* IV, 1113, note 36. Cf. 1055. Hajo Holborn, *Ulrich von Hutten* (Paperback reprint, Harper and Row, 1965).

54. *LB* X, 1639 F–1640 A, 1668 C–D.

55. *EE* IV, 1161, p. 380.

56. *EE* IV, 1203, p. 494, l. 26 and VIII, 2188, p. 216.

57. *Corpus Reformatorum, Melanchthonis Opera* I, No. 624, col. 1083–84.

58. *LB* X, 1645 A–1646; *EE* IV, 1188, p. 448.

59. *EE* IV, 1155, note. Ferguson, *Opuscula Inedita*, p. 332.

60. *Ibid.*, pp. 338–61.

61. On the burning *EE* IV, 1203, p. 494; on the bull and edict *EE* V, 1313, p. 127; Dürer's exclamation *Dürer-Schriftlicher Nachlass*, ed. Hans Rupprich (Berlin, 1956), p. 171.

62. *EE* IV, 1218, ll. 32–34.

63. *LB* X, 1663 A, to Hutten.

64. *LB* X, 1538 A, to Luther.

65. *EE* IV, 1195, ll. 27–29.

66. *EE* IV, 1217.

67. *EE* IV, 1143.

68. *EE* IV, 1219.

69. Theodor Brieger, "Aleander und Luther 1521," *QFRG* I (1884), p. 263. Kalkoff, *Anfänge*, pp. 11–12.

70. Otto Clemen, "Die Lamentationes Petri," *ZKG* XIX (1898), pp. 431–34.

71. *EE* IV, 1236, pp. 586–87.

72. *EE* IV, 1225, ll. 248–49.

73. *EE* IV, 1196, ll. 631–33.

74. *EE* IV, 1239.

CHAPTER EIGHT

1. *LB* X, 1663 C; *EE* IV, 1242, p. 599; X, 2792.

2. *EE* V, 1289, l. 33, and note.

3. R. H. Bainton, *Here I Stand* (New York), 1950, Ch. XII.

4. *EE* V, 1369, l. 38.

5. L. von Muralt und W. Schmid, *Quellen zur Geschichte der Täufer in der Schweiz* (Zürich, 1952), I, 73.

6. *EE* V, 1313.

7. *EE* V, 1324 and 1338.

8. *EE* V, 1352, p. 260.

9. Werner Kaegi, "Hutten und Erasmus," *Historische Vierteljahrschrift* XXII (1924–25), 200–78.

10. *EE* V, 1496, ll. 3–6, and 1444, n. 2.

11. *EE* V, 1356.

12. *EE* V, 1342, pp. 220 ff. Basel, Feb. 1, 1523. Cf. 1331, p. 160.

13. Ed. Böcking, *Ulrichi Hutteni Opera* II (Leipzig, 1859), pp. 180–248.

14. *LB* X, passages in this order: 1637–38, 1661 B, 1643 F, 1650 D, 1651 D–E, 1654 A–F, 1658 A, 1663 A–B, 1672 C–D.

15. *EE* V, 1415, l. 55.

16. *EE* V, 1263, ll. 43–49

17. *EE* V, 1324.

18. *EE* V, 1352, p. 258.

19. *EE* V, 1384, p. 328, ll. 46–47.

20. *EE* V, 1313, pp. 126–28.

21. *EE* V, 1340. In May 1523 Duke George had written to Henry VIII that the crux of the controversy lay in the doctrine of predestination, the denial of free will, and the neglect of good works. Felician Gess, *Akten und Briefe zur Kirchenpolitik Herzog Georgs von Sachsen*, I, 1517–27 (Leipzig, 1905), No. 509. My thanks to John Headley for the reference.

22. *LB* IX, 1197–1214 B, Easter 1522.

23. Thompson, *Colloquies*, pp. 101, 69, 6–7, 216, 156–57.

24. *EE* V, 1384, ll. 90–91.

25. *EE* V, 1367, p. 293, June 3, 1523.

26. *LB* V, 557–88, July 1524, and *EE* V, 1474.

27. *EE* V, 1334, Jan. 5, 1523, selected lines.

28. R. H. Bainton, "Erasmus and *das Wesen des Christentums*," *Glaube, Geist und Geschichte, Festschrift Benz* (Leiden, 1967), 200–06.

29. The longest list is in the annotation on I Tim. I: 13, *LB* VI, 926–28.

30. *EE* VIII, 2134, ll. 110–12. Cf. *EE* IV, 1039, p. 118. Conrad Bittner, "Erasmus und Luther und die Böhmischen Brüder," *Rastloses Schaffen, Festschrift Fr. Lammert* (Stuttgart, 1954), 107–29.

31. *EE* IV, 1183, p. 439.

32. *EE* IV, 1039, p. 118.

33. Thompson, *Inquisitio de Fide* (New Haven, 1950).

34. *WA* I, 353–54, No. 13. English in H. J. Hillerbrand, *The Reformation in its Own Words* (New York, 1964), p. 55.

35. *WA* VII, 3, p. 33. Bonn, ed., p. 23.

36. *De Libero Arbitrio* in *LB* IX. I have used the critical edition of Johannes Walter, *Quellenschriften zur Geschichte des Protestantismus* VIII (1935), abbreviated as *QS*. The *Hyperaspistes* is in *LB* X. Luther's *De Servo Arbitrio* is in the Weimar edition XVIII. I have used the critical edition of Clemen (Bonn, 1913), referred to as

Bonn. I have frequently cast the review of these tracts into direct discourse and have, therefore, used quotes, though many of my summary formulations are not direct citations.

37. *Bonn,* p. 126.

38. *LB* IX, 913 B, 924 C, *Sola Fides* 630; V, 310 B, 327 B.

39. *QS,* pp. 25 and 59.

40. *Bonn,* p. 186.

41. *QS,* p. 26; *LB* X, 1327 E, 1487 A–B, 1528 E. Cf. *EE* VII, 1804, l. 94, where Erasmus says he is deterred by the authority of the Apostle Paul from believing that man can acquire *meritum de congruo* without special grace.

42. *LB* X, 1286 A–E.

43. *QS,* IIIc12, p. 75.

44. *Ibid.,* p. 84.

45. *Ibid.,* p. 56; *LB* X, 1286 B–E.

46. Heiko A. Oberman, *The Harvest of Medieval Theology* (Harvard, 1963), 167–68.

47. *QS,* pp. 80–81.

48. *Bonn* 214. The sophisticated distinctions include that between the *potentia absoluta* and the *potentia ordinata,* that is, between God's absolute power and his established procedure, which is normally dependable. Luther distinguished rather between the hidden God, who allows natural disasters and predetermines destiny, and the revealed God disclosed in Christ.

49. *Bonn,* p. 291.

50. Oberman, *op. cit.*

51. *Supra,* p. 173.

52. *QS,* IV, 13, p. 87.

53. *Ibid.,* p. 3.

54. *Bonn,* p. 100.

55. *Ibid.,* p. 138.

56. *QS,* p. 50 ff., on Exod. 9:12–16 and 33:19.

57. *QS,* p. 17.

58. *Ibid.,* p. 8.

59. *Ibid.,* p. 8, n. 8.

60. *LB* IX, 532 E; X, 1650 D; *EE* V, 1273, p. 44.

61. *Bonn,* p. 111.

62. *Ibid.,* pp. 115, 117.

63. *EE* IV, 1000, p. 28, ll. 45–46; V, 1342, p. 227; *LB* V, 289 B; IX, 448 E.

64. For this and many other designations see Georg Gebhardt,

Die Stellung des Erasmus von Rotterdam zur römischen Kirche (Marburg
a. L., 1966), pp. 114–30.

65. *LB* V, 1171 F.
66. *LB* V, 488 D–E.
67. *LB* V, 322 F.
68. *LB* V, 495 C.
69. *LB* V, 509 F.
70. *LB* V, 498 B.
71. *EE* VI, 1729, ll. 27–28; *LB* IX, 1112 D.
72. *LB* V, 1171 B–C, 1175 A; *LB* IX, 947 C. Thompson,
Inquisitio, p. 100 ff.
73. *LB* V, 496 A.
74. Colloquy, "The Godly Feast," Thompson, *Colloquies,* p. 68.
75. *LB* V, 1175 B.
76. *LB* V, 284 B, 293, 309 F, 528 D, 529, 542 D, 545–46 B.
77. *EE* VI, 1717, p. 352; 1729, p. 372.
78. *LB* V, 1162 F.
79. Klaus Oehler, "Der Consensus omnium" . . . . *Antike und
Abendland,* X (1961), 103–29.
80. Matt. 11:25.
81. *WA* VII, 317.
82. *EE* VII, 1893, p. 216.
83. Matt. 5:32 and 19:9.
84. *LB* IX, 961.
85. *De Sermone Domini in Monte secundum Matthaeum,* Lib. 1, cap.
46.
86. *LB* VI, 691 D.
87. *LB* V, 435.
88. *QS,* Ib2, p. 14.
89. *EE* V, 1352, p. 258.
90. *EE* XI, 3120.
91. *EE* IV, 1219, p. 544. The controversy flared again just before
the death of Erasmus. Luther in 1534 attacked his *Catechism.*
Erasmus replied, while still asserting that he had never called
Luther's doctrine heretical. *LB* X, 1537; the whole tract, 1537–
58.

CHAPTER NINE

1. *EE* V, 1358, p. 276.
2. *EE* V, 1448, p. 458.

3. *EE* V, 1503.

4. *EE* III, 925, note 13.

5. Nathaniel Weiss, "Louis de Berquin, son premier procès 1523," *BSPF* LXVII (1918), p. 180.

6. *EE* VIII, 2188, p. 213.

7. *EE* VI, 1581, p. 105; 1679, ll. 54–55; VIII, 2188, p. 213.

8. Margaret Mann Phillips, "Louis de Berquin et 'L'Enchiridion' d'Érasme," *Rev. du Seizième Siècle*, XVIII (1931), pp. 89–103.

9. *EE* VI, 1697, note 24.

10. *EE* VI, 1579, p. 83, l. 89.

11. *EE* VI, 1581, p. 100.

12. *LB* IX, 814–954.

13. *EE* VI, 1634.

14. *LB* IX, 1106–07.

15. *LB* IX, 1109 A.

16. *LB* I, 995–96.

17. *EE* VII, 2061, pp. 513–14. On the controversy compare *EE* VI, 1706, 1794; VII, 1805, 1948, 2021. On Erasmus in the controversy: Angiolo Gambaro, "Il Ciceronianus di Erasmo da Rotterdam," *Scritti Vari* I (Torino, 1950), 129–84. Benedetto Croce, *Anedotti di Varia Letteratura* (Naples, 1942), 131–40, 327–28, 364. Scott Izora, *Controversies over the Imitation of Cicero* (New York, 1910). Giorgio Petrocchi, *La Dottrina linguistica del Bembo* (Messine, 1959). Giorgio Santangelo, "Le Epistole 'De Imitatione' di Giovanfrancesco Pico della Mirandola e di Pietro Bembo," *N. Coll. di Testi Uman.* XI (Firenze, 1954).

18. Marcel Bataillon, *Erasmo y España* (Buenos Aires, 1950), I, 294.

19. *LB* X, 1678 D.

20. *EE* VII, 1967.

21. *LB* IX, 1015–94.

22. *EE* VII, 1875, ll. 153–55.

23. *EE* X, 2637, p. 4, Introduction.

24. *EE* VII, 1846, July 16, 1527.

25. *EE* VII, 1920.

26. *EE* VI, 1790.

27. *EE* V, 1284.

28. *EE* V, 1291.

29. Thompson, *Colloquies* p. 326.

30. *EE* VII, 2059, October 1, 1528.

31. *EE* V, 1344.

32. *EE* V, 1388.

33. *EE* VI, 1721.

34. *EE* VII, 1854.

35. *EE* VI, 1692; VII, 2048, 2066, 2077. Summary *EE* III, 925, n. 13.

36. Thompson, *Colloquies*, 296–97, 343, 347, 355, 371, 421.

37. *EE* VII, 1889; V, 1276, n. 9.

38. *EE* V, 1510, p. 570.

39. *Tischreden, WA* III, 3392b, *rex amphiboliarium*; 1, 822, *cimex*.

40. Walther Koehler, "Zwingli und Luther," *QFRG* VI (1924), 51–56 with passages from the *Enchiridion* and the Paraphrases on Matt. 26, Mark 14, John 6, and Acts 2.

41. Ernst Staehelin, "Das Lebenswerk Johannes Oekolampadius," *QFRG* XXI (1939).

42. *EE* V, 1510, 1496, p. 548.

43. Th. Burckhardt-Biedermann, *Bonifacius Amerbach und die Reformation* (Basel, 1894), p. 207; and *AK* III, 1253, ll. 51–53.

44. *EE* VII, 1977, ll. 70–73.

45. K. R. Hagenbach, *Joh. Oeklampad und Oswald Myconius* (Elberfeld, 1859), p. 16.

46. *Zwingli Briefe* No. 707, *CR* XCVI, 63.

47. Rudolf Wackernagel, *Geschichte der Stadt Basel* III (Basel, 1924), p. 490, cf. 496.

48. Niklaus Paulus, *Protestantismus und Toleranz im 16 Jhr.* (Freiburg i.B., 1911), p. 196.

49. Wackernagel, *op. cit.*, III, pp. 487, 497, 472.

50. Burckhardt-Biedermann, *op. cit.*, p. 63 f.

51. *EE* VI, 1756.

52. Wackernagel, *op. cit.*, pp. 494, 501, 507, 509-11.

53. *EE* VIII, 2248, p. 317 and *AK* III, 1405.

54. *EE* VIII, 2201.

55. *EE* VI, 1618, 1620.

56. *EE* VI, 1539, ll. 99–101.

57. *EE* VI, 1708, p. 341.

58. *EE* VII, 1893, ll. 77–80.

59. *EE* VI, 1717, ll. 50–56.

60. *EE* VI, 1637, pp. 209–10.

61. *EE* VI, 1638, 1639.

62. *LB* X, 1560 B.

63. *LB* X, 1562 B.

64. *LB* X, 1567 B. Cf. *EE* VI, 1708.

65. *EE* V, 1459, p. 482. Cf. 1523.

66. *EE* V, 1353, p. 268.

67. *EE* VI, 1554, ll. 28-29.

68. *EE* V, 1433, l. 11.

69. *EE* VIII, 2134, p. 113.

70. England, *EE* VII, 1878, 1998; France, V, 1319, 1375; Spain, VI, 1697; Vienna, VII, 2005; Poland, VII, 1805, 2054.

71. Casimir v. Miaskowski, *Erasmiana, Die Korrespondenz des Erasmus von Rotterdam mit Polen* (Paderborn, 1901).

72. *EE* V, 1342, p. 217.

73. *EE* VII, 1926.

74. *EE* VI, 1586; V, 1388, 1408.

75. *EE* V, 1342.

76. *EE* III, 2196, l. 127.

77. *EE* VIII, 2328, ll. 11-12.

78. *EE* VIII, 2202. Reedijk, *Poems* pp. 435-36. On his departure, *EE* VIII, 2149, Introduction.

CHAPTER TEN

1. *EE* IX, 2473, l. 35.

2. *EE* IX, 2459, ll. 4-6 and XI, 3090, p. 276.

3. *LB* V, 620 F, 629-30; 667 A-668 F, 631-33.

4. *LB* IX, 964 E.

5. Psalm 133:1.

6. *LB* V, 676-77.

7. *LB* VI, 691-703.

8. *H* 207-08.

9. *LB* IX, 955-65.

10. *LB* VI, 702 C; and IX, 958 E.

11. *LB* IX, 963 B; and VI, 697 F.

12. *LB* VI, 702 E.

13. *LB* V, 700 D.

14. *LB* IX, 962 F.

15. *H*, 207-08.

16. *H* 207.

17. *LB* VI, 695 E.

18. *LB* VI, 701 E.

19. *LB* VI, 693 B, 701 C-D.

20. *LB* IX, 961; and VI, 692.

21. *LB* VI, 691 D.

22. *LB* V, 716 D, 712 C, 711 C–D.

23. *EE* IV, 1233.

24. Thompson, *Colloquies*, pp. 217–23.

25. *EE* V, 1404.

26. *EE* VIII, 2215, p. 277.

27. *EE* II, 409.

28. *EE* IV, 1247.

29. *EE* IV, 999, p. 19.

30. Jean-Claude Margolin, "Érasme et la Musique," *De Petrarche à Descartes* IX (Paris, 1965), p. 27, and the entire work.

31. *LB* V, 1101 D. Cf. Charles Garside Jr., "Zwingli and the Arts", *Yale Historical Publications*, Miscellany 83 (New Haven, Conn., 1966).

32. *LB* V, 420.

33. W. P. Walker, "Musical Humanism in the Sixteenth and Early Seventeenth Centuries," *Music Review* II, 1 (1941), 1–13.

34. *Supra* p. 245.

35. *LB* IX, 1155 D–E.

36. *LB* V, 159 E, 309 D; and 1100–01 A.

37. *LB* VI, 731 F, Annotation on I Cor. 14 in 1519.

38. *LB* V, 488 B.

39. Matt. 15:8, Mark 7:6 [from Is. 29:13], *LB* IX, 899.

40. *LB* V, 390 F.

41. *LB* V, 488 B–C.

42. *LB* IX, 902.

43. *LB* IX, 617–18.

44. F. Saxl, "Holbein's Illustrations to the Praise of Folly," *Burlington Magazine* LXXXII–LXXXIII (1943), 275–79.

45. *EE* II, 584; III, 601, 669, 683, 684.

46. *EE* III, p. 169, n. 9. Allen's notes on Holbein *EE* V, 1452, p. 470.

47. *EE* VI, 1759. Cf. Alois Gerlo, *Erasmus et ses Portraitistes* (Brussels, 1950), and Paul Ganz, "Die Erasmusbildnisse von Hans Holbein," *Gedenkschrift* (Basel, 1936), p. 260 ff.

48. *EE*, see Index under *Dürer*.

49. *EE* VI, 1558, p. 46.

50. *LB* I, 928 E. Cf. Erwin Panofsky, " 'Nebulae in Pariete'; Notes on Erasmus' Eulogy of Dürer," *Warburg and Courtauld Inst. Journal* XIV (1951), 34–41.

51. *EE* V, 1342, pp. 212–15.

52. *EE* VII, 1809.

53. *LB* 1, 1061–64. Cf. L. Elaut, "Érasme traducteur de Galien," *BHR* XX, 1 (1958), 36–44.

54. *LB* I, 537–44.

55. *LB* I, 543.

56. *EE* III, 788, 818.

57. *LB* I, 539 F.

58. Linacre, *EE* VI, p. 47; Cop, *EE* I, 50 and 124; another doctor, *EE* VI, 1759.

59. *EE* III, 869, 891, 893. .

60. H. N. Cole, "Erasmus and his Diseases," *Jr. Am. Med. Ass.* CXLVIII, 7 (1952).

61. A. Werthemann, *Schädel und Gebeine des Erasmus von Rotterdam* (Basel, 1930).

62. *EE* IV, 1196, ll. 443–44; *EE* I, 296, ll. 53–55, and note 53.

63. Eduard His, "Selbstkarikaturen des Erasmus," *Basler Zeitschrift für Geschichte und Alterumskunde* XLV (1946), 211–13.

64. William S. Heckscher, "Reflections on seeing Holbein's Portrait of Erasmus at Longford Castle." *Essays on the History of Art Presented to Rudolf Wittkower* (Phaidon, 1967), 128–48, plus plates.

65. Thompson, *Colloquies*, "The New Mother," (*Puerpera*). Cf. Jean-Claude Margolin, "L'Idée de Nature dans la Pensée d'Érasme," *Vorträge der Aeneas-Silvius-Stiftung an der Universität Basel* VII, (1967).

66. *EE* VI, 1800.

67. *EE* II, 586, ll. 191–93.

68. *LB* V, 813–14. See use of Ethiopian script on p. 369.

69. Elizabeth Feist Hirsch, "Damião de Gois," *International Archives of the History of Ideas* XIX (The Hague, 1967).

70. *LB* V, *Modus Confitendi* 145–71; *Modus Orandi* 1099–1133.

71. *LB* V, 155 E.

72. *LB* VII **3 verso.

73. *EE* I, 95, l. 6.

74. Paul Althaus, *Forschungen zur Evangelischen Gebetsliteratur*, (Gütersloh, 1927, reprint Hildersheim, 1966).

75. *LB* V, 1201.

CHAPTER ELEVEN

1. Karl Heim Oelrich, "Der Späte Erasmus," *RGST* LXXXVI (1961); *AK* IV, 1519, 1533, 1605.

2. Pierre Mesnard, "Zasius et la Réforme," *ARG* LII, 2 (1961), 145–62.

3. *EE* V, p. 1, note 9; *AK* II, 971, ll. 29–31.

4. *EE* VIII, 2158, p. 164, 2188, p. 120. Cf. Augustin Renaudet, *Études Érasmiennes* (Paris, 1939), 313–14.

5. *EE* IX, 2561.

6. *EE* IX, 2579, ll. 2–5.

7. *EE* X, 2826, p. 253.

8. Allen says that the first public step towards the divorce was taken on May 17, 1527. *EE* VII, 1932, note 64. Erasmus said on May 14, 1533 that the case had been going on for eight years (*EE* X, 2810, l. 16) which takes it back to 1525. For a review of Erasmus' varying judgments as to the proper solution see Allen *EE* X, 2846, p. 271.

9. Garrett Mattingly, *Catherine of Aragon* (Boston, 1941).

10. *EE* VIII, 2256.

11. *EE* VII, 2040.

12. William Walker Rockwell, *Die Doppelehe des Landgrafen Philipp von Hessen* (Marburg, 1904), pp. 295 and 301.

13. Erasmus reviewed the measure of his involvement to Sadoleto, *EE* VIII, 2315, p. 432. Several pages are devoted to Erasmus by Hans Thieme, "Die Ehescheidung Heinrichs VIII. und die europäischen Universitäten," *Juristische Studiengesellschaft Karlsruhe* XXXI (1957).

14. Charles W. Ferguson, *Naked to Mine Enemies* (Boston, 1958), p. 436.

15. *EE* XI, 3090, p. 277; and *EE* Index, under the names.

16. *EE* XI, 2979, 2997. Note comment on XI, 3052, l. 23.

17. *EE* V, 1347, p. 242; VI, 1729, 1735, 1759; XI, 3101.

18. *EE* III, 902, written in 1518.

19. *EE* X, 2638, 2639, 2679, 2680, 2682; XI, 3052. An especially venomous anonymous tract with respect to which Erasmus suspected Aleander was entitled *Racha*. Long lost, it has been discovered and described but not published by Eugenio Massa, "Intorno ad Erasmo: una Polemica che si Credeva Perduta," *Storia e Letteratura Classical and Medieval Studies in honour of Berthold Louis Ullman*, ed. Charles Henderson Jr. II (Rome, 1964), 436–53. Whether it was by Aleander is still an open question.

20. *EE* IX, 2513, ll. 434–37.

21. *EE* XI, 2988.

22. *EE* XI, 3033, 3050, 3063.

23. *EE* XI, 3048, l. 92 and 3007, p. 112.

24. *EE* IX, 2443, pp. 162–63.

25. C. Reedijk, *The Poems*, no. 131.

26. Loretto, see *EE* Index; Walsingham, see Thompson, *Colloquies* p. 296; Zasius' remark, *AK* III, 1030.

27. *EE* IX, 2615, ll. 283–85.

28. Th. Burckhardt-Biedermann, *Bonifacius Amerbach und die Reformation* (Basel, 1894).

29. *EE* IX, 2631.

30. *LB* IX, 906 C; X, 1575–76. Cf. Bainton, *Concerning Heretics*, pp. 30–42.

31. *EE* X, 2886.

32. Kenneth S. Strand, *A Reformation Paradox* (Ann Arbor, 1960).

33. *EE* IX, 2615, ll. 366–67, and *EE* Index under *Franck*. Cf. Eberhard Teufel, *"Landräumig" Sebastian Franck* (Neustadt an der Aisch, 1954). For the hearings before Rath see *Quellen zur Geschichte der Täufer* VII, eds. Krebs und Roth, *Elsass* I (1959), pp. 359, 543.

34. *De Bello Turcico LB* V, 346–68.

35. *EE* VI, 1644.

36. *EE* VI, 1901, ll. 36–38.

37. *LB* X, 1577–87.

38. *EE* VII, 1901, pp. 232–33, ll. 94–96, referring only to the preceding sentence.

39. *EE* VIII, 2149 ll. 40–41, April 13, 1529.

40. *EE* VIII, 2134, ll. 211–13.

41. *EE* VIII, 2341.

42. *EE* VIII, 2134, ll. 213–15.

43. *LB* VII ** 3 verso.

44. *LB* IX, 445 and 558.

45. Peter Rassow, "Die Kaiser-Idee Karls V," *Historische Studien* 217 (Berlin, 1932). Ch. II. Erasmus' pessimism as to a council, *EE* X, 2516, 2761.

46. *EE* VIII, 2355, p. 496.

47. *EE* IX, 2357.

48. *EE* IX, 2358.

49. *EE* IX, 2366.

50. *EE* IX, 2375, p. 26.

51. Karl Heinz Oelrich, *op. cit.*

52. *LB* V, 388 D ff.

53. *LB* V, 501 E, 503 F–504 A.

54. *LB* V, 469–506 *De Amabili Ecclesiae Concordia.*

55. *LB* V, 1133–96

56. *LB* V, 1176 A.

57. *LB* V, 1172 F–1173 A; 1175 A; 1172 A.

58. *LB* V, 1144 B–C.

59. *LB* V, 1187 C; 1188 A.

60. *LB* V, 1193 D–E.

61. *LB* V, 1160 E–F.

62. Rudolf Padberg, "Erasmus als Katechet," *Untersuchungen zur Theologie der Seelsorge* IX (Frieburg i.B., 1936).

63. *LB* V, 788 A, 791 A, 813 F, 815 D, 822 A, 828 C, 831 D, 832 A, 982 A–B.

64. Passages culled from *LB* V, 1293–1318.

65. *EE* X, 2897, p. 347.

66. *EE* X, 2906, l. 79f.

67. *EE* XI, 3049, l. 68f.

68. Burckhardt-Biedermann, *op. cit.* pp. 98–103, 395–400.

69. Cornelis Reedijk, "Das Lebensende des Erasmus," *Basler Zeitschrift* VII (1958), 23–66.

70. *EE* XI, 3025, end of May, note 18.

71. *EE* XI, 3029.

72. *EE* XI, 3037, August 10, 1535.

73. *EE* XI, 3049, l. 163.

74. *LB* V, 770.

75. *EE* XI, 3085, ll. 21–24.

76. *EE* XI, 3073.

77. *EE* XI, 3095, l. 26.

78. *EE* I, pp. 53–54 and 70. Cf. Reedijk, *Lebensende.*

79. *EE* XI, 3141, p. 354. I have lost the reference to the article which explained the discrepancy in terms of the time difference. But that there was such a difference is verified in the following articles brought to my attention by Dr. Hans Guggisberg: M. Fallet-Scheurer, "Die Zeitmessung im alten Basel," *Basler Zeitschrift für Geschichte und Altertumskunde* XV (1916), 237–366, and Hans Stohler, "Die Sonnenuhren am Basler Münster und die alte Basler Stundenzählung," *ibid.* XLI (1942), 253–318.

EPILOGUE

1. Peter G. Bietenholz, *History and Biography in the Work of Erasmus of Rotterdam* (Geneva, 1966) collects a number of passages with this theme.

2. I Kings 19:4, 14.

3. Marcel Bataillon, *Erasmo y España* (Buenos Aires, 1950). 2 vol., p. 365.

4. Andreas Flitner, *Erasmus im Urteil seiner Nachwelt* (Tübingen, 1952).

5. Much interest in Erasmus has been evident of late in Eastern Europe, partly for his own sake and partly with reference to his historical influence country by country. Margolin in his bibliography of Erasmus for the years 1950–61 lists eleven entries for Poland, five for Russia, four for Czechoslovakia, two for Hungary, and one each for Yugoslavia, Rumania, and Turkey.

6. Werner Kaegi, "Erasmus im achzehnten Jahrhundert" in *Gedenkschrift* (Basel, 1936), pp. 205–27.

7. James Kelsey McConica, *English Humanists and Reformation Politics* (Oxford, 1965).

8. Margaret Mann Phillips, "Erasmus and Propaganda: A Study of the Translations of Erasmus in English and French," *Modern Language Review* XXXVIII (1942) 1–17

9. Roland H. Bainton, *Here I Stand*, p. 214.

10. *EE* III, 967, p. 592.

11. *Supra* p. 235.

12. *EE* VI, 1640.

13. *EE* VI, 1581, p. 103.

14. *EE* III, 983, p. 609. Luther may be necessary, *EE* V, 1523, p. 597.

15. *EE* V, 1342, ll. 705 and 996–97.

Bibliography

*

ADAMS, ROBERT P., *The Better Part of Valor* (Seattle, 1962). Deals with the peace literature of the Renaissance.

ALDRIDGE, JOHN WILLIAM, "The Hermeneutic of Erasmus," *Basel Studies of Theology* 2 (Zürich, 1966).

ALLEN, PERCY S., *Erasmus' Services to Learning* (London, 1925). *Erasmus Lectures and Wayfaring Sketches* (Oxford, 1934).

ALLEN, MRS. P. S., "Erasmus on Peace," *Bijdragen van Vaderlandsche Geschiedenis en Oudheidkunde* VII (1936), 235–40.

ALTHAUS, PAUL, *Forschungen zur Evangelischen Gebetsliteratur* (Gütersloh, 1927, reprint Hildersheim, 1966).

APPELT, THEODORE CHARLES, *Studies in the Content and Sources of Erasmus' Adagia* (Chicago, 1942).

AUER, ALFONS, *Die vollkommene Frömmigkeit des Christen* (Düsseldorf, 1954), a study of the *Enchiridion*.

AUGUSTIJN, CORNELIUS, *Erasmus en de Reformatie* (Paris, 1962).

AULOTTE, R., "Une Rivalité d'Humanistes: Érasme et Longueil, Traducteurs de Plutarque," *BHR* XXX, 3 (1968), 549–73.

AXTERS, STEPHANUS, *Geschiedenis van de Vroomheid in de Nederlanden*, Vol. III, *De Moderne Devotie 1380–1550* (Antwerp, 1956).

BAINTON, ROLAND H., "Castellio Concerning Heretics," *Records of Civilization*, XX (1935, reprint Octagon Press, 1965), chapter on Erasmus and religious liberty.

"The Complaint of Peace of Erasmus, Classical and Christian Sources," *ARG* XLII (1951), reprinted in *Collected Essays* I (Boston, 1962).

"The Unity of Mankind in the Classical-Christian Tradition," *Albert Schweitzer Jubilee Book* (Cambridge, Mass., 1945), reprinted in *Collected Essays* III (Boston, 1964).

"The Paraphrases of Erasmus," *ARG* LVII, 12 (1966), *Festschrift* Bornkamm.

"Erasmus and Luther and the Dialogue *Julius Exclusus*," *Festschrift* Lau (Leipzig, 1967).

"Erasmus and the *Wesen des Christentums,*" *Glaube, Geist, Geschichte, Festschrift* Benz (Leiden, 1967).

BAINTON, ROLAND H., "The Responsibilities of Power according to Erasmus of Rotterdam," *The Responsibility of Power, Festschrift* Holborn (New York, 1967).

"Erasmo e L'Italia," *Rivista Storica Italiana* LXXIX, 4 (1967), 944-51.

"Continuity of Thought of Erasmus," *American Council of Learned Societies,* XIX, 5 (May, 1968).

"Erasmus and the Persecuted," Commemorative Volume (Louvain, 1969).

BARON, HANS, "Zur Frage des Ursprungs des deutschen Humanismus," *HZ* CXXXII (1925).

BARTOS, F. M., "Erasmus und die böhmische Reformation," *Communio Viatorum, Ecumenical Institute Comenius Theological Faculty,* Prague, 1 (1958), 116-23, 246-57.

BATAILLON, MARCEL, *Erasmo y España,* 2 vols. (Buenos Aires, 1950), enlarged over the French edition of 1937, more important for the influence of Erasmus in Spain than for his biography.

BERGES, WILHELM, *Die Fürstenspiegel des hohen und späten Mittelalters* (Leipzig, 1938).

BIERLAIRE, FRANZ, "Érasme et Augustin Vincent Caminade," *BHR* XXX, 2 (1968), 357-62.
La Familia d'Erasme (Paris, 1968).

BIETENHOLZ, PETER G., *History and Biography in the Work of Erasmus of Rotterdam* (Geneva, 1966).

BITTNER, KONRAD, "Erasmus und Luther und die Böhmischen Brüder," *Rastloses Schaffen, Festschrift* Fr. Lammert (Stuttgart, 1954), 107-29.

BLOM, N. VAN DER, "Die letzen Worte des Erasmus," *Basler Zeitschrift für Geschichte und Altertumskunde* LXV, Nr. 2 (1965), 195-214.

BLUDAU, AUG., "Die Beiden Ersten Erasmus-Ausgaben des Neuen Testaments und ihre Gegner," *Biblische Studien,* VII, 5 (Freiburg i. Br., 1902).

BOLGAR, R. R., *The Classical Heritage* (New York: Harper & Row Torchbook, 1964).

BORGHI, LAMBERTO, *Umanesimo e concezione religiosa in Erasmo di Rotterdam* (Florence, 1935).

BORNKAMM, KARIN, "Das Verständnis christlicher Unterweisung in den Katechismen von Erasmus und Luther," *Zt. f. Theologie und Kirche* LXV (May, 1968), 204–30.

BOUYER, LOUIS, *Autour d'Érasme* (Paris, 1955), vindicates his orthodoxy.

BRUNS, IVO, "Erasmus als Satiriker," *Deutsche Rundschau*, CIII–IV (1900), 192–205.

BURCKHARDT-BIEDERMANN, TH., *Bonifacius Amerbach und die Reformation* (Basel, 1894).

CANTIMORI, DELIO, "Note su Erasmo e l'Italia," *Studi Germanici*, II, 2 (1937), 145–70. See also *Gedenkschrift*.

CAPRAREIS, VITTORIO DE, "Per la datazione dei due Lettere di Erasmo," *Rivista Storica Italiana*, LXIV (1952), 222–31.

CASPARI, FRITZ, *Humanism and the Social Order in Tudor England* (Chicago, 1954).

CHAMBERS, R. W., *Thomas More* (Ann Arbor, 1958).

CLEBSCH, WILLIAM, "John Colet and the Reformation," *Anglican Theological Review*, XXXVIII (1955).

CLEMEN, OTTO, "Die Lamentationes Petri," *ZKG* XIX (1898), 431–34.

COLE, H. N., "Erasmus and his Diseases," *Journal of the American Medical Association* (February 16, 1952), CXLVIII, 7.

CONSTANTINESCU BAGDAT, ELISE, *La "Querela Pacis" d'Érasme* (Paris, 1924), translation and Introduction.

COPPENS, JOSEPH, "Les Idées reformistes d'Érasme dans les préfaces aux Paraphrases du Nouveau Testament," *Scrinium Lovaniense* (Louvain, 1961), 345–71.

Courants Religieux et Humanisme à la fin du XVe et au début du XVIe Siècle. Colloque Strasbourg May, 1957 (Paris, 1959).
See Renaudet on Erasmus at Paris; Bataillon on "évangelisme" in Spain; Halkin on the *Devotio Moderna*; Margaret Mann Phillips on the philosophy of Christ in the *Adages*; Walker on Origen in France; Dagnes on the "évangelisme" of Lefèvre; and other articles of less interest for Erasmus.

CRAHAY, ROLAND, "Recherches sur le Compendium Vitae attribué à Erasme," *BHR* VI (1939), 1–19 and 135–53.

DAHLMANN, HELFRIED, "Clementia Caesaris," *Neue Jahrbücher für Wissenschaft und Jugendbildung*, X (1934).

DELARUELLE, LOUIS, "Guillaume Budé," *Bibliothèque de l'École des Hautes Études* (Paris, 1907).

DELITZSCH, FRANZ, "Die Entstehung des Erasmischen Textes

des Neuen Testaments, insonderheit der Apocalypse," *Hand-schriftliche Funde* (Leipzing, 1861).

DIBBELT, HERMANN, "Erasmus' Griechische Studien," *Das Gymnasium* LVII (1950), 55–71.

DOLAN, JOHN P., *Erasmus, Handbook of the Militant Christian* (Notre Dame, Indiana, 1962), translation and Introduction to the *Enchiridion*.

DOLFEN, CHRISTIAN, *Die Stellung des Erasmus von Rotterdam zur scholastischen Methode* (Osnabrück, 1936).

DRERUP, ENGELBERT, *Die Schulaussprache des Griechischen*, 2 vols. (Paderborn, 1930), on Erasmus 1, 46–75.

DROZ, E., "Pierre de Vingle, l'Imprimeur de Farel," *Aspects de la Propagande Religieuse* (Geneva, 1957), 61–64, on a French translation of the *Enchiridion* published at Lyons.

DRUMMOND, ROBERT B., *Erasmus*, 2 vols. (London, 1873).

DULIEU, LOUIS, "Les 'Théologastres' de l'Université de Paris au Temps d'Érasme et de Rabelais," *BHR* XXVII, 1 (1965) 248–71.

ELAUT, L., "Érasme traducteur de Galien," *BHR* XX, 1 (1958), 36–44.

EMERTON, EPHRAIM, *Desiderius Erasmus* (New York, 1899). Emerton claims that Erasmus taught the essential rightness of the natural, the value of individual judgment, and the revolt of the mind against arbitrary limitations.

ETIENNE, JACQUES, "Spiritualisme érasmien et théologiens louvanistes" (Louvain, 1956), *Université Catholique Louvaniensis*, Diss. III, 3.

EXNER, HELMUT, "Der Einfluss Erasmus auf die Englische Bildungsidee," *Neue Deutsche Forschungen*, XIII (Berlin, 1939).

FAREL, COMITÉ, *Guillaume Farel* (Neuchatel, Paris, 1930).

FERGUSON, CHARLES W., *Naked to Mine Enemies* (Boston, 1958).

FERGUSON, JOHN, *Moral Values in the Ancient World* (London, 1958), see chapter on *Homonoia*.

FERGUSON, WALLACE K., "Renaissance Tendencies in the Religious Thought of Erasmus," *JHI* XV, 4 (Oct., 1954), 499–508.
"The Church in a Changing World: A Contribution to the Understanding of the Renaissance," *AHR* (Oct., 1953).
Erasmi Opuscula (Hague, 1933).

FERRET, P., *La Faculté de Théologie de Paris—Moyen Age*, IV (Paris, 1897).

FEUGÈRE, GASTON, *Érasme* (Paris, 1874), makes Erasmus a prudent sceptic.

FLITNER, ANDREAS, *Erasmus im Urteil siener Nachwelt* (Tübingen, 1952), down to the eighteenth century.

FRANCKE, KUNO, "Erasmus als Denker und Künstler," *Internationale Monatsschrift für Wissenschaft Kunst und Technik*, VI (1912), 270–91.

FRICKE, DIETMAR, *Die Französischen Fassungen der Institutio Principis Christiani des Erasmus von Rotterdam* (Geneva, 1967).

FROUDE, JAMES ANTHONY, *Life and Letters of Erasmus* (London, 1894), written in a lively style with appreciation for the anti-dogmatic aspect of Erasmus.

FUCHS, HARALD, "Augustin und der Antike Friedensgedanke," *Neue Philologische Untersuchungen*, III (1926).

GAMBARO, ANGIOLO, "Il Ciceronianus di Erasmo," *Scritti Vari*, I (Torino, 1950), 129–82.

GANZ, PAUL, "Die Erasmus Bildnisse von Hans Holbein," *Gedenkschrift* (Basel, 1936).

GARROD, H. W., "Erasmus and his English Patrons," *The Library*, V, Ser. IV, 1 (June, 1949), 1–13.

GARSIDE, CHARLES, "Zwingli and the Arts," *Yale Historical Publications*, Miscellany 83 (New Haven, 1966).

GEANOKOPLOS, DENO JOHN, *Greek Scholars in Venice* (Cambridge, Mass., 1962).
"Erasmus and the Aldine Academy of Venice," *Greek, Roman and Byzantine Studies* (1960), 107–34.

GEBHARDT, GEORG, *Die Stellung des Erasmus von Rotterdam zur Römischen Kirche* (Marburg a. L., 1967), reproduction from typescript. A full collection of the statements of Erasmus primarily in his later period as to why he would not leave the Church of Rome.

Gedenkschrift zum 400 Todestage des Erasmus von Rotterdam (Basel, 1936). Allen's essay in *Wayfaring Sketches* is repeated; Huizinga writes on the national feeling of Erasmus; Pfeiffer traces the fortunes of the *Antibarbari*; Ruegg compares the *Moria* with the *Utopia*; Croce describes the relations of Erasmus to the Neapolitan circle; Cantimori calls attention to the comparative lack of influence of Erasmus in Italy; Sabbadini deals with Ciceronianism; Gertrud Jung studies Erasmus in relation to Vives; Liechtenhan deals with Erasmus' political hopes; Staehelin takes up Erasmus and Oecolampadius; Scherrer discusses Erasmus as handled by Murner; Kaegi writes on Erasmus in the eighteenth century; Husner describes the library of Erasmus; and Ganz deals with the Holbein portraits.

GEIGER, LUDWIG, "Studien zur Geschichte des französischen Humanismus," *Vierteljahrschrift für Kultur und Litteratur der Renaissance I* (Berlin, 1886), 1–48.

GELDER, EMMO, H. A. VAN, *Erasmus Schilders en Rederijkers* (Groningen, 1959), anticipations of Erasmian ideas in the Netherlands, impact of Erasmus on the popular drama.

GELDNER, FERDINAND, "Die Staatsauffassung und Fürstenlehre des Erasmus von Rotterdam," *Historische Studien*, CXCI (1930).

GERLO, ALOIS, *Erasmus et ses Portraitistes* (Brussels, 1950).

GILMORE, MYRON P., *Humanists and Jurists* (Cambridge, Mass. 1963).
The World of Humanism (New York, 1952).

GODET, MARCEL, "La Congrégation de Montaigu 1490–1580," *Bibliothèque de l'École des Hautes Études*, No. 198 (Paris, 1912).

GRAY, HANNA H., "Renaissance Humanism: the Pursuit of Eloquence," *JHI* XXIV (1963), 497–511.

GUARNESCHELLI, JOHN, *Erasmus' Concept of the Church 1499–1524* (unpublished dissertation Yale University, 1965).

GUNDERSHEIMER, WERNER L., "Erasmus and the Christian Cabala," *Journal of the Warburg and Courtauld Institutes* XXVI (1963), 33–53.

HÄGGLUND, BERNT, "Theologie und Philosophie bei Luther und in der Occamistischen Tradition," *Lunds Universitets Årsskrift*, N. F. Avd. I, Bd. LI, 4 (1955).

HAGENBACH, K. R., *Joh. Oekolampad und Oswald Myconius* (Elberfeld, 1859).

HARBISON, E. HARRIS, *The Christian Scholar in the Age of the Reformation* (New York, 1936).

HECKSCHER, WILLIAM S., "Reflections on Seeing Holbein's Portrait of Erasmus at Longford Castle," *Essays in the History of Art presented to Rudolf Wittkower* (London, 1967), 128–48 plus plates.

HEEP, MARTHA, "Die Colloquia Familiaria des Erasmus und Lucian," *Hermaea*, XVIII (1927).

HENDRIKS, OLAF, *Erasmus en Leven* (Bussum, 1946).

HERDING, OTTO, "Isokrates, Erasmus und die *Institutio Principis Christiani*," *Dauer und Wandel der Geschichte*, Festgabe für Kurt von Raumer (Münster, 1966).

HERMANNS, MARIA, *Erasmus v.R., und seine ärtzlichen Freunde* (Würzburg, 1937).

HIRSCH, ELIZABETH FEIST, "Damião de Gois," *International Archives of the History of Ideas*, 19 (The Hague, 1967).

HIS, EDUARD, "Selbstkarikaturen des Erasmus," *Basler Zeitschrift für Geschichte*, XLV (1946), 211–12.

HOFER, JOHANN MICHAEL, *Die Stellung des Desiderius Erasmus und des Johann Ludwig Vives zur Pädagogik des Quintilian* (Erlangen, 1910).

HOOGEWERFF, G. J., "Het Bezoek van Erasmus aan Kardinal Domenico Grimani," *Nederlandsch Historisch Institut Mededeelingen* (Rome), Ser. 3, t. 5 (1947), xxvi–xliii. Taxes Erasmus with inaccuracy.

HUIZINGA, JOHANN, *Erasmus* (New York, 1924; London, 1952). Shows fine feeling for the Erasmian spirit of moderation.

Erasmus, Gedenkrede (Oct. 24, 1936), reprinted in *Parerga* (Basel, 1945).

"Erasmus über Vaterland und Nationen," *Gedenkschrift* (Basel, 1936), 34–49.

HUSNER, FRITZ, "Die Handschrift Scholien des Er.v.R. zu den Hieronymusbriefen," *Festschrift Gustav Binz* (Basel, 1935).

HYMA, ALBERT, *The Christian Renaissance* (New York, 1924).

The Youth of Erasmus (Ann Arbor, 1930).

"Erasmus and the Oxford Reformers," *NAKG* XV (1932), 69–92, 97–134. Claims rightly, I think, that the English influence on Erasmus has been exaggerated.

"The Continental Origins of English Humanism," *HLQ* IV (1940–41), 1–25.

"Erasmus and the Reformation in Germany," *Medievalia et Humanistica*, VIII (1954).

IHM, GEORG, *Der Humanist Rudolf Agricola* (Paderborn, 1893).

IMBART DE LA TOUR, PIERRE, *Les Origines de la Réforme*, II, *L'Église Catholique et la Crise de la Renaissance* (Melun, 1946²).

IONGH, ADRIANA WILHELMINA, *Erasmus Denkbeelden over Staat en Regeering* (Amsterdam, 1927).

JAYNE, SEARS, *John Colet and Marsilio Ficino* (Oxford, 1963).

JOACHIMSEN, PAUL, "Der Humanismus und die Entwicklung des deutschen Geistes," *Deutsche Vierteljahrschrift für Literatur und Wissenschaft* VIII (1930), 419–80.

"Renaissance, Humanismus und Reformation," *Zeitwende*, II (1925), 402–25.

KAEGI, WERNER, "Erasmica," *Schweizerische Zeitschrift für Geschichte*, VII (1957).

"Hutten und Erasmus" *Historische Vierteljahrschrift*, XXII (1924–25), 200–78, 461–514. See *Gedenkschrift*.

"Vom Mythos Basels," *Discordia Concors Festchrift Edgar Bonjour* (Basel, 1968), 133–52.

KAERST, J., *Die Antike Idee der Oekumene* (Leipzig, 1903).

KAISER, WALTER, *Praisers of Folly* (Cambridge, Mass. 1963).

KALKOFF, PAUL, "Die Anfänge der Gegenreformation in den Niederlanden," *SVRG* Pt. 1, LXXIX (1903), Pt. II, LXXXI (1904).

"Erasmus und Luther und Friedrich der Weise," *SVRG* CXXXII (1919).

"Die Vermittlungspolitik des Erasmus," *ARG* I (1903–4), 1–83.

KISCH, GUIDO, *Erasmus und die Jurisprudenz seiner Zeit* (Basel, 1960).

KLEIN, ROBERT, "Le thème du fou et l'Ironie Humaniste," *Umanesimo e Ermeneutica, Archivo di Filosofia* (Anno 1963, N.3), 11–25.

KOEHLER, WALTER, "Zwingli und Luther," *QFRG* VI (1924).

KOHLS, ERNST WILHELM, "Das Geburtsjahr des Erasmus," *Theologische Zeitschrift* XXII (1966), 91–121 and 347–59. Argues for 1466.

Die Theologie des Erasmus, 2 vols. (Basel, 1966), through the *Enchiridion*.

"Ubi sunt qui ante nos?" *Reformatio et Confessio Festschrift* Maurer (Berlin, 1965).

"Die theologische Position und der Traditionszusammenhang des Erasmus mit dem Mittelalter in 'De libero arbitrio,'" Walther von Loewenich zum 65. Geburtstag, *Humanitas-Christianitas* (Witten, 1968).

KRISTELLER, P. O., "An Unknown Humanist Sermon on St. Stephen by Guillaume Fichet," *Mélanges Eugène Tisserant, Biblioteca Vaticana*, VI (1964).

Renaissance Thought, two parts (New York, paper 1955 and 1965).

Eight Philosophers of the Italian Renaissance (Stanford, 1964).

"Two Unpublished Letters of Erasmus," *RN* XIV, No. 1 (Spring, 1961), 6–14.

KRODEL, GOTTFRIED, *Die Abendmahlslehre Er.v.R.* (unpublished dissertation, Erlangen, 1955, microfilm Harvard.)

KRUITWAGEN, B., *Erasmus en zijn Druckers* (Amsterdam, 1923).

LECLER, JOSEPH, *Histoire de la Tolérance au siècle de la Réforme*, 2 vols. (Aubier, 1954), also in English, section on Erasmus, *Toleration and Reformation*, tr. T. L. Wilson, 2 vols. (New York, 1960).

LINDEBOOM, J., *Erasmus, Onderzoek naar zijne Theologie en zijn godsdienstigen Gemoedsbestaan* (Leiden, 1909).

LUBAC, HENRI DE, *Exegèse Médiévale*, Sec. Partie II (Aubier, 1964), 427–87, on Erasmus and the Humanists.

LUPTON, J. H., *Life of John Colet* (1887, reprint 1961). Lupton edited many of Colet's works.

MAJOR, EMIL, *Erasmus v.R.* (Basel, 1926), iconography.

MANGAN, JOHN JOSEPH, *Life, Character and Influence of Desiderius Erasmus of Rotterdam*, 2 vols. (New York, 1927), highly unsympathetic, useful for the translation of letters.

MANN, MARGARET, see Phillips.

MANSFIELD, BRUCE E., "Erasmus in the Nineteenth Century: The Liberal Tradition," *St. R.* XV (1968), 193–219.

MARC'HADOUR, GERMAIN, *L'Univers de Thomas More* (Paris, 1963).

MARGOLIN, JEAN-CLAUDE, *Douze Années de Bibliographie Érasmienne* (Paris, 1963).
Érasme et la Musique (Paris, 1965).
Érasme par lui-même (Paris, 1965).
"Érasme Declamatio de Pueris Instituendis," *Travaux d'Humanisme et Rennaissance*, LXXVII.
"L'Idée de Nature dans la Pensée d'Érasme," Vorträge der Aeneas-Silvius-*Stiftung an der Universität Basel*, VII (1967).

MASSA, EUGENIO, "Intorno ad Erasmo: Una Polemica che si Credeva Perduta," *Storia e Letteratura, Classical and Medieval Studies in honor of Berthold Louis Ullman*, ed., Charles Henderson Jr., vol. 2 (Rome, 1964).

MATTINGLY, GARRETT, *Catherine of Aragon* (Boston, 1941).

MAURER, WILHELM, "Das Verhaltniss des Staates zur Kirche nach humanistischer Anschauung vornehmlich bei Erasmus," *Aus der Welt der Religion* (1930).

McCONICA, JAMES KELSEY, *English Humanists and Reformation Politics* (Oxford, 1965), contends that the English Reformation implemented Erasmian ideas.

MEHL, OSKAR JOHANNES, "Erasmus contra Luther," *Luther Jahrbuch* (1962), 52–64.

MEISSINGER, KARL AUGUST, *Erasmus* (Berlin, 1948). Erasmus as a mediator, emphasis on the *Carmen Alpestre*.

MESNARD, PIERRE, *L'Essor de la Philosophie Politique au XVIe Siècle* (Paris, 1936).

"Zasius et la Réforme," *ARG* LII, 2 (1961), 145–62.

"Humanisme et Théologie dans la Controverse entre Érasme et Dorpius," *Filosofia* XIV (Torino, 1963), 885–900. Thinks Dorp had a point in reproaching Erasmus for undue reliance on rhetoric to the neglect of dialectic.

MESTWERDT, PAUL, "Die Anfänge des Erasmus," *Studien zur Kultur und Geschichte der Reformation* II, (Leipzig, 1917). Valuable for the influence of the *Devotio Moderna* and of Valla and Pico on Erasmus.

METZGER, BRUCE M., *The Text of the New Testament* (Oxford, 1964).

MIASKOWSKI, CASIMIR, *Erasmiana, Die Korrespondenz Erasmus . . . mit Polen* (Paderborn, 1901).

MILES, LELAND, *John Colet and the Platonic Tradition* (La Salle, Indiana, 1961).

MILLER, CLARENCE, "Current English Translations of the Praise of Folly," *Philol. Quarterly*, XLV, 4 (1966).

MORE, THOMAS, *Utopia*, ed Surtz and Hexter, *Complete Works of St. Thomas More*, IV (New Haven, 1965).

MURRAY, R. H., *Erasmus and Luther* (London, 1920).

NEWALD, RICHARD, *Erasmus Roterodamus* (Freiburg i. Br., 1947). Emphasizes his friendships, literary productivity, and independence of spirit.

NIGG, WALTER, *Der christliche Narr* (Zürich, 1956).

NOLHAC, PIERRE DE, *Érasme en Italie* (Paris, 1898).

NULLI, SIRO ATTILIO, *Erasmo e il Rinascimento* (Turin, 1955). So hostile to the Christian in Erasmus as to present a distortion.

NURSE, PETER H., "Érasme et des Périers," *BHR* XXX, 1 (1968), 53–64.

OBERMAN, HEIKO, *The Harvest of Medieval Theology* (Cambridge, Mass., 1963).

OEHLER, KLAUS, "Der Consensus omnium als Kriterium der Wahrheit, in der antiken Philosophie und der Patristik," *Antike und Abendland*, X (1961), 103–29.

OELRICH, KARL HEINZ, "Der späte Erasmus und die Reformation," *Reformations-geschichtliche Studien und Texte* LXXXVI (Münster, 1961).

PADBERG, RUDOLF, "Glaubenstheologie," *Festgabe für Franz X. Arnold* (Freiburg i, Br., 1958), a study of Erasmus' *Paraphrase* of Matthew.

"Erasmus als Katechet," *Untersuchungen zur Theologie der Seelsorge*, IX (1956).

PANOFSKY, ERWIN, " 'Nebulae in Pariete', Notes on Erasmus' Eulogy on Dürer," *Warburg & Courtauld Institutes Journal* XIV (1951), 34–41.

PAQUIER, JULES, *Jérôme Aléandre* (Paris, 1900).

"Érasme et Aléandre" *Mélanges . . . de l'École française de Rome*, XV (1895), 351–74.

PASTOR, LUDWIG VON, *The History of the Popes*, 40 volumes (1891–1953), vol. VI.

PAULUS, NIKLAUS, *Protestantismus und Toleranz im 16ten Jahrh.* (Freiburg i. Br., 1911).

PAYNE, JOHN B., *Erasmus: His Theology of the Sacraments* (Richmond, Va., 1969).

PFEIFFER, RUDOLF, "Humanitas Erasmiana," *Studien der Bibliothek Warburg*, XXII (1931).

"Die Einheit im geistigen Werk des Erasmus," *Deutsche Vierteljahrschrift für Literatur und Wissenschaft*, XV (1937), 473–87. See *Gedenkschrift*.

PHILLIPS, MARGARET MANN, "Louis de Berquin et L' 'Enchiridion' d'Érasme," *Rev. du Seizième Siècle*, XVIII (1931), 89–103.

Érasme et les Débuts de la réforme française 1517–36 (Paris, 1934).

"Erasmus and Propaganda," (English and French translations), *Modern Language Review*, XXXVII (1942), 1–17.

Erasmus and the Northern Renaissance (Reprint 1959). The most satisfactory general biography.

PINEAU, J.-B., *Érasme sa pensée religieuse* (Paris, 1923). Accuses Erasmus of moralism and scepticism.

PIZZI, CLEMENTE, *L'Umanisto Andrea Ammonio* (Florence, 1934).

POHLENZ, MAX, "Antikes Führertum" (Cicero and Panaitios), *Neue Wege zur Antik* II, 3 (1934).

Nachrichten von der Gesellschaft der Wissenschaften zu Göttingen philol. hist. Kl. LXXXI, 1 (1933), 53–92.

PORTER, H. C. AND THOMPSON, D. F. S., *Erasmus and Cambridge* (Toronto, 1963).

POST, R. R., *Geschiedenis van Nederland*, Deel II (Amsterdam, 1935).

Valuable for the background of wars in the Netherlands during the youth of Erasmus.

"Erasmus en het laat-middeleeuwsche Onderwijs," *Bijdragen voor Vaderlandsche Geschiedenis en Oudheidkunde*, VII (The Hague, 1936).

De Moderne Devotie (Amsterdam, 1940).

"De Roeping tot het Kloosterleven en de 16e Eeuw," *Medelingen der Koninklijke Ned. Akad. van Wetenschappen Afd. Letterkunde N. Reeks*, Deel 13, 3 (1950).

Statistics. See chapter 1, note 2 for his articles on the date of Erasmus' birth.

RASSOW, PETER, "Die Kaiser-Idee Karls V (1528–40)," *Historische Studien*, 217 (Berlin, 1932).

RAYMOND, MARCEL, "Les 'Découvertes' d'Érasme en Angleterre," *BHR* XIV (1952), 117–23.

REEDIJK, CORNELIS, "Een Schimpdicht, van Erasmus op Julius II," *Opstellen . . . Kossman* (Hague, 1958), 186–207.

"Erasmus' Verzen op het Overlijden van Hendrik van Bergen, Bisschop van Kamerijk," *Het Boek*, XXX, 3 (Hague, 1949–50), 297–305.

"Een Voorstel tot Adoptie: Erasmus' Epistola Iocosa de Utendo Aula," *Het Boek*, XXXI, (signed 1954), 315–26.

Poems of Desiderius Erasmus (Leiden, 1956).

"Das Lebensende des Erasmus," *Basler Zeitschrift*, LVII (1958), 23–66.

REICKE, BO, "Erasmus und die neutestamentliche Textgeschichte," *TZ* XX (1966), 245–65.

REINHARDT, K., *Kosmos und Sympathie, neue Untersuchungen über Poseidonius* (München, 1926).

REITZENSTEIN, R., *Werden und Wesen der Humanität in Altertum* (Strasbourg, 1907).

RENAUDET, AUGUSTIN, *Études Érasmiennes* (Paris, 1933).
Préréforme et Humanisme à Paris (1494–1517) (Paris, 1953).
Érasme et l'Italie (Geneva, 1954).
"Jean Standonck," *BSPF* LVII (1908), 1–81.
"Mélanges" (in honour of) *BHR* XIV (1952), has the article by Raymond already listed.

RICE, EUGENE, *The Renaissance Idea of Wisdom* (Cambridge, Mass., 1958).

RITTER, GERHARD, "Erasmus und der deutsche Humanistenkreis

am Oberrhein," *Freiburger Universitäts Reden*, Heft XXIII (1937).

Machtstaat und Utopie (München, 1943), revised as *Die Daemonie der Macht* (Stuttgart, 1947?), English: *The Corrupting Influence of Power*, tr. F. W. Pick (Hadleigh, Essex, England, 1952).

ROGGE, JOACHIM, "Zwingli und Erasmus," *Arbeiten zur Theologie*, XI (1962).

SAXL, F., "Holbein's Illustrations to the Praise of Folly," *Burlington Magazine* LXXXII–III (1943), 275–79.

SCHÄTTI, KARL, *Erasmus von Rotterdam und die Römische Kurie* (Basel, 1954).

SCHLINGENSIEPEN, HERMANN, "Erasmus als Exeget," *ZKG* XLVIII, 1 (1929), 16–57.

SCHMIDT, K. L., "Prudentius und Erasmus über die Christuskrippe mit Ochs und Esel," *Theol. Zeitschrift*, V (Basel, 1949).

SCHNEIDER, ELIZABETH, *Das Bild der Frau im Werk des Erasmus v.R.*, (Basel, 1955).

SCHÖNFELD, HERMANN, "Die kirchliche Satire und religiöse Weltanschauung in Brandt's Narrenschiff und Erasmus' Lob der Narrheit," *Modern Language Notes VII* (1892), 139–49.

SCHOTTENLOHER, O. H., "Erasmus im Ringen um die humanistische Bildungsform," *RGST* LXI (1933), 1–106. "Johann Poppenruyter und die Entstehung des Enchiridion," *ARG* XLV, 1 (1954), 109–16.

SCHULZE, MARTIN, *Calvin's Jenseits-Christentum* (Görlitz, 1902), parallels with Erasmus.

SCHWARTZ, W., *Principles and Problems of Biblical Translation* (Cambridge, Eng., 1955).

SCOTT, IZORA, *Controversies over the Imitation of Cicero* (New York, 1910).

SEEBOHM, FREDERIC, *The Oxford Reformers* (London, 1896).

SIMONE, FRANCO, "Robert Gaguin ed il suo cenaculo umanistico 1478–85," *Aevum Rassegna di Scienze storiche, linguistiche e filologiche*, XIII (1939), 410–76.

SKARD, EILIV, "Zwei religiös-politische Begriffe Euergetes-Concordia," *Det Norske Videnskapsakademi Oslo*, Avh. II Hist. Filos. Kl. No. 2 (1931).

SMITH, PRESERVED, "Key to the *Colloquies*," *HTS* XIII (1927). Many plausible suggestions as to the identification of interlocutors in the Colloquies.

Erasmus (New York, 1923). In the rationalist tradition, excellent on new factual data.

SOWARDS, J. K., "Erasmus and the Apologetic Textbook: a Study of the *De Duplici Copia Verborum ac Rerum*," *Studies in Philology*, LV (1958).

"The Two Lost Years of Erasmus," *Studies in the Renaissance*, IX (1962), 161–86.

SPITZ, LEWIS W., *The Religious Renaissance of the German Humanists* (Cambridge, Mass., 1963), excellent on the indebtedness of Erasmus to the piety of the *Devotio Moderna* and to the Neoplatonic tradition.

STAEHELIN, ERNST, "Briefe und Akten zum Leben Oekolampads," Bd. I, *QFRG* X (1927). Bd. II, *QFRG* XIX (1934).

"Das Theologische Lebenswerk Johannes Oekolampads," *QFRG* XXI (1939).

STANGE, CARL, *Erasmus und Julius, eine Legende* (Berlin, 1937).

TARELLI, C. C., "Erasmus' Manuscripts of the Gospels," *The Journal of Theological Studies* XLIV (Oxford, 1943).

TELLE, EMILE V., *Erasme de Rotterdam et Le Septième Sacrement* (Geneva, 1954).

TEUTLER, THOMAS N., "Forgiveness and Consolation in . . . Er." *Studies in the Renaissance* XII (1965), 110–33.

THIEME, HANS, "Die Ehescheidung Heinrichs VIII, und die europäischen Universitäten," *Juristische Studiengesellschaft Karlsruhe*, Heft, 31 (1957), 3–23.

THOMPSON, CRAIG, *Ten Colloquies of Erasmus* (Liberal Arts Press, N.Y., 1957).

Colloquies of Erasmus (Chicago, 1965).

Translations of Lucian by Erasmus and St. Thomas More (Ithaca, N.Y., 1940).

"Inquisitio de Fide," *Yale Studies in Religion*, XV (New Haven, 1950).

"Erasmus as Internationalist and Cosmopolitan," *ARG* XLVI, 2 (1955), 167–95.

THOMSON, J. A. K., "Erasmus in England," *Bibliothek Warburg Vorträge* (1930–31), 64–82.

THUASNE, LOUIS, *Roberti Gaguini Epistolae et Orationes*, Tom. I (Paris, 1903).

THÜRLEMANN, INES, *Erasmus von Rotterdam und Joannes L. Vives als Pazifisten* (Unpublished Dissertation, Freiburg, Switzerland, 1932).

TIMMERMANNS, B. J., "Valla et Érasme défenseurs d'Épicure," *Neophilologus* XXXIII–XXIV (1937–39), 414–19.

TREINEN, HANS, *Studien zur Idee der Gemeinschaft bei Erasmus von Rotterdam . . .*, (Saarluis., 1955).

VALLESE, GIULIO, *Da Dante ad Erasmo* (Naples, 1962).

VAN RHIJN, M., *Studiën over Wessel Gansfort en zijn Tijd* (Utrecht, 1933).

VILLOSLADA, RICARDO G., "La Universidad de Paris 1507–1522," *Analecta Gregoriana*, XIV, Series Fac. Hist. Eccl. Lectio B. (No. 2), Cap. II.

VOCHT, HENRI DE, in *Monumenta Humanistica Lovaniensia* (Louvain).

I *Literae . . . ad Franciscum Craneveldium* 1522–28 (1928).

IV (1934). On Erasmus, Vives, Dorp, Goes, et al.

VII *Acta Thomae Mori* (1947).

IX *Jerome de Busleyden* (Turnhout, 1950).

X (1951), XI (1953), XII (1954), XIII (1955), *Collegium Trilingue Lovaniense.*

Voordrachten gehoreden ter Herdenking van den Sterfdag van Erasmus (Rotterdam, 1936).

WACHTERS, H. J. I., *Erasmus* (Amsterdam, 1936), a solid recital.

WACKERNAGEL, RUDOLF, *Geschichte der Stadt Basel III* (Basel, 1924). The documents on which he drew have since been published in the *Aktensammlung zur Geschichte der Basler Reformation . . .* ed. Dürr and Roth, 6 vols. (Basel 1921–50).

WALKER, D. P., "Musical Humanism in the Sixteenth and Early Seventeenth Centuries," *Music Review* II, I (1941), 1–13.

WALTHER, DANIEL, "Marguerite d'Angoulême and the French Lutherans," *Andrews University Seminary Studies* (Berien Springs, Michigan) II (1964), 137–55.

WEINSTOCK, HEINRICH, *Die Tragödie des Humanismus* (Heidelberg, 1953), thinks that Erasmus was not a religious figure, let alone a Christian.

WEISS, NATHANIEL, "Louis de Berquin son premier procès . . ." (1523), *BSPF* LXVII (1918), 162–83.

WERTHEMANN, A., "Schädel und Gebeine des Erasmus von Rotterdam," *Verhandlungen der Naturforschenden Gesellschaft*, XL (Basel, 1928–29), 313–93.

WIESEN, DAVID S., *St. Jerome as a Satirist* (Ithaca, N.Y., 1964).

WIND, EDGAR, " 'Aenigma Termini' the emblem of Erasmus," *Journal of the Warburg Institute*, I (1937–38), 66–69.

Pagan Mysteries in the Renaissance (New Haven, 1958), on *Festina Lente*.

WOODWARD, WILLIAM HARRISON, *Desiderius Erasmus Concerning the Aim and Method of Education* (Cambridge, Mass., 1904).

ZICKENDRAHT, KARL, *Die Streit zwischen Erasmus und Luther über die Willensfreiheit* (Leipzig, 1909).

MODERN ENGLISH TRANSLATIONS OF ERASMUS

Adagia, The Adages of Erasmus, translated and edited by Margaret Mann Phillips (Cambridge, England, 1964).

Ciceronianus, translated and edited by Izora Scott (New York, 1908).

Colloquia. See under Craig Thompson, in the general bibliography.

De Copia Verborum, translated by Donald B. King and H. David Rex (Milwaukee 1963).

De Immensa Misericordia Dei, The Immense Mercy of God, W. P. A. Project, Sutro Library (San Francisco, 1940).

De Libero Arbitrio, Discourse on the Freedom of the Will, translated and edited by Ernest F. Winter (New York, 1961).

De Pueris Instituendis, Concerning the Aim and Method of Education, translated with Introduction by William Harrison Woodward (Cambridge, England, 1904).

Enchiridion, translated and edited by Matthew Spinka in "Advocates of Reform," *Christian Classics* XIV (Philadelphia, 1953).

Enchiridion, The, translated and edited by Raymond Himeleck (Bloomington, Indiana, 1965).
Handbook of the Militant Christian, translated and edited by John P. Dolan (Notre Dame, Indiana, 1962).

Encomium Artis Medicae, Dutch and English translation (Amsterdam, 1907).

Encomium Moriae, The Praise of Folly, translated and edited by Hoyt Hudson (Princeton, 1941).

Epistolae, The Epistles of Erasmus, a selection translated and edited by Francis M. Nichols, 3 vols. (London, 1901–08).
A number are translated in *Luther's Correspondence and other Contemporary Letters*, Preserved Smith, 2 vols. (Philadelphia, 1913 and 1918).

Institutio Principis Christiani, The Education of a Christian Prince, translated and edited by Lester K. Born in *Records of Civilization* XXVII (New York, 1936).

Julius Exclusus, translated by Paul Pascal with notes by J. Kelley Sowards (Bloomington, Ind., 1968).

Querela Pacis, Our Struggle for Peace, translated and edited by José Chapiro (Boston, 1950).

Scholar's Facsimiles, of Paynell's translation, ed. W. J. Hirten (New York, 1946).

The Complaint of Peace (Open Court, Chicago, 1917).

Vitae, Lives of Jehan Vitrier . . . and John Colet, translated by J. H. Lupton (London, 1883).

Selections: *Christian Humanism and the Reformation*, John C. Olin (New York, 1965).

Erasmus and the Humanists, translated and edited by Albert Hyma (New York, 1930).

CRITICAL EDITIONS

Antibarbari in Albert Hyma, *Youth of Erasmus* (Ann Arbor, Michigan, 1930).

Apotheosis Capnionis, translated and edited by Giuilio Vallese (Naples, 1949).

Ciceronianus, edited by Jo. Carolus Schönberger (Augsburg, 1919).

Colloquies, see Van der Haeghen, *Bibliotheca Erasmiana*, 7 vols. (Gand, 1897–1912), III, p. 110.

Declamatio . . . in Laudem Artis Medicae, edited by E. Merck (Darmstadt, 1960).

De Libero Arbitrio, edited by Jo. Walter, *Quellen zur Gesch. d. Prot.* VIII (1910, reprint 1935).

De Pueris Instituendis, translated and edited by Jean-Claude Margolin, *Travaux d'Humanisme et Ren.* LXXVII (Geneva, 1966).

Dilutio eorum quae Iodocus Clithoveus scripsit adv. declamationem Ded. Eras. Roterod. suasoriam matrimonii, critically edited by Emile V. Telle (Vrin, Paris, 1968).

Dulce Bellum Inexpertis, edited by Yvonne Rémy et René Dumil-Marquebreucq (Brussels, 1953).

Enchiridion, Paraclesis, Ratio, in *Ausgewählte Werke*, edited by Hajo and Annemarie Holborn (München, 1933).

Encomium Moriae, edited by I. B. Kahn (Hague, 1898).

Erasmi Epistolae, edited by P. S. and H. M. Allen, 12 vols. with Index (Oxford, 1906–58).

Erasmi Opuscula, edited by Wallace Ferguson (Hague, 1933), doubtful works.

Erasmus von Rotterdam Ausgewählte Schriften, in eight volumes, edited by Werner Welzig (Darmstadt 1967—). Volume III came out in 1967 reprinting the Holborn edition of the *Methodus* and *Ratio*; volume I in 1968 reprinting similarly the *Enchiridion.*

Inquisitio de Fide, translated and edited by Craig Thompson, *Yale Studies in Religion* XV (New Haven, 1950).

"La Correspondence d'Érasme et Guillaume Budé," translated with notes by Marie-Madeleine de la Garanderie, *De Pétrarche à Descartes* XIII (Paris, 1967).

Poemata, The Poems of Desiderius Erasmus, edited by Cornelis Reedijk (Leiden, 1956).

Querela Pacis, edited by Ferdinand Geldner, *Quellen z. Gesch. d. Humanismus u. d. Ref. in Facsimile Ausgabe* (München, n.d.).

BIOGRAPHICAL AIDS

There are fuller bibliographies than mine in Cornelis Augustijn, *Erasmus en de Reformatie* (Amsterdam, 1962), and in the works of Gebhardt, Kohls, and Treinen listed in the Bibliography.

Karl Schottenloher, *Bibliographie zur deutschen Geschichte im Zeitalter der Glaubensspaltung,* Bd. VII covers recent literature, 1938-1960. *Studies in Philology* devotes in each issue a section to Erasmus. Also the reader is referred to Jean-Claude Margolin, *Douze Années de Bibliographie Erasmienne* (1950-1961) and J. V.-M. Pollet. "Erasmania," *Rev. des Sciences Rel.,* XVII (1952).

Abbreviations

*

AK	Alfred Hartmann, *Die Amerbach Korrespondenz*, vols. II, III (Basel, 1943——).
ARG	*Archiv für Reformationsgeschichte*
ARH	*American Historical Review*
BHR	*Bibliothèque d'Humanisme et Renaissance*
BSPF	*Société de l'Histoire du Protestantisme français, Bulletin*
EE	*Erasmi Epistolae*, ed. P. S. and Mrs. Allen, 12 volumes (1906–58)
H	Holborn, Hajo and Annemarie, *Ausgewählte Werke*
HLQ	*Huntington Library Quarterly*
HTS	*Harvard Theological Studies*
HZ	*Historische Zeitschrift*
JHI	*Journal of the History of Ideas*
LB	*Lugduni Batavorum*, the Leiden edition of the works of Erasmus, edited by Leclerc, 1703 (reprinted 1963).
NAKG	*Nederlands Archief voor Kerkgeschedenis*
QFRG	*Quellen und Forschungen zur Reformationsgeschichte*
QS	*Quellenschriften zur Geschichte des Protestantismus*
RGST	*Reformationsgeschichtliche Studien und Texte*
RN	*Renaissance News*
SVRG	*Schriften des Vereins für Reformationsgeschichte*
St. R.	*Studies in the Renaissance*
TZ	*Theologische Zeitschrift*
WA	*Weimar Ausgabe* of Luther's works
ZKG	*Zeitschrift für Kirchengeschichte*

Acknowledgments for Line Illustrations

*

p. 15: Universitäts-Bibliothek Basel

p. 16: Yale University, Beinecke Library

p. 21: Yale University, Beinecke Library. Louis Guicciardini, *La Description de Tous les Pais-bas* (1582)

p. 27: Courtesy, Maison d'Érasme, Bruxelles, Belgium. Daniel Van Damme, *Ephéméride Illustrée de la Vie d'Érasme* (Anderlecht, 1936)

p. 37: Yale University, Beinecke Library

p. 48: Daniel Van Damme, *Ephéméride Illustrée de la Vie d'Érasme* (Anderlecht, 1936). Bibliothèque Nationale, Paris.

p. 52: Oeffentliche Kunstsammlung Kunstmuseum, Basel. *Praise of Folly*

p. 61: Yale University, Beinecke Library

p. 63: Oeffentliche Kunstsammlung Kunstmuseum, Basel. *Praise of Folly* facsimile

p. 69: Yale University, Beinecke Library

p. 74: Oeffentliche Kunstsammlung Kunstmuseum, Basel. *Praise of Folly*

p. 92: Oeffentliche Kunstsammlung Kunstmuseum, Basel. *Praise of Folly*

p. 96: Yale University, Beinecke Library

p. 103: J. Ph. Bergomensis, *Supplementum Chronicarum* (Venice, 1503)

p. 108: Yale University, Beinecke Library

p. 109: Franz Joseph Dölger, *Die Fisch-Denkmäler in der frühchristlichen Plastik, Malerei und Kleinkunst,* IXOYC Vol. IV (Aschendorffsche Verlagsbuchandlung, Münster, Westfalen, 1927)

p. 111: Courtesy, Maison d'Érasme, Bruxelles, Belgium. Daniel Van Damme, *Ephéméride Illustrée de la Vie d'Érasme* (Anderlecht, 1936)

p. 113: The New York Public Library Picture Collection

p. 117: Oeffentliche Kunstsammlung Kunstmuseum, Basel. *Praise of Folly*

p. 120: Oeffentliche Kunstsammlung Kunstmuseum, Basel. *Praise of Folly* facsimile

p. 122: Oeffentliche Kunstsammlung Kunstmuseum, Basel. *Praise of Folly*

p. 133: Yale University, Beinecke Library

p. 139: Henry de Vocht, *Jerome Busleyden* (Turnhout, 1950). Courtesy, Editions Brepols s. a. Brussels

p. 141: Courtesy, Maison d'Érasme, Bruxelles, Belgium. Daniel Van Damme, *Ephéméride Illustrée de la Vie d'Érasme* (Anderlecht, 1936)

p. 147: *Oratio Legationis Francisci Regis Franciae* (Strassburg, 1519)

p. 156: Oeffentliche Kunstsammlung Kunstmuseum, Basel. *Praise of Folly*

p. 161: Daniel Van Damme, *Ephéméride Illustrée de la Vie d'Érasme* (Anderlecht, 1936) Oeffentliche Bibliothek der Universität, Basel.

p. 173: Yale University, Beinecke Library. Hartmuth Schedel, *Weltchronik* (Nürnberg, 1493)

p. 183: Yale University, Beinecke Library

p. 187: Louvain, Librairie Universitaire Uystpruyst. Henry de Vocht, *Acta Thomae Mori* (Louvain, 1947)

p. 201: Yale University, Beinecke Library. Hans Curjel, *Hans Baldung Grien* (München, 1923)

p. 203: Yale University, Beinecke Library

p. 205: Abte Sainte Baste, Arras, France. Arras Codex, ca. 1560

p. 215: Yale University, Beinecke Library

p. 223: The Pierpont Morgan Library

p. 233: Oscar Thulin, *Martin Luther* (Berlin, 1958)

p. 249: Yale University, Beinecke Library

p. 251: Yale University, Beinecke Library

p. 255: Augsburg, Steyner (1526)

p. 258: Oeffentliche Kunstsammlung Kunstmuseum, Basel. *Praise of Folly*

p. 262: *Ulrich Zwingli: zum Gedächtnis der zürcher Reformation, 1519-1919* (Zürich, 1919)

p. 263: Comité Farel, *Guillaume Farel*, (Editions Delachaux & Niestlé, Neuchâtel, 1930)

p. 269: Wilhelm Speiser, *Bilder zur Basler Geschichte* (Basel, 1940)

p. 281: Kupferstichkabinett der Oeffentlichen Kunstsammlung, Basel

p. 286: Oeffentliche Kunstsammlung Kunstmuseum, Basel. *Praise of Folly*

p. 287: Oeffentliche Kunstsammlung Kunstmuseum, Basel. *Praise of Folly*

p. 291: A. Werthemann, *Schädel und Gebeine des Erasmus* (Basel, 1930), Birkhäuser Verlag Basel

p. 293: Yale University, Beinecke Library

p. 294: Eduard His, *Selbstkarikaturen des Erasmus. Basler Zeitschrift fur Geschichte* XLV (1946) Historische und Antiquarische Gesellschaft zu Basel

p. 305: Yale University, Beinecke Library. *Freiburg im Breisgau,* Badischen Architecten-und-Ingenieur-Verein (Freiburg i. Br., 1896)

p. 331: From Sebastian Münster, *Cosmographia,* reproduced in Marcel Bataillon, *Érasme en Espagne* (Paris, 1925)

Index

*

Also available in Fount Paperbacks

Memories, Dreams, Reflections
C. G. JUNG

'Jung's single-minded humility, his passion to unearth truth, is one of the loveliest impressions to emerge from this absorbing and many-sided book.'
The Times

Myths, Dreams and Mysteries
MIRCEA ELIADE

'A penetrating and sympathetic scrutiny of the mythologies that vivify ancient communities and tell us so much of the perennial meaning and destiny of man.'
The Times Literary Supplement

Silent Music
WILLIAM JOHNSTON

Silent Music is a brilliant synthesis which joins traditional religious insights with the discoveries of modern science to provide a complete picture of mysticism – its techniques and stages, its mental and physical aspects, its dangers, and its consequences.

The Varieties of Religious Experience
WILLIAM JAMES

'A classic of psychological study . . . fresh and stimulating . . . this book is a book to prize.'
The Psychologist

The Religious Experience of Mankind
NINIAN SMART

'Professor Smart's patient, clear and dispassionate exposition makes him a tireless and faithful guide.'
Evening News